URBAN SPACE

URBAN SPACE

A BRIEF HISTORY OF THE CITY SQUARE

Second Edition

JERE STUART FRENCH

California State Polytechnic University—Pomona
Illustrations by Michael Doty

KENDALL/HUNT PUBLISHING COMPANY
Dubuque, Iowa

Cover photo courtesy of ENIT

Copyright © 1978, 1983 by Kendall/Hunt Publishing Company

Library of Congress Catalog Card Number: 83–81687

ISBN 0–8403–3109–6

Printed in the United States of America

B   403109   01

For C. L. French

in memory

Contents

Foreword

It is good to see Jere French following up his book URBAN GREEN with a balancing, broader, and more inclusive treatment of URBAN SPACE. This is important because it widens and strengthens the bridge many on both sides have been endeavoring to build between urban environment as structure and as landscape. Green urban parks, expanding out through the cultivated greenery of suburban and rural surrounds into the ultimate greenery of wilderness, are seen as the traditional concern of landscape architects. Urban spaces, largely structurally defined and therefore assumed to be architectural, have not been considered a landscape focus, in spite of excellent urban design works by many landscape architects.

Townscapes, coined by Gordon Cullen, is one of the better semantic bridges. But there is still a stubborn and persistent tendency, based on history and professional licensing, to separate landscape design from urban design. Therefore it is good to see Jere, a landscape architect, writing of urban space in terms of architecture as a parent of urban design.

For we are not interested in inter-professional competition. There is enough of that in daily practise, where each profession tries more and more to cover the total environment. What we are interested in is a design approach which is based on the realities of human experience, a Gestalt approach. The environmental experience for each person, or any group, at any given time and place is derived from everything they perceive around them, conditioned by the accumulation of previous experience. Buildings, streets, trees, water, rocks, people all combine to produce holistic impacts. Architectural, landscape, or other preconceptions may warp or over-simplify such arrangements, establish unnecessary constraints, and limit the range of potential design alternatives. Every effort to see urban space as a series of whole concepts in which structural and natural elements can interact in diverse combinations to produce unprecedented results is an advance in the state of the art.

Urban structure intensifies inward from suburban fringes toward the center, in reverse parallelism to green open space patterns. At the scale of San Gimignano the contrast between structured town and green surround is refreshing and stimulating. At the scale of any large city the analogous contrast is untenable and unbearable. We need to develop much more complex, subtle and sophisticated design concepts for urban spaces; concepts which can expand to include total building/circulation/open space relations within urban areas. This book is a big step in that direction. Having defined, evolved, imposed, expanded, and implied order we do now need to redefine it.

Garrett Eckbo

Preface

The difficulties in writing about architecture, or any of the graphic arts for that matter, stem from the obligation of translating two and three dimensional physical form into a lineal, literary form.

Some authors manage to avoid this problem by resorting primarily to description, a method which requires supportive graphics in order to clarify their meaning. What is lost in translation to words is therein restored by photos and drawings.

Another approach often taken in writing about architecture, particularly architectural history, seems to depend largely on the use of general information—dates, names, personalities, love-life; in short a colorful, albeit incidental, sort of accounting of things.

When we add another dimension—time, the problems of describing works of architecture increase even further. I have tried to avoid these pitfalls when possible, and to address myself mainly to ideas. In dealing with urban space—a subject even more elusive than architecture—the need to understand ideas and the concepts of spatial organization emerges as my principal goal. Urban space must be seen as *volume*—the thing contained, while the container serves primarily to charge that volume with the qualities of shape, scale, rhythm, movement. Kakuzo Okakura says it best:

> The reality of a room is to be found in the vacant space enclosed by the roof and walls, not by the roof and walls themselves. The usefulness of a water pitcher dwells in the emptiness where water might be put, not in the form of the pitcher or the material of which it is made. Vacuum is all-potent, all containing. In vacuum alone motion becomes possible. One who could make of himself a vacuum into which others might freely enter would become master of all situations. The whole can always dominate the part. (The Book of Tea).

- JSF

Credits and Acknowledgments

Drawings—Michael Doty

Photos—Illustrated London News, Göste Glase, Reportagerud, Eduard Renner, ENIT, Schröder, San Francisco Convention & Visitors Bureau, French National Tourist Office, Schneiders, Lindau-Schachen, Werbe V. Verkehrsant, Foto Sachsse, Willy Pragher, Otto Fazler, Andres & Company, Mattelay & Campbell—Copeland, Los Angeles Planning Department, Ed Rondot, Stadtbildstelle, Wolff & Tritschler, Stegerer, Ernst Tremel, Gertrud Herbrick, Derkelvesant, Giuliano Carraro, Quilici, Frank Leslie's Illustrated Newspaper 1867, Beehive Press, History of Kotohira, Ito's 'Minka', T. Uesugi, Phoenix Civic Plaza Director, Patrick W. Sturn, Philadelphia City Planning Commission, Janice Wilkman, San Antonio Chamber of Commerce, Downtown St. Louis Inc., Fred P. Swiss, James Gilray, L. Rudolph Barton, and Tita Thomas.

Photos not credited are the author's.

Plates—landscape architecture students
Cal Poly U., Pomona.

I am indebted to Professor Takeo Uesugi for developing the material used in Chapter Eight.

Urban Space is what we make it—no better, no worse.

ONE

Perception: the Meaning of Urban Space

This book is about the city, and particularly about city spaces. It is an attempt to familiarize environmental designers (architects, landscape architects, planners) with some of the problems we face in planning cities. There is also the hope that something of the *value* of cities will rub off along the way. These vast collections of people and structures are mentioned by scholars and historians as perhaps man's greatest accomplishment. But it is the *ideal* of urbanization they refer to, not the scruffy gridiron of streets, decaying buildings and poisoned air most of us suffer through daily. More to the point perhaps, civilization would seem to be man's greatest accomplishment, and our cities—for better or worse—the indicators of any civilization's success.

In order to test this thought it is well to study the record of city building left to us from the past, to discover what was accomplished, and more importantly to understand the essential purposes served by the city. We can peruse the available books, study the maps, and literally dig out the foundations of the past in order to know them for what they were. We may put together again the walls of Antioch and Tyre and marvel over their technique in vaulting and proportion, not to repeat it in our own time, one assumes, but to know it in theirs. We walk in Brunelleschi's shoes through the ruins of Rome and search again for the technology that built the Pantheon, so that the pain of his efforts might comfort us in ours, and the measure of his imagination and genius might inspire us to seek the same in ourselves.

In the study of cities there is room for the anthropologist, the sociologist, the political scientist and others who seek the underlying cultural pattern which produced the physical form. This is likewise the concern of the environmental designer if he hopes to contribute meaningfully to the shape of the city.

For the most part the visible structure of a city—its buildings, parks, monuments, streets and squares—reflects the real values of its people. There won't be parks unless people continue to want them. Nor will civil legislation by itself eliminate urban ills. What happens in the city is usually what people want—or better, deserve. Bruno Zevi, the modern Roman architect, tells us that the physical structure of the city is an indicator of its political status. Tyranny is reflected in the heavy, imposing buildings, the formality and symmetry of streets and open spaces, the monumentality of structural mass as witnessed by imperial Rome, together with Mussolini's reincarnation of that ideal. It is the imposition of state over everything else. Society builds in its own image, and the city is a mirror of its values. Do we build theatres, like the Classic Greeks, or colosseums, like the ancient Romans? Look around your city. To what powers are its monuments raised?

The shape of the city has changed considerably over the many centuries, in accordance with changes in social, political and technical developments, but only during the last century—since the oncoming of the Industrial Revolution—have changes in the urban fabric become so rapid and alarming as to make us take sharper notice. For the first time in history man is beginning to question the validity of his "greatest accomplishment," even to the point of abandonment. Predictions of ensuing chaos abound as our largest cities grow more unmanageable, more unserviceable, more dangerous. Some say that modern man—at least in America—has already rejected cities; one result has been the tendency more and more to live on the edges of urbs, leaving the center to poverty and even anti-urban elements.

Is this direction irreversible? Yes and no. If modern cities are failing to keep their promise of old it might be because modern man has predestined that failure. And the decline of the city is most evident in the United States, where the frontier ethic still prevails and the private property syndrome continues to nurture Americans on a diet of xenophobia and compartmentalization. The single family residence, here in the last quarter of the twentieth century, is still America's dream house, and the private automobile the preferred means of transportation. While the picture is changing somewhat—even dramatically in places—it comes more as a grudging surrender to economic realities than a brave new direction in urban life.

In spite of a persistence for low density, American cities are frequently found to be overcrowded—232,000 for instance, packed into two and a half square miles of Harlem. Americans tend to equate density with poverty on a straight line scale—greater personal space means greater wealth, and the reverse. This is one of the reasons used by middle America for fleeing from the center—in addition to the more frequently cited explanations of crime, better schools, and the like. So the return to city center becomes more difficult to sell in the face of increased density, and all the rest.

Success to many of us is readily equated to personal space—a piece of land of our own. What belongs to everybody seems to belong to nobody. A frontier society, fearful of intruders, rigorously protective of private property and independent choice cannot easily adapt to an open, give-and-take urban structure, more common to Europe or the Middle East. Therefore, the American city has grown and developed through most of the twentieth century without any real sense or even acceptance by the people who occupy it. Zoning, for example, is primarily an American device for keeping commercial, industrial, and residential areas from mixing together—supposedly to protect them from each other. The results, however, tend to provide

for an even greater degree of isolation, separation, and mixed densities. Following a devastating explosion in Central Los Angeles in the Summer of 1974, which demolished an entire city block, it was reported that "by some miracle no one was killed," and only one person injured—the night watchman. It was no miracle at all, since no one *lived* in that section of the city, just a mile from the great towers of the downtown center. Large tracts of Central Los Angeles, as well as other American city centers, have for years been converting residential to commercial and industrial zoning.

And where do the uprooted residents go? Into the suburban fringe if they can make it—otherwise to the already crowded high density inner city sinks (ghettos and slums).

As our cities continue to grow and sprawl—increasing the costs of services from decreasing sources of energy and material, it becomes more than ever before the clear task of the environmental designer to produce better answers to the increasing problems of urban life today, and to provide us as well with a blueprint for future urban needs—for the city that can conserve energy and space, where density may be high without overcrowding, and where people have a variety of opportunities for work and leisure without having to travel many miles in each direction.

To do this we will have to learn again to *like* cities, to really look forward to the opportunities, events, and life style only the city provides. Architects, business leaders, teachers, and universities will have to return to the heart of the city again—to lead the way back from the suburbs. And to accomplish any kind of mass migration back to the center, all kinds of inducements will have to be offered. Crime in the streets must be controlled, if street life is ever to flourish. Libraries, theatres, museums, and sports palaces add considerably to urban life, but we must also include the day to day advantages people enjoy in suburbia—quiet walks on tree lined streets, nearby tennis courts, a garden to tend, a private place to sit in the sun, a place to ride bicycles and romp with kids and dogs. Good department stores, unique restaurants, and night clubs will continue to draw people to the inner city from the fringe areas where such things exist only in somewhat pallid form, but, once drawn, how will we keep them there? The city really does have it all, in terms of variety, educational opportunity, culture, and entertainment. What it lacks mostly is space.

Clean up the downtown, reduce crime, embellish the amenities and we still face the original cause of the exodus—crowding, lack of privacy, the simple pleasures. But there is still plenty of available space in the city if we can find it—and then convert it to practical use. The problem is that due to our economic policies, tax laws and even private property itself, land is literally wasted. Inoperative gas stations gobble space at downtown intersections. Decaying, uninhabited slums abound, their absentee owners resisting the improvements which would increase their taxes, while all the time the useless land increases in paper value. Sterile new tenements, built more with the idea apparently of imprisoning welfare recipients than housing them, rapidly decay in an atmosphere of dark resentment and neglect.

The environmental designer can't improve the economy, reduce inflation, or find jobs for the unemployed, but he needs to know the problems facing modern American cities if he hopes to assist in their restoration. And his major contribution will likely be made in terms of urban space—public open space so desperately needed in the high rise-bounded, auto-choked streets of most American cities, and beyond the streets in the public parks and squares. It is upon this aspect of the urban fabric that we shall concentrate our study. Here in the public spaces of downtown we must eventually come face to face with the society created by this structure—ourselves.

Comprehending urban space is not a simple task, but if we are to succeed in designing future urban growth and arresting decay we must become familiar with the intricacies of spatial organization as well as the complexities of urban life, and the dynamic quality of its structure. In the city nothing remains constant.

Planning for urban space is the most complex of the environmental arts, combining the spatial and graphic aspects of architecture with the infinite variety of the city and its people—a multi-faceted client. There is also a great lack of any sense of control—unlike architecture, the walls that form city spaces are themselves usually independent structures, unrelated to the whole.

Let us then consider architecture, the parent to urban design, as a useful tool in illustrating the complexities of spatial organization. The architect deals with a great number of determinants, not the least of which are weather, topography, soil, surrounding structures, and availability of materials. When cost and function are added it is clear that much more than aesthetics is involved in the design of a building, and many more hands than the architect's are used in its making. He may view it as a work of art, but to others it may represent very different values.

Frustrated as he may become in trying to blend beauty and imagination into a low cost, high density housing project, budgetary and practical functions represent only the most obvious limits to design which are imposed upon the architect. According to Erne Goldfinger, noted British architect, the really significant determinants of architectural design are inherent to its particular spatial qualities. Unlike painting, sculpture, and other graphic arts, architecture is an art form determined primarily by the element of containment—walls, floors, ceiling. Certainly a building has sculptural (external) quality, but the final assessment of its value rests upon its spatial (internal) statement. And this is both aesthetic and functional, if indeed the two can be separated.

Goldfinger goes on to describe the space thus contained as a product of not merely vision alone, but of all our senses.

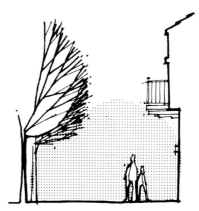

We perceive enclosure three dimensionally through the effect of stereoscopic vision, but our auditory and olfactory senses are also brought into usage in order to better determine the *quality* of the space. The air itself gives significant clues. Is it clean, fresh and breezy, or moist and humid, windy or still, hazy, smoggy, rank or close. Inside a building or in a courtyard, the quality of the air greatly effects our perception of the enclosure. In the same way, sounds add to our sense of perception. Footsteps, voices bouncing off walls and back to us relay a feeling for those enclosing walls, the texture of their surfaces, coverings, and incidental furnishings. These are the indicators we rely on at night to tell us of our surroundings. And the blind, of course, know all too well how to gauge surroundings from sound. Odors enrichen the perception of space—give another dimension to its meaning and purpose. Primitive societies, we have learned, as well as Oriental and Middle Eastern cultures, retain a higher degree of sensitivity to auditory and olfactory stimuli than do their American and Western European counterparts. This becomes evident in a comparison of street layout and public spaces. Visual organization—the street, building fronts, and spatial modulators are not so carefully attended. The basic elements of enclosure common to Western cities are often missing or subordinate to more flexible, everchanging controls in Eastern societies. People—the crowds in the bazaar—become the enclosing agents, along with their wares, animals, stacks of goods, the ever present protective drapes, which move softly in the breeze, adding color and movement to the total picture.

Temporary stalls with their variety of aromas, the odor of horses, camels, people—the sounds of vendors, beggars, musicians, all add to the display of the senses. We can include the *feel* of the hot sun on our faces and the *touch* of the many draped materials to complete a picture of sensory awareness.

Middle Eastern cultures, lacking a strong dependence upon stationary structure for the determination of enclosure readily exploit senses which the western world denies or misuses. Modern technology at work in the western city, with its resultant noise and pollution, is certainly a major factor in the failure to use our audial and olfactory senses more successfully. To some degree certainly, the sounds and odors emanating from the automobile have reduced our ability to judge enclosure by smell and sound. A visit to Venice quickly assures us of how much of our senses we have surrendered to the automobile. The narrow, twisting streets are scaled to people on foot. No auto exhaust, roaring motors or speeding wheels threaten comfort or safety, and we can hear voices and footsteps, the stirring of breezes, even the song of a bird. And we can experience the aromas being wafted from restaurants, cafes, markets, storage houses, and even the slightly fishy odor of the canals. Voices bouncing from a stone wall carry clearly for a hundred feet or more, and the traveler to this city may find himself spending his first hour or so trying to adjust to this exhilarating experience. Piazza San Marco, the principal and historic square in Venice, benefits more no doubt from the absence of automobiles than from all the other qualities so glowingly ascribed to it by scholars and architectural critics. For without their noisy intrusion it has managed to remain true to its purpose and its sense of scale.

In his treatise on the perception of space, Goldfinger goes on to argue that enclosure, while being the prime function of architecture, is nevertheless perceived only *subconsciously* most of the time. That is to say, we are aware at all times of the spatial order surrounding and enclosing us, and we may be pleasantly or adversely affected by it, without paying it much attention. These enclosing agents—walls, ceiling, floor—represent the outer shell of our spatial awareness, offering an overall sense of *being,* that is at one with the environment. The *quantity* (size)

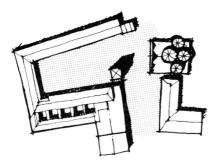

and the *quality* (shape, color, detail) of this enclosure affect our psychological reaction to it—mainly comfort, but at times quite a few other things as well. *Being,* in the sense of our relationship to enclosure, is constant, and is directly responsive to our own personal means of measuring scale. We know instantly and inherently when the enclosure of walls, buildings, hills, or trees is too horizontal, too vertical, too great or too small, and we respond to it instinctively. We may be uncomfortable here alone in this space. We are limited in the kinds of things we want to do. We feel comfortable only on the edges, or near areas which offer some psychological protection (fountain, sculpture, umbrella). The enclosing agents may be tall, impersonal buildings—all glass, giving us a fishbowl feeling in the center of the space they form. There is usually need in such cases for an inner means of enclosure—another set of enclosing agents to provide us with a sense of scale and intimacy proper to psychological need. The immediate surroundings which establish the primary space in a square may be created in very subtle terms—a step down, a change in pavement, umbrellas, awnings, trees (as a suggestion of ceiling), planters, free standing screens, benches, and the like. In the living room of a house it is not the walls which direct an activity so much as the arrangement of furniture, the decorative appointments, lighting, and even the momentary groupings of people. These are the real dimensions of human enclosure, as described by the Middle Eastern marketplace. We should think of this shifting, inner dimension of space as *primary,* while the walls of the room represent the *secondary* enclosing agents.

You can demonstrate the *effect* of primary and secondary enclosure by observation—the empty living room in contrast to a lively cocktail party in the same room. Now the walls of the room are less apparent as personal, immediate space comes into being. In the crowded room the sounds, cushioned by people's bodies, are softer, less hollow. The best functional use of the space is sought—if subconsciously—in order to maximize efficiency of purpose. People gather in the places where conversation is easier, and in so doing form an immediate space of their own—their bodies being the enclosing agents. Furniture arrangements which are not satisfactory to the demands of the occasion are unused, or moved about to achieve the right spatial

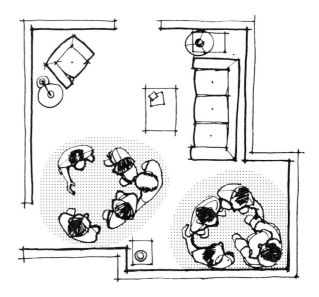

relationship. And it is up to the designer to understand the needs placed upon such a room and to establish the proper enclosing agents. Walls, without thought to furniture, doors without thought to circulation invariably create difficulties in the use of the room and in the efficiency of its primary space. If those walls of our living room can be seen as the enclosing buildings of the square, then the primary space left to the urban designer is the key to its quality and usefulness, as the furniture, decor, lighting and grouping of people become the benches, planters, fountains, umbrellas, and grouping of people in the square.

Goldfinger explains to us that all of the senses are used in determining the quality of space and that space is experienced subconsciously—and usually at two levels. But there are other aspects in spatial awareness which need to be considered. Edward T. Hall's, *The Hidden Dimension,* explores the differences in spatial experience on an ethnic, or nationalistic level. That is to say, people from different cultural backgrounds perceive space differently. For example, Americans and Western Europeans depend more on solid, durable walls to achieve separation while Middle Easterners, lacking a strong architectural heritage rely on the subtle and momentary agents of enclosure that we noted earlier. The bazaar in Arab cities reflects this dynamic organization through the manipulations of merchants and craftsmen, angling for advantageous locations in the active, busy marketplace, thus creating a constantly shifting order of enclosure.

Westerners, and particularly Americans, do not tolerate the density or the organic quality of enclosure associated with Middle Eastern and Oriental cultures. But, as Hall demonstrates, even Western nations vary considerably from one another in their comprehension and uses of personal space.

Take time, as Hall has done, to observe people in groups. How close do they come to one another in face to face encounter? Try it yourself. At what point do you become uncomfortable? What is the distance you maintain and protect—your own personal space?

History reveals differences in spatial perception as well, and in rare instances we find these recorded in books written by form givers of the past. Leone Battista Alberti and Andrea Palladio developed rules for proportions to be used in the design of squares which were derived from musical harmonies as well as newly discovered methods of orthographic projection. Their efforts to develop method for the organization of external space were joined by many others, down through time, including such great design scholars as Giacomo da Vignola, Francois Blondel, and Le Corbusier.

By studying the history of urban space we also can become acquainted with the successful solutions of the past—those that have stood the test of time. And in doing so we can learn how designers met the problems of enclosing space, within the limitations and according to the dictates of their times. We will come to understand the degree to which they succeeded in their efforts only by understanding first the problems they faced and the methods at their disposal.

History never pauses in its reminder to us that *change* is the most significant and most constant factor in urban space. Political and social changes have an effect, of course, and age itself is a process of change, but unlike the other graphic arts—even architecture—the form and quality of external space is constantly in the process of movement. The shadows creep along the opposite facade, air currents blow against our face and stir the leaves, light varies with the sun and cloud cover, we are warm then cold. Our senses, you will remember, record a multitude of conscious and subconscious stimuli and we experience the space as a composite of all things present therein. We become familiar with the patterns of regular change—be they daily or seasonal, but in the end it is the passing of time which renders the square obsolete, or forces changes in form in order to keep up with changing needs and uses. Our study will record the shifting nature of urban space through history—as well as the square which has resisted change, resolving public needs in other ways. The square which is little changed through hundreds of years of usage might suggest to us that it was perhaps a nearly perfect solution originally and could not be improved upon even through time. Or perhaps *time,* for that particular place, has been standing still. A look through history might help us to know.

Although the great squares of the past call attention to themselves over the years, the *nature* of urban space remaims illusory, surprising, and often accidental. Gordon Cullen, in *Townscape,* reminds us that while a single building is architecture, two buildings is a townscape. No matter their relationship to one another, the space between them, planned or otherwise, is experienced as a tangible volume.

Some architects refer to this volume between buildings as *negative space,* just as planners often refer to open areas in the city as *voids.* The terminology speaks for itself, but regardless of intent—or lack of it—the placement of buildings (walls, trees,

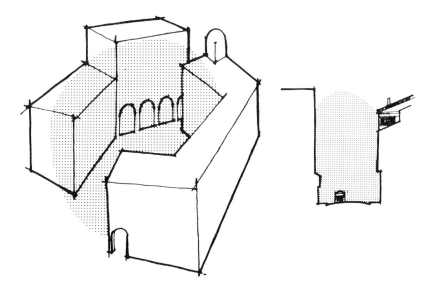

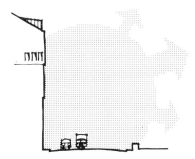

plant masses) alters or creates external space. And the meaning of such volumetrics is not always apparent at the outset, the *realization* of space coming only with the completion of the enclosing structures. The great, vertical shaft of space created by the twin towers of New York's World Trade Center is a striking example (as was the Rockefeller Center complex before it). The buildings that grew up around Grand Central Station enclosed a volume above the station that was commensurate with their size and distance from one another, until the Pan Am building was erected between them, at once rendering the major, viable space into several narrow *voids*—vertical slivers of space without meaning or value. In fact, the long range appraisal of high density, high rise urban design will most likely be made on the basis of developing and maintaining an appropriate ratio of mass to space. A ratio of some sort will always be present, as Cullen insists, whenever we have two or more buildings in some proximity to one another. Unfortunately, the space thus created is rarely considered to be more important than the buildings which create it, but it is nevertheless the more important contribution to the overall visual prospect of the city. The walls are thus the form givers of the greater space, and only when planned as such does the city begin to take on an identity which is both functional and

humanly pleasing to experience. The buildings of the Rue de Rivoli in Paris were designed with the external scale and volume of the streetscape in mind. Just the opposite is represented by Wilshire Boulevard in Los Angeles—a continuing Parade of grand, unrelated three dimensional billboards, each insisting on independent attention, using the space between them only as a means of separating and further individualizing the structures—a true example of *negative space* in use.

What quality or homogeneity the streetscape may achieve is usually dependent on some kind of city ordinance designed to protect air rights. For example, the skyscraper of the early twentieth century so threatened the quality of street space that a step-back ordinance was enacted in New York, and later in other major American cities, to prevent their streets from becoming

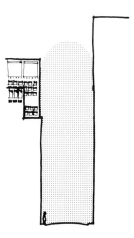

narrow, dark canyons. A walk through New York's financial district, where many of our first skyscrapers were built, will serve to demonstrate the logic of the step-back. In order to recreate that original straight line severity post-war architects surrendered volume at the base, as in the case of the Seagram Building, taking the entire step-back at the ground line, or in the pyramidal Trans-America Building in San Francisco, by rendering the step-back in an unbroken sloping line.

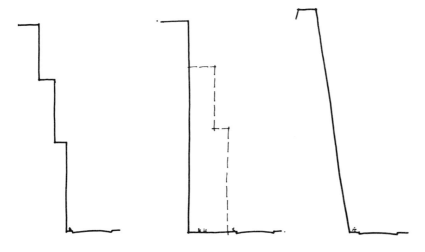

It has proven necessary then to regulate the forces which act upon the quality of public open space in the city. It would seem to make better sense, economically and aesthetically, to control the quality of public space by more direct means. By original design. In the rebuilding of Rotterdam, for instance, the planners began by first laying out plans for the entire city—streets, parks, and building masses. Then a larger, scale model was built so that they could carefully study the spatial quality created by the planned building complexes. Heights and set-backs of all structures were studied and finally determined from the standpoint of the volume of external space created, before actual construction commenced.

Following Rotterdam's post-war reconstruction, other cities in Europe took up the challenge of direct planning methods on a similarly large scale, and in the United States, from about 1950, the cities of Pittsburgh, Boston, Philadelphia, Hartford, and St. Louis have all engaged in massive planning and redevelopment of their central core areas.

The design of urban space is a two-fold process, you'll remember. After the mass/space ratio is resolved and the enclosing structures placed to best advantage in forming the external space, the *quality* of that space must be achieved, through precise detailing and placement of primary enclosing agents. At any rate the practice of designing urban space is not yet as exacting as we can expect, and in our study of its past record we shall encounter certain pitfalls in the planning of the square—including designs that were uncompromising and therefore shortlived, those that had merit once but should not be tried again, and schemes which ridiculed human scale and dignity—then as now. There is also the danger of borrowing horizontally—that is, from other contemporary cultures where concepts of personal space as well as climatic factors and building styles differ greatly.

Middle Eastern people tolerate a higher degree of density and require less in the way of tangible separation. Germans, according to Hall, need heavy doors and solid walls between them, while the English operate successfully by means of *implied* personal space, effectively shutting out everything beyond their range of understood boundaries.

We are at ease in public restrooms only when provided with real physical separation (modesty panels) between urinals, an idea difficult to comprehend in France and Italy. In Sweden public nude bathing is thought by most Americans to be in common vogue. Not so. Rigid practicality and a love for naturalness are responsible for the popularity of nude bathing, but the quality of aloofness in the Swedish character takes them to hidden spots and private stretches to practice it. In densely crowded Japan, however nude bathing is only possible through a cultural development of many centuries—an act of will to insure the dignity of individual privacy when it is physically impracticable. No one *looks* at anyone else unless directly engaged in conversation by that person. Japanese simply do not see private acts performed in public places. This understanding of privacy in public view is so well developed that when visiting in Western homes Japanese guests are reluctant to close doors—in fear of offending their hosts.

Urban spaces, from any time in history or any society on earth can tell us much about the quality of life enjoyed by its people. Some spaces are clearly the result of democratic usage, others suggest military purpose, pomp, and the monumentality of government. Some civic spaces afford people an opportunity to sit and talk, others provide only for listening. For some of us the importance of urban space is found simply in the space itself—breathing room in the crowded city. For others it is the opportunity for human exchange. This was brought home to me one early summer evening in the John F. Kennedy Plaza in Philadelphia, while a band played nostalgic tunes and people danced—yes, really danced, even selecting their partners from the crowds of onlookers!

People haven't changed as much as cities have, and for that reason public open space remains a vital requirement of urban life. The automobile has driven man from the streets of the city, and the depersonalization of modern commerce in most cities has further reduced our willingness to penetrate the urban fabric—beyond the minimum obligations of work. What public gathering places we still hold onto are all the more important in our struggle against further de-humanization. And the measure of a city's worth—in terms of its respect for the needs of its people—ought to be gauged by the quality of public space it manages to provide.

TWO

Form: The Structure of Urban Space

Urban space is generally represented by three broad categories: the street, the park, and the square. There are, of course, other kinds of public spaces which could be included in a dialogue on public open space, such as: school grounds, college campuses, incidental public spaces associated with libraries, court houses, sports parks, theatres, and the like. We shall not concern ourselves with the latter examples here because the public spaces involved are secondary to some other activity or their usage is limited, not available to the general public.

For that matter we can also eliminate private grounds and gardens, amusement parks, and the like. Naturally, all of these forms of open space have their purpose and use to the city, and in any overall accounting respective to urban space they should be noted. Disneyland, Tivoli Gardens, Versailles, and other such wonders of private endeavor add to the enrichment of a city's recreational/cultural development, but they do not represent any sense of civic trust, or concern for the quality of urban life. They are in fact *escape* oriented—a means of avoiding the realities around us. And of course, they aren't free. Public open spaces—the streets, parks and squares, open to all and maintained with pride, represent the reality of urban life at its best.

Before beginning an historic account of the development of public open space it will be necessary to make a few analytical comparisons—to develop the framework of our study. For instance, the differences between street and square seem very obvious to us—not worth the trouble to explain. But that wasn't always the case. The original public square—the marketplace—grew out of main street, simply through a widening process. Now

we see them as having quite opposite functions: one a gathering place, a coming together and stopping; the other a system of dispersal, of traffic and movement. The square, or gathering place, can be seen to augment a host of urban activities, some of the common forms being:

> *trade*—buying and selling, depository and manufacture of goods.
>
> *information*—from earliest times a place of social activity where news can be desseminated.
>
> *recreation*—passive activities, games, teaching, lunch and conversation, sociability.
>
> *protection*—in times past a place for preparing of the militia, training and drill, a place to gather in time of danger.
>
> *piety*—the open space before the church for worship, holy inspiration and prayer.

Squares may include several activities, as we will see in the example of the Classic Greek *agora*, but for the most part they tend to be somewhat more specific as to use. (We have no trouble determining the purpose of the market square, crowded with fruit stands and vendors, or the church square, filled with after-service activities.)

The city park, another kind of urban space altogether, differs from the square in lots of ways that are pretty obvious—but mainly in its basic purpose. The park is a *retreat*—a respite from the city, with its attendant complexities of sight and sound. An escape into a green oasis, away from hard edged gray geometry and congestion. The square, to the contrary, thrives on the rich tapestry of civic chaos. It may be a retreat from the street, but only a short one, for safety's sake. The city is never more than a holler away. The square is its heart and the beat should be felt.

There are many kinds of squares, respective of a great variety of need and endeavor. In the *Ten Books of Architecture,* Alberti wrote: "there ought to be several squares laid out in different parts of the city, some for the exposing of merchandises to sale in time of peace; others for the exercises proper for youth: and others for laying up stores in time of war, of timber, forage, and the like provisions necessary for the sustaining of a siege.[1]

These were needs Alberti saw in the urban life of Florence, about 1475. They are not so different today—only more complex, in keeping with the nature of the modern technological city. Generally we recognize the following kinds of squares in American cities:

market square	collegiate square
parade ground	civic center
green	mall
parvis (church square)	traffic island
residential square	

The market square, representing trade, is, of course, the first and *oldest* primary open space in the city. Its history has evolved from classic times when the exchange of goods had become an established factor in the growth and development of a city. Although contemporary sources refer to several market squares in ancient Rome, each catering to a specialized market, and writers of the Renaissance period, like Alberti, describe separate spaces for wood, metal, cloth, vegetables and so on, the single emporium, centrally located and readily accessible, has been the general rule down through history. This should be expected if we are to facilitate the exchange of goods. And in country towns throughout Europe—even in the United States in many places—or wherever technology has not completely overhauled basic economic nature, market day still functions in the manner of its time honored purpose. Today's shopping center represents the modern form into which the market square has evolved, and although it usually contains an element of central pedestrian space, it is largely a corruption of the original market square in that *center* is no longer a relevant term, the shopping center having fled to the suburban fringe.

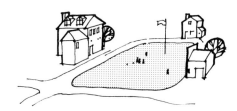

The *parade,* or parade ground evokes memories of Sunday concerts and uniformed bands during the long, hot summers in country towns across the midwest. The memory is firsthand perhaps to only the seasoned citizenry, and even so it represents only a vestige of its still earlier role—that of protection. Towns of the American frontier, as well as cities throughout history which were dependent upon their own resources for self-preservation, necessarily developed some form of home guard. Here the

1. Alberti, *The Ten Books of Architecture,* p. 173.

militia, the minutemen, the Indian fighters drilled and took their target practice, just as their counterparts had done before them. Little need for such activity remains today, with the exception of occasional ritual (Buckingham Palace's changing of the guard), and today the parade grounds, *place d'armes*, and *plaza de las armas* that remain are given over to some other function. (In English new towns the word parade indicates a secondary or neighborhood shopping street, an altogether different meaning.)

A similar kind of space, typical of all colonial New England towns, is the village *green*. It was the true American *agora*, organically formed as needs suggested, functioning as marketplace, gathering and social use, facing the church and important houses, and sufficiently ample for military drill.

The *parvis* is the name given to the church square and is usually located on the front side. This provides an opportunity for gathering before and after services, or in the case of St. Peter's Square in Rome, for receiving the papal blessing. It also allows for an uninterrupted view of the entry facade of the church or cathedral, providing a setting or frame for the structure. The parvis may be connected to or associated with secular spaces when, for example, church and city hall both face onto the same square. When the church or cathedral is placed high up on a hill, as was typical in the middle ages, the parvis is unrelated to other civic spaces.

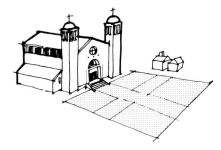

The urban space we refer to as the *residential square* is, of course, related to housing. Its beginnings in the seventeenth century mark the advent of informal public space—primarily the neighborhood park and the back yard. And in the beginning it was indeed a very informal kind of place—used for storage, parked carriages, and domestic activities. It wasn't until later that the enclosed area, nearly always surrounded by apartment buildings, acquired some kind of informal treatment, including trees, plant beds, sculpture, and the general qualities of a typical geometric garden. We shall concern ourselves particularly with the residential squares of Bath and Edinburgh where they eventually became an intrinsic aspect of the total planning scheme in those cities, during the late eighteenth and early nineteenth centuries.

The *collegiate square* is associated with schools and universities and generally is outside the scope of our study, due to limitations on public entry. Historically the collegiate square is thought of as a *closed* square, much for this reason; and to this day the squares of Oxford and Cambridge retain portcullis and barbican, as insurance against tourists, one supposes. But the major open space of medieval universities is with us as well, only somewhat modified, in the form of the *campus* (lat. "field").

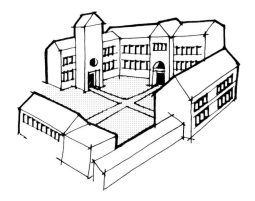

The modern *civic center* is represented in different times and places by such terms as *piazza della Signoria, radhausplatz, place d'hotel,* and the like, all generally meaning "government square." It is indeed the seat of local government, and facing the square we usually find the city hall, court house and regulatory facilities such as police or militia, jail and fire department. Andrea Palladio in the sixteenth century specified the buildings and the activities of government square, and most new world towns can be traced to their national origins (French, English, Spanish) by the strict adherence to prototypical planning of the town center. The modern American civic center may comprise a greatly varied complex of functions, including fire and police stations, library, court house, jail, post office, city hall, and art museum.

avenues of the radial system, and is usually represented by the round-about or *rond-point,* often accented by an obelisk, fountains or planting—depending on nationalistic design criteria. The traffic island is the opposite extreme of the collegiate square, by being the most open of all urban spaces, around and through which the constant flow of modern traffic swirls. As such it has usually become isolated from pedestrian usage—a forlorn vestige of times when men and carts could mingle in the crossroads without danger. Picadilly Circus and Charing Cross in London are two such vestiges of the past, while the *Place de l'Etoile* in Paris is a nineteenth century harbinger of future traffic—a traffic island to accommodate modern traffic a half century before its arrival.

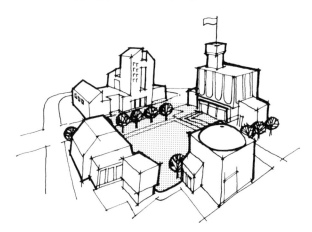

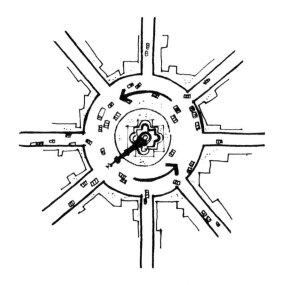

The *mall* is generally regarded as being a long, rectangular pedestrian space—a corridor through the city connecting major spaces or complexes of buildings at either end. Some of our present malls were originally mere city streets, but having been uplifted and reconsecrated through cosmetic design treatment now enjoy an elevated status and purpose. Nevertheless, the attenuated shape and the suggestion of *movement* rather than *place* keep the mall in the category of street rather than square.

The *traffic island,* for lack of a better term, is a meeting place for streets—a sorting out and dispersal of traffic flow. It is the most common form of connection in the network of streets and

These various public spaces have occurred throughout the history of urban development, and with little change in form or function continue to occur in cities today. With the exception perhaps of the parade all are found in some useful modern context.

Streets are the arteries—the lifelines of the city, carrying away its waste and bringing in a wealth of needs and luxuries. In principal there are only three kinds of street systems, all very old

but to have them wind about sometimes to the right, sometimes to the left, near the wall and especially under the towers upon the wall; and within the heart of the town, it will be handsomer not to have them straight but winding about several ways, backwards and forwards, like the course of a river. For thus, besides that by appearing so much the longer, they will add to the idea of greatness of the town, they will likewise conduce very much to beauty and convenience, and be a greater security against all accidents and emergencies. Moreover, the winding of the streets will make the passenger at every stop discover a new structure, and the front door of every house will directly face the middle of the street.[2]

and all still in use today in the modern city. The oldest *planned* system of street layout is the gridiron, dating back some 10,000 years in recorded history. Streets have always been the first matter of business in city building and it is worth noting that with only the simplest of means for making measurements early civilizations understood the basic organizational logic inherent to rectilinear planning.

But, a more natural order surely prevailed earlier, as evidenced from a variety of sources of primitive village layout, and later in situations where topography, or other considerations, took precedence over man-made order.

In fact, uneven, rough terrain was usually seleced for building sites because of advantages for defense. The whole of the Middle Ages is represented by *organic* street systems and heavy walls for protection, until the development of national powers and mobile armies reduced the need for cities to provide for their own protection. On the subject of street systems Alberti wrote:

> If it is only a small town or a fortification it will be better, and as safe, not for the streets to run straight to the gates;

Later, for reasons generated by a greater need to improve the flow of traffic, the radial system evolved. It is associated originally with Baroque planning, particularly seventeenth-century Rome and, later, Washington, D.C., and Paris (where all three street systems prevail). At either end of the *Champs*

2. Alberti, p. 75.

Elysees, the backbone of the city, are seen the definitive examples of radial (*Place de l'Etoile*) and gridiron (*Place de la Concorde*) systems, each with its grand array of vistas, which make possible a series of visual connections through the city.

Generally, as Alberti recognized in the fifteenth century, some form of organic street plan tends to be most applicable to cities of variable terrain (San Francisco notwithstanding), but even without the necessity of accommodating nature, planners have long appreciated the aesthetic advantages provided by curving streets. Promoted by John Wood and his followers who laid out the crescents at Bath and Edinburgh, and Frederick Law Olmsted's free flowing scheme for a subdivision at Riverside, Illinois, with its intermingling of streets and park corridors, there followed a plethora of curvilinear street plans, laid out over flat terrain or curving themselves like contour lines into the hillsides—giving a rice paddy look to the landscape of post-war American subdivision development. The curving layout escaped some of the monotony of gridiron regularity, while trapping the unwary in a disorienting maze of confused directions.

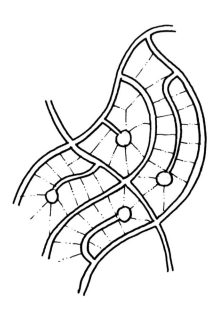

City parks are distinguished from squares primarily by *purpose.* The square is a gathering place, a centralized concept, a nucleus of urban activity. The city park evolved from the opposite need—respite for traffic, commerce, and crowds. As escape, parks are seldom seen in small rural towns, and only came into popular use in the cities after industrial growth had separated citizens from early access to the countryside. The park became, and still is, a glimpse of nature—idealized, romanticized after the eighteenth century English naturalist movement.

Size is also a factor, major city parks being as large as 4,000 acres, and on down to a minimum of five to ten acres for a neighborhood park. The values and purposes change when the park gets smaller than that, losing its prime function of retreat and separation from urban surroundings. It becomes in effect an open, green square.

The historic development of the public square can be traced through a series of *natural* and *behavioral* factors, resulting in distinction of physical form and functional purpose. These factors are outlined as follows:

Behavioral Determinants	Natural Determinants
Economic	Climatic
Political	Geographic
Social	Vegetative
Religious	Geologic
	Topographic

Economic

From Chapter one we learned that urban space is subject to constant change, minute-by-minute, daily, seasonal, over-the-years. The sun's steady movement and its accompanying shadow patterns, the light from the sky, the sun's angle and temperature changes, groups of people, crowds or empty space, changes in the surroundings, the enclosing agents and their specific activities all have their effects on urban space. The *Piazza della Fiore*, a market square in Rome, goes through a daily metamorphosis. In the early morning it is open, quiet and tranquil. One is aware only of the simple beauty of its medieval and Renaissance enclosure. Then rather suddenly it springs to life with the arrival of the merchants—clothing salesmen, food vendors, craftsmen—all unfolding and setting up their stalls, defending against the sun with bright colored cloth awnings and drapes. It becomes a carnival—a hubbub of noise and color, excited crowds, housewives shopping for the dinner, children running about, until dusk when the color and clutter clear away leaving it just as it had been in the early morning light. This is the way of the market square, still functioning as a daily market—not only in historic Rome, but in modern Stockholm and Los Angeles as well. In this simple view, it represents the basic economic factor which helped to develop the archaic village of Athens into a great classic city, and the mountain citadels of Europe's Dark Age into the powerful trade centers of the Middle Ages, and eventually London's Covent Garden and Paris' *Les Halles*—two well-known central markets of the eighteenth and nineteenth centuries. These are examples of purely economic institutions, and they illustrate this factor in simplest terms. In most modern examples the economic determinant is not so obvious, but it is always there—and is associated with *every* aspect of the square's design, particularly *form, shape, size* and *location*.

Political

We associate the political factor with a specific kind of square—the civic center, but more significantly, we have learned to recognize the political nature of a society—or a particular government—by its respect for and usage of public space. The Greeks used public space wisely, as a basic tenet of their understanding of government, while the Persians of classic times disregarded it. Imperial Rome used open space in a larger, more formal way. Here, and in totalitarian cultures generlly, public space has been used as a means of collecting and ordering the masses. The great square at Nurnburg which Adolph Hitler built, as well as the wide, formal streets and grand spaces Mussolini envisioned for his modern Rome, are examples.

The political structure of any society can be ascertained to some extent by its handling of public space, you will recall. Formality, grandness of scale and proportion tend to deny a sense of individuality or variety of endeavor, replacing these with a ritualistic order and mass response—a characteristic of a despotic political structure. Informal arrangement, scaled to a level of individual participation, suggest a quality of urban space respectful of democratic institutions.

Social

The social factor in design represents the effects of class structure and the horizontal as well as vertical mobility existing in the system. Upper, middle, and lower classes have usually been represented in the make-up of society through history, but in greatly varying percentages and mobility. During the Middle Ages we know, for example, that the majority of people existed at the bottom rung (the legs and trunk of society), while the nobility (representing the arms) and the clergy (the head) made up the rest. The rise of a middle class in medieval society (the *Bourgeoisie*) is first noted by the accompanying rise in trade, and the growing dependence on commerce as a source of revenue and power.

Today, most of us in the United States are middle class. Through a continuing process of growth and change in economic and political institutions, our society has seen the virtual disappearance of both lower and upper classes. Trade unions and the right to vote, along with the elimination of titles and the introduction of the graduated income tax have seen to it, and, after countless centuries, there are no more slaves. So here we are, a vast middle class, rubbing elbows and sharing public conveniences—a significant fact to keep in mind in the planning of urban space.

Religious

We shall discover the degree of importance which religion plays in any urban structure by observing the placement of the church, in respect to the form of the city—often at the highest point—like the Parthenon, Chartes Cathedral, or Sacre Coeur in Paris, with *fleche* and towers silhouetted against the sky. We also find the church dominating the central marketplace, sharing the square with civic buildings or in possession of its own square, adjacent or connected to the central square. The church square has an important part to play in the development of city space, as we shall see.

Now consider the five natural determinants as they apply to urban form.

Climatic

Climatic conditions, particularly precipitation and temperature change, rank as the most important on the list of natural factors. In planning urban space we must ask questions like, "how many days of sunshine can we expect anually? What is the temperature range—seasonally and daily? What is the direction and velocity of prevailing winds?" We must plan for snowfall, runoff from storms, the treachery of ice and the heat of an August day. Aside from the physical qualities inherent in conditions of weather, there are some subtle but significant emotional aspects to consider too. Fountains, for example, and water display in general are most useful in the dryer, warmer climatic zones. In the cool, wet climate of London, however, the great, gushing fountain at Trafalgar Square—like the Halprin Fountains in Portland, Oregon—only serves to remind a cold, sodden public of the nature of their discomfort. Fountains came to English parks and squares after the Renaissance, along with classic architectural styles, which for similar reasons did not adapt well to the northern climates, and required the addition of a great many chimneys and fireplaces to keep them warm. The high ceilings and large windows of Georgian and Palladian structures in the North, with their problems of heat loss and inefficiency, illustrate

an early example of style succeeding over organic design logic. In our own times we can, of course, find many better examples, suggesting that technology is often called upon to replace reason.

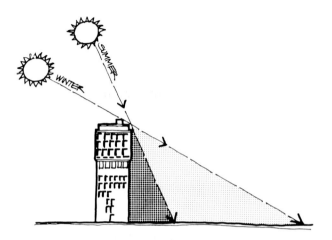

Geographic

The geographic factor affects climate by way of sun angle—the further North the lower that angle, hence the cooler the temperature, the fewer hours there are of sunlight, the longer the shadows that we see cast across the square. We can determine the angle of the sun seasonally, or daily, from available charts, as it moves across the southern sky. Roof overhangs, trees and other kinds of screening devices can be placed precisely to control the sun. Looking south we can watch the sun rise to our left, reach its zenith at noon and sink to our right. But when we face east or west we must abide the sun's rising (or setting) directly before us (a little to the left or right depending on the season) and no amount of screening can blot it out, short of solid walls. Facing north we see the sun only as it rises and sets during the summer. The low angle made by the sun in northern latitudes makes it necessary to reduce the probability of shadow, which during the winter months can totally engulf a city square. For this reason northern cities tend to be spread out, with fewer tall buildings but wider streets, just as cities nearer the equator usually have a denser, more vertical structure, with narrower streets and fewer open areas. The angle of the sun, including the varying hours of daylight, assure that no single design concept for urban space can be universally applied.

Vegetative

The vegetative factor refers to plant material—shrubs, grasses, and trees, particularly as they relate to usage in parks and squares. Irrespective of the basic design form of the space— be it geometric or curvilinear or amorphous—the type of plant material and its maintenance often play the major role in portraying the character of the place.

But it is from the much more significant standpoint of *ecosystematic* design, and the seeking of balance between environmental and technological demands that the vegetative factor plays the greater role in urban design. We may view the use of plant material in the city at two levels then. In the *narrower* view we are simply concerned with the aesthetic use of plants and their function as a contrasting element to the gray angularity of the surrounding city. For example, such concerns as: in colder climates do we use primarily deciduous trees to allow the winter sun to come through? What are the shade requirements for street trees in order to protect against the glare and heat of summer or the tropics? Do shrubs, vines, and ground covers reduce heat and glare (which bounces off glass and paved surfaces)? Does grass offer a softer underfoot without substantial increases in maintenance costs?

But in the *broader* sense vegetation in the city can play a major environmental role, relative to:

noise reduction	control of airborn pollutants
visual screening	microclimatic change
temperature reduction	wind control
regulating humidity	retention of soil water

We are learning only lately something of the awesome effects that technology has wrought on climate. The vast conurba-

tions of today, spreading over hundreds of square miles, deprive those areas of most natural ecological processes. The absence of trees affects weather, preventing or even causing rain, upsetting the stability of air layers, and greatly increasing temperature highs, especially in tropical cities. Bangkok has experienced radical climatic change following the removal of its vast network of tree-lined canals. (This gigantic error was perpetrated by U.S. Army and Air Force engineers because of an alleged "bad odor," during the Viet Nam conflict when upwards of 100,000 American personnel were stationed in Bangkok.) The overlaying of paved surfaces prevents natural percolation of surface runoff, most of which ends up being channeled into rivers or storm drains, resulting in a continuous lowering of the water table and a need to import water to the city from greater and greater distances. Most airborn pollutants, particularly dust and industrial waste, are reduced by the natural filtering of foliage, just as noise and wind are lessened in the city by judicious planting. Choosing the proper trees and other plants can play an important part in energy conservation, but that's another story.

Geologic

The geologic factor is concerned with soil and subsurface structure. It involves drainage, compaction, stability for construction—basically the chemical and physical make-up of the ground we build on and grow in. We need to know what it can support—in the way of architecture and plant life. It is also importantly related to producing materials for construction. Stone, brick, slate, tile, cedar, redwood, adobe, fir all come from the

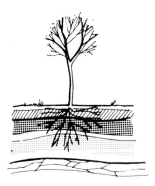

ground, and are usually cheaper in areas where plentiful. The conditions of nature have long been a factor in the materials as well as the methods of building.

Topographic

Topographic conditions reflect the slope of the land. Is it hilly, mountainous—or flat? Many medieval towns, built on hilltops, have squares which are stepped or steeply sloped, as in Arezzo, Italy, or St. Paul de Vence in southern France. Approaching a square from above or below makes a difference in how we perceive that space. Generally, it is advantageous to arrive from above. It is physically easier, if on foot, and gives us visual command of the space, telling us what we need to know about it—locations of things, circulation patterns, places to rest.

From below the space remains aloof, challenging, unattainable. It is for this reason that temples, cathedrals—most religious shrines, have been located on elevated sites since the earliest times. Even in the central square the entrance to the church is usually found to be a flight of steps above the square.

Determination of Form

The form of the square, as well as its size, location, and overall shape, are to a large extent determined by the natural and behavioral characteristics cited above. Within these limitations the finite determination of form must emerge, dependent upon the outer enclosing agents and the inner structure of the square. Most of these, regardless of historic precedent, fall into two rather general categories:

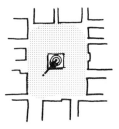

(1) *Centric.* When the volume of space is generated from the center, created by a series of sight lines or directional forces beginning at or terminated by a central point such as an obelisk, statue or fountain, the space is referred to as *centric.* The directional forces may radiate outward from the center along streets or

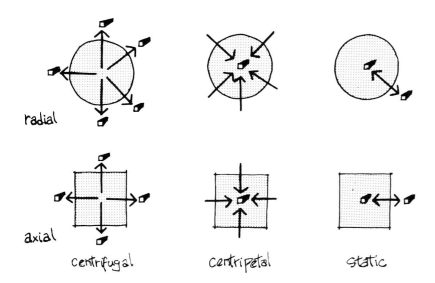

radial

axial

centrifugal   centripetal   static

being *static*. This is more likely in *axial* designed squares. You can stand at the central point and determine for yourself whether the square seems to be exploding outward, down predetermined avenues to distant termini, or whether it draws towards itself, where a final visual crescendo of space and form is enacted.

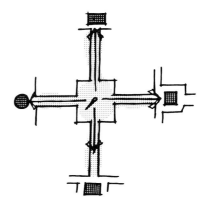

malls which are themselves visually terminated by other squares or *eye-catching* forms. This type of centric square is *centrifugal* and *radial*. When the visual forces are reversed, the *radial* square is said to be *centripetal*, or directed inward.

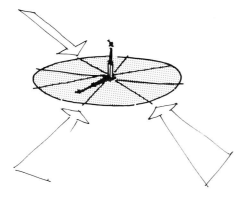

The other type of centric square (axial) depends upon a single axis or double axis, crossing through the central point. The visual forces may be outward—away from the center or inward, depending upon the emphasis at either end of the various sight lines, or the directional forces may be counterbalanced, the result

The centric square is usually carefully planned, and the subject of a later chapter, where it will be dealt with in greater depth.

There is another, less precise form of centric space which derives from empirical form determination: the *amorphous space*, ill formed, without character or aesthetic value generally, having been formed by accident of urban evolution, is without spatial order. Its enclosing structures are unrelated in scale, location, or detail. There is generally a lack of organization—no volumetric order to the space. Amorphous spaces can be saved by designing a centric system which de-emphasizes the dissimilar enclosing elements and develops a strongly centripetal spatial form. Gianlorenzo Bernini accomplished this on several occasions simply by careful location of a single obelisk. This device is referred to by Paul Zucker as the *nuclear* square.

(2) *Enclosed.* The second type of space is basically the opposite, in that its success depends upon an *open center* and a strongly defined enclosing structure. We can refer to this as *enclosed* space, the volumetrics of which depend almost entirely upon the scale and detail of the surroundings (architectural

detailing, fencing, walls, trees, and shrubbery), the overhead (awnings, trees, umbrellas) and the grid pattern or other detailing in the ground plane. The *enclosed* square is solid and obvious. There is usually a clear line of demarcation between what is square and what is not, and unless there are other devices available by which to give it direction and scale it may seem to be static. Forces of movement may be generated within the square, by the inner details, the rhythm and build-up of visual forces in the architectural detailing, or the use of color and value emphasis. But the strongest means of developing direction in a basically open space is by use of a dominating structure—a tower, a free-standing *campanile* or a major building at one end of the square. This may be the city hall, the parish church, a library, or anything substantial. The important thing is its visual dominance, which allows the other enclosing buildings to play subordinate roles.

Now a sense of direction exists, and if the dominant structure or form resides at the terminus of the *long axis* (a), the strength of the square is fused into a single spatial statement. When the major structure resides at the end of the *short axis* (b), the open space may be split visually, like an amoeba, into two smaller spaces of equal size, by the force of the axial sight line alone. This is called *duality*, and it is enforced by strengthening the termini at each end of the long axis by porticos and fountains, as:

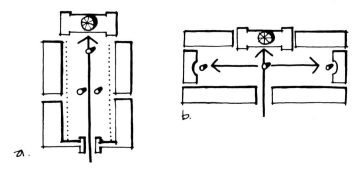

Where a single building dominates the square, and generates direction by visual forces, Zucker uses the term *dominated* square. Most open squares profit by the domination of one

building over the others, thereby avoiding a uniformly static sense of enclosure. The problem of over-dominance may arise occasionally, in which case the building takes over completely and the square is relegated to the subordinate role of providing a setting for viewing the structure. We can judge this possibility for ourselves in our own cities, or by studying some well-known examples, such as the Piazza San Marco, in Venice.

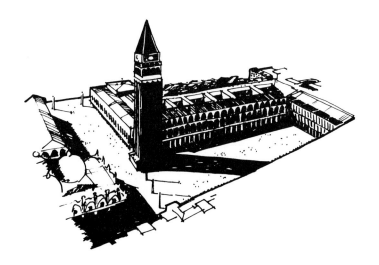

Does the facade of St. Mark's Cathedral dominate to the detriment of the square, or does it merely add emphasis as the dominant enclosing agent?

The enclosed square is also charged by the existence of a vertical element, like the tower or *campanile* mentioned earlier. It can become the means of giving direction or emphasis to the square. More significantly it may also add an element of *vertical* balance. The square normally tends to be horizontal in line, due to the nature of the enclosing buildings. A tower, campanile, or other vertical element works as a directional counterbalance, not overcoming the horizontal emphasis but reducing its force. Without vertical relief the quality of the square suffers from dullness.

The balancing of directional forces in the square by addition of a singular vertical element is variously expressed through history. *Centric* as well as *enclosed* squares usually possess some form of vertical element, the difference being in point of location. Look again to the Piazza San Marco, where the campanile functions not only as the vertical balancing agent, but as pivotal point between merging spaces, and as a tool of overall urban scale, bringing the square into relationship with the city as a whole.

A similar and perhaps better example is the Washington Monument in its relationship to a series of horizontal sight lines and visual termini.

There is also seen in this balance of directional forces a symbolic sexual relationship—the open horizontal square being feminine, the upright solid form being masculine. This idea of male symbolism is carried out by *campanile*, tower, obelisk, sculpture, church spire, monumental column, pyramid, dome, and even the single jet of a fountain. Does it result from aesthetic balance—a need to regulate vertical and horizontal dimensions for the sake of visual beauty? Or does it emanate from a more primitive emotional need—a *yin* and *yang* relationship of life's forces? We don't know for sure, but we do know how strongly we are affected by it and how necessary it has apparently always been to society, from the evidence of primitive villages to our most sophisticated modern spaces.

What are the reasons behind the various shapes found in squares? A square can be square, hence its English name. But the various names derived from Latin (*platea*; place or widened street), are more cautious, and refer to location rather than shape: *Place* (French), *Piazza* (Italian), *Praça* (Portuguese), *Plaza* (Spanish), *Plateia* (Greek). A square (or place) can be *circular* (radius point, no axis), *elliptical* (three radius points, major and secondary axes), *octagonal* (sympathetic to radial usage, but having *three* equal axes), *rectangular* (possessing major and secondary axes), *square* (two equal cross axes), and *amorphous* (organic, dialectic). The form a square takes is related to its function—as a singular urban space or as part of a system of interrelated streets and squares. Shape is determined by the particular purposes for that square, as explained earlier in this chapter, and by the dictates of taste. Geometric forms tend to limit the possibilities for changes, and to complete themselves in our mind's eye even when interrupted or altered by other forms. Amorphous forms blend readily into the fabric of their surroundings, giving way easily to change, but adding little to the drama of man-made creation. The form of the square may eschew change in urban design or it may enhance it, but nothing we do in the design of urban space will eliminate change—or freeze time at its robust pinnacle, as Baroque architecture attempted, for the elements of nature and man prescribe against it, and are forever engaged in its progress.

THREE

Time: The Development of Spatial Order

The history of human settlement is divided broadly into three eras:

The Hunter state
The Agrarian state
The Industrial state

These divisions refer to primary *economic* methods employed to sustain society and life, and should not be confused with the more common *political* eras:

ancient
middle (Medieval)
modern

History has been studied and divided many different ways, but for our part economic divisions are the most appropriate in describing the growth and development of settlement patterns—from village to market town to city.

Hunter State

The Hunter state is measured from the dawn of man's existence until roughly 10,000 B.C. In basic economic terms it is the period of man's nomadic life—when he was required to pursue his food and clothing. In order to survive he was obliged to follow the wild herds and likewise to follow the seasons in search of bark and berry or edible root, to gather fuel and food in the manner of nearly all animal life. Little or no settlement was involved in the life of a family tribe—only temporary encampment for protection. No roots, and therefore no civilization.

Agrarian State

The second era in man's history describes a major economic change in his pattern of living. The Agrarian period, from 10,000 B.C. to 1800 A.D. finds man in virtual control of his supply of food and clothing. It is the time of man the producer, through the development of farming—hunter turned shepherd, gatherer turned planter. Now he could settle down somewhat, build permanent housing, enjoy a safer, more comfortable life style—and begin to multiply.

Village life is the obvious result of a stable social order. For protection and convenience, neolithic culture produced a variety of permanent shelters arranged to meet basic needs. During the twelve thousand years of the Agrarian state, cultural growth was considerable—from rough, protective settlements to the great cities of Europe and the Orient, which reached the pinnacle of existence by the close of the eighteenth century. What they had in common—rude settlement and great cosmopolitan city—was their similar dependence upon agriculture as the primary economic force of their times.

25

Tools were greatly refined, of course, over this long period, but it took the harnessing of new sources of power to change dramatically the basic economic structure of society, and usher in the present era.

The Industrial State

The Hunter state lasted conservatively five hundred millenia and changed the face of the earth very little. The Agrarian state in only twelve millenia left its considerable mark, through agriculture, grazing, mining, and the depletion of forests. The Industrial state in one-fifth of one millenium has wrought tremendous change, not only to the surface but the air above and the mineral resources beneath. In only one hundred and fifty years man reached the peak of wastefulness, and now faces exhaustion of most traditional resources. To survive, the Industrial state must produce its own safeguards, its own means of salvation from the dangers of its own causing.

Our study of urban space deals with the growth of community—from agrarian village to present industrial urban organization. It involves recognition of behavioral and natural factors which affect the development and form of all environmental design, as well as urban space in particular. Changes of a technological nature—man's inventiveness—are also involved in the process shaping our environment.

The various social sciences we study in order to better equip ourselves to become environmental designers include psychology, sociology, political science, anthropology, and philosophy. These form the basis of the behavioral factors discussed in Chapter Two. The natural sciences required of an environmental designer include biology (botany), ecology, and the earth sciences. Geography has characteristics of behavioral and natural factors.

In the design of his environment man has always reflected these factors—consciously or unconsciously—in his solutions. In a similar way the student makes use of behavioral and natural sciences to properly equip himself for engaging in the design process.

Environmental Process

From the earliest recorded times man has applied method to his search for solution to environmental problems. Mostly trial-and-error to begin with, method eventually became the primary consideration in the practice of architecture and the environmental arts, and students have been subjected to variations and innovations in method as long as there have been schools to teach them. The seventeenth century *philosophers* invented "modern method," followed by "scientific method" and the works of Isaac Newton and Christopher Wren. Under Napoleon III both the *Beaux Arts* and the *Ecole de Polytechnique* methods were simultaneously in vogue, producing very different solutions during the reconstruction of Paris under Baron Haussmann. In more recent years Frank Lloyd Wright's *organic* method is often compared against Le Corbusier's *modular*. And today there are the computer generated processes. In Landscape Architecture we are familiar with the work in methodology developed by Angus Hills of Great Britain, Ian McHarg, Phil Lewis, and Julius Fabos.

Process, or method, is the means by which we develop solutions to problems, and all process, from the complex Cartesian systems of the seventeenth century to the computer aided programs used by contemporary urban designers, eminate from two basic root forms: *empirical* and *rational*.

Empirical process, like scientific method, is generated by trial-and-error. In terms of urban design it is achieving a solution to the form of the square over a long period of usage and infinite corrective adjustments. Empirical method should not, however, be confused with *irrational* approach, by which success is achieved accidentally, obliquely. Nor is it somehow connected with the school of art by that name. Empirical method does at times involve accident, but can be very scientific and precise. Its prime arguments are (1) that the complexities of spatial design wrought by continual change, both short and long range, are sufficient to require the integral of *time*, and (2) that change, being a prime factor inherent to all urban space, continual adjustment to design solutions becomes necessary. Adherents to empirical method argue that the design for a plaza, with all of the various natural factors of change at work, can only be perfectly correct during one moment of the day—and seasonally, only one time of the year (or twice, considering both vernal and autumnal equinoxes). Finally, applying the third dimension in time, the plaza is successful only so long as it remains contemporary—that is, meeting the immediate needs of the society for which it was designed. Is the *Place de la Concorde*, that gigantic fulcrum of Parisian axes, as meaningful today, choked with high speed traffic, as it was in the eighteenth Century? Does the self-conscious natural charm of Brooklyn's Prospect Park carry the same hopeful message to the crowded surroundings that it did in the 1870s?

Rational process is certainly clearer, and an approach with which students often feel more comfortable. A rational solution is a singular commitment of process to form—done at one time for all time. It assumes a logic for continual usefulness based on a principle which we can call the "unchanging nature of man." Physically, emotionally, intellectually, any change in man's nature is so gradual as to be inconsequential in respect to the design of a specific place, like the foregoing plaza. Proponents of rational process would point out that a design failure results from a poor or incomplete program—that the criteria were not properly assembled, causing misapplication of data, resulting in the wrong solution. In other words, if the program is complete, if the factors relating to the need are carefully gathered and assessed, and if a mature physical design emerges, based on the accuracy and priority of these factors, then the solution will continue to succeed as long as basic conditions remain the same. And change be damned. But even the rationalists concede that the times during which Michelangelo designed the *Piazza del Campidoglio* were far different from our own. The empirical view, respecting change, would note that the *Campidoglio* no longer functions as the Capitol of Rome, that the beaurocracy of statecraft long ago outgrew the modest facilities leaving us a relic to history, nearly without modern function. Nor is the style of the High Renaissance any longer in vogue, nor the centric piazza, crowned by the equestrian Marcus Aurelius.

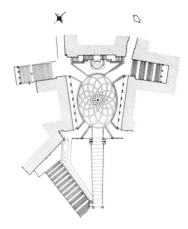

But the rationalist would certainly point to the perfection of spatial balance and scale—as correct today as in the sixteenth century because man's perception of space and scale have not changed. Proportion, scale, form, rhythm, value—these are timeless qualities of design, not to be confused with "style" and "taste" which vary in the utmost.

r CLASSIC		e MEDIEVAL				r RENAISSANCE				e INDUSTRIAL	
Greek e	*Roman* r	*Early* *Christian* e	*Byzantine* r	*Romanesque* e	*Gothic* r	*Early* *Ren.* e	*High* *Ren.* r	*Baroque* e	*Neo-* *Classic* r	*19 C.* e	*20 C.* r

Each environmental period that we study, each ethnic, geographic, volumetric stipulation we are required to consider makes us ever more aware of these two fundamental approaches to design process. Of course, these views represent the extreme examples of empirical and rational process. Most work reflects a mixture, with one or the other tending to dominate.

Using western culture for illustration we can, by considerable oversimplification, trace the major and secondary epochs of environmental design history, as they reflect these tendencies toward process.

The small letters "r" and "e" represent dominance by either rational or empirical processes. You will note that the major divisions in environmental design history alternate regularly, as do the secondary periods. Developmental epochs in design tend to be empirical, suggesting a *search* for form or style. Rational periods reflect an *acceptance* of style and a search for perfection, or at least improvement. Historians refer to three definitive periods in any art form as *archaic* (learning), *classic* (achieving), and *baroque* (embellishing).

Looking at the chart we can see that while the Classic Period in art is generally regarded as being rational, the Roman half is even more so. The Middle Ages reflect primarily an empirical quality in design process, although Gothic is less so than Romanesque, and, the most rational of all periods, the Renaissance has its internal variations, Early Renaissance and Baroque being developmental.

Builders of Romanesque churches and cathedrals were still struggling with form and engineering technique in searching for the ideal means of expressing in stone the essence of their faith. In the Gothic Cathedral that struggle had nearly ended. A solution to spatial relationships, which Bruno Zevi calls "dimensional

contrast," had been found. The Renaissance, on the other hand, is a highly rational period in history, beginning with an experimental century during which architects were making a transition from Gothic to Classic, blending the old with the even older to form a neoclassic style from an empirical method. About that time Leone Alberti came along with his rulebook, followed in the sixteenth Century by a host of other architectural rulemakers, and the neoclassic structure of the Renaissance settled into a rather strict, formal mold. Then in the second half of the period—the seventeenth and eighteenth centuries—we see the formula repeated.

We can also see from the chart that periods of dominant design process tend to alternate, regardless of actual lengths of time involved; again an oversimplification, but nonetheless an indicator of cyclical behavior.

In this chapter we have dealt with the economic divisions in history, as they relate to the determination of form and the design processes. Using the four behavioral factors in relationship to environmental form and process, we can summarize as follows:

Economic factors evolve from three basic historic states— nomadic, agrarian, industrial. Urban space originated in the economic factor, trade—the result of settlement, during which a basis for civilized culture was established. The need for a division of labor led to specialization, and to refinement and surplus—the necessary ingredients of trade. With the development of surplus goods and foodstuffs, along with refinement in craftsmanship, a village found itself in the enviable position of mercantilism. The farmers, leatherworkers, weavers, potters, carvers brought wealth to the village through trade advantage. The market square resulted from the importance of trade in respect to the well-being of the village—on its way to becoming a market town.

Political factors help to delineate the quality, scale, and form of architecture, from tyranny to democracy, according to Zevi. The existence of a square, no matter its particular shape or function, suggests an open society, free to use the space for a variety of purposes, in addition to its being a market. The functions of government have faced the square, from the *bouleterieon* of Athen's ancient *agora* to the civic center of today. Government square has through history readily assumed the form dictated by process, and the natural and behavioral determinants of form, including the need for parade grounds, dissemination of information to the populace, and engaging in public meetings.

Religious factors led to the situating of towns through the establishment of monastic orders. As *process*, religious fervor has made heavy demands on the skills of artisans and builders. The architecture of the Middle Ages, Gothic, is different from the following age, the Renaissance, for primarily religious reasons. The difference lies in another kind of empirical/rational debate,

namely: *spiritualism* vs. *humanism*. The growth of religion is mirrored in the art and architecture of the world. The gradual change from fear to faith, and eventually to compassion and love of mankind marks the emergence of modern theology throughout the world. The location of towns and the use of open space result from the theological dictates of Christianity, Islam, Judaism, Hinduism, Buddhism, and other modern faiths, which not incidentally, are also formgivers.

Social factors, in terms of design process, are tied to the class structure of society. A free society may mean one thing socially and another politically. Ancient Athens was politically democratic—for the 40 percent of the population who weren't slaves. Society, regardless of political institutions is primarily a matter of class structure. Is there a titled class, or simply an upper class? Does the upper and middle class make up only 15-20 percent of the population (as in nineteenth century England) or does the middle class alone make up 90 percent of the total, (as in modern United States which includes upper middle, middle middle, and lower middle)? Is there a classless society in existence, as Marx promised, and if so, what can we expect will be its impact on design process and the form of urban space?

Keep these factors in mind as we study several basic periods in history, and apply the means of measurement dealt with in these first chapters to the quality of urban space as it unfolds through time.

Agra, 1865 (Illustrated London News)

The basic elements of enclosure common to Western Cities are often misleading or subordinate to more flexible, ever-changing controls in Eastern societies. People, the crowd in the bazaar, become the enclosing agents, along with their wares, animals, stacks of goods . . . . the sounds of vendors, the feel of the hot sun on our face, the smell of food preparation, people and oxen, the touch of the many colored draperies complete a picture of sensory awareness.

Stockholm (Göste Glase)

Stockholm Berzelii Square (Reportagerud)

London. Trafalgar Square

People are the most important ingredient to the square, giving scale, color, dynamics, and at times acting as the walls—the primary enclosing agents of the immediate space. A public festival in Stockholm, a sidewalk cafe, Londoners sitting on a fountain or tourists in Trafalgar Square—all help to create a kind of shifting enclosure.

A square is often structured around a central element, which acts as a fulcrum to spatial balance. A church on one of the sides may tend to dominate and give direction to the space. A square of indistinct form may depend on such central objects as fountains or sculpture to give spatial definition, and dominance from within.

Frankfurt. Bernhard Square (Renner)

Bergamo. Piazza Vacchio (ENIT)

Rome

Sculpture in the square. What he sees at eye level is what is most important to the participator as he passes through a space.

Augsburg
(Schröder)

Stuttgart

Stockholm

Female symbolism. The representation of Yin and Yang balance in the square. Public space is by nature horizontal, open, receptive—idealized feminine characteristics.

Los Angeles Mall

San Francisco
Ghirardelli Square
(S.F. Conv. & Visitors Bur.)

Male symbolism. To achieve a sense of balance in line and mass the design of the square has often required a contrasting vertical element. Is it sexual symbolism in a Yin and Yang relationship or mere aesthetic judgment?

Bologna (ENIT)

Augsburg (Schneiders, Lindau-Schachen)

Paris
Place Vendome
(French Nat. Tour. Office)

Bonn. Marktplatz (Foto Sachsse Bonn, Werbe—U. Verlsehrsamt Bildarchia)

The rathaus (1737-8) stands before the marketplace as the dominant enclosing structure, a typical combination since the empirical development of classic Greek towns. The square's flexibility of function is pictured on these pages. Note the organizing functions of the obelisk (right).

The open square as Beethoven knew it; and (below) the square as it continues to function on market day.

(O. Fazler)

A typical empirical market square, faced by church and city hall. When social interaction is counted all four behavioral factors are found here.

Freiburg. Markplatz (W. Pragher)

Thirsk, Yorks. The market square. Note the obelisk, acting as identifying agent, central organizer, and masculine/vertical balancing agent.

Florence. Sta. Croce (ENIT)

The use of the parvis for storing automobiles denies the space to various human activities, and is aesthetically disturbing to the facade of the church as well.

The government square in Hamburg (right) is dominated by the Rathaus. This photo demonstrates the square's continuing use in formal gatherings and military protocol.

Hamburg. Rathausplatz (Andres & Co.)

The parvis in front of Alberti's famous facade. Here the space is sufficiently generous to site the structure properly. Note male and female symbolism.

Florence. Piazza S. Maria Novella (ENIT)

Savannah, Ga. Monterey Square (Mottelay
& Campbell—Copeland) Beehive Press

The square (left) during the American Civil War
shown in its functions as a parade ground for
drilling confederate infantry soldiers.

The government square has served as a parade or
drill ground since medieval times, as suggested
here by way of an historic re-enactment in
Florence.

Florence—Piazza della Signoria (ENIT)

Grand military review of troops of the Sondefund,
in Freiburg, 1848.

Freiburg, Ger. (Illustrated London News)

Los Angeles. The Arco Towers. Prodigy of Mies' rectangular simplicity, the towers enclose a shaft of space both awesome and repelling. Its verticality and scale prevent any sense of human relationship despite the trees and fountain. (L.A. Planning Dept. Ed Rondot)

Los Angeles. The new high-rise structures dwarf the library (lower right). In both pictures note the use of female/horizontal organizers in the squares, where vertical enclosing agents here dictate a reverse of the standard centric form. (Ed Rondot)

FOUR

Order Defined: Classic Spatial Heritage

Given the form determinants and a design methodology it is possible to analyze objectively the contributions to urban space made by various groups of people through history. Cities leave records in stone and steel respective of their accomplishments—their values in general, and that kind of record can be very useful in assessing culture. We know something of the role that religion played in medieval society simply from the abundance of church architecture. We know something of the quality and fervor of Christianity as well, from the very style of that architecture. Ancient Egyptian society was also motivated along religious lines, but the evidence left in stone describes a very different theology. The Egyptian form givers attempted to mislead posterity by propagandizing a social and political order that never existed, carving a hypothetical culture into the monuments they left behind. It is not uncommon, therefore, for the established order to hope occasionally to influence history. A good detective must look beyond the monumental façades and colonnades and look deeper into the way things worked.

Primitive cultures are usually more straight forward in respect to the evidence they leave. The societies at Machu Picchu, and Pomeiock left no books or other records of their cultures with which to confuse us. Machu Picchu, high in the Andes Mountains of Peru, is a miracle of building technology, employing methods for lifting and placing huge stones which continue to baffle modern scientists and engineers. Visitors marvel at the technical and artistic skill demonstrated by these mute walls, and by the level of social order that the organization of buildings suggests. Near the center of the city there is a large, grassy open space. No one knows how it was used by the ancient

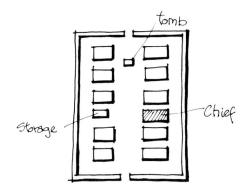

Incas who lived here, but it was most certainly a gathering place of some kind—in short, a square. Open space at their centers is not uncommon for most primitive societies. Sometimes the arrangement of enclosing agents is quite regular, as the Indonesian village of Toba Batak (above) suggests, while the plan for Gbande (below), a primitive fortified village in Liberia, is more organic in its organization. In most such examples a clearly em-

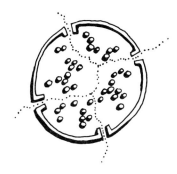

49

pirical order is present and functioning in the arrangement of living quarters.

In about 1585 John White, an English explorer, made a sketch of the village of Pomeiock in North Carolina. In this restruction we can easily ascertain the physical organization, use of the central space, means of circulation and function of the protective encircling pallisade. Such examples from the past—or

from societies distant from our own—may reveal the physical workings of their towns and villages, but we must be careful in making judgments from the evidence we find. Our concern will be to ascertain the establishment of order, and to measure it both in terms of existing conditions and in respect to artistic values. We cannot allow our own cultural biases to influence our judgment. Let us look to *their* values, and then try to determine the degree of success achieved by those efforts.

The establishment of order in urban design is obviously an early achievement in town building, as primitive planning and ancient records suggest, and the use of some form of open space is noted as an apparent necessity in most societies possessing a functioning social order. In classic Greek cities (500 B.C.) the organization and function of urban open space was carried beyond basic levels of social organization, and given purpose and value unknown to earlier societies. Paul Zucker, in *Town and Square*, explains the occurrence of planned urban space in ancient Greece by means of philosophic speculations: (1) by *sociological* criteria—the evolution of society from masses of people to collections of individual citizens capable of self- determination, and (2) by *aesthetic* criteria—the evolution of visual sensibilities, whereby the populace began to initiate a placement of value on appearance.

For whatever reason, the Greek builders of the Classic period are singled out for evaluating the meaning of public open space beyond elemental purpose, just as they are credited with evolving the concept of the city—a clear result of the level of maturity reached by that society. For it is certain that contemporary Egyptian cities lacked planned squares, as did the cities of the fertile crescent and their Persian followers—despite other cultural attainment. These societies produced formal, gridiron cities devoted primarily to *religious* and *political* custom. The major structures were palaces and temples. There is little indication of social or economic activity in their development outside basic agrarian need. Totalitarian government, as stated earlier, abhors public open space, where citizens might freely intermingle. The plans of Khorsabad, Ur, Persepolis, and Thebes reveal no such spaces, except for ritual—and here totalitarian societies have always been alike, from Rameses to Hitler.

The unique qualities of ancient Greek social order derive from a varied ancestry. Involved in this development were the ancient Minoans, short, olive skinned Mediterranean people, whose culture progressed uninterruptedly from about 3000 B.C. on the island of Crete. The eventual spread to the mainland produced the Mycenaean civilization, both of which are referred to generally as Aegean.

From about 2000 B.C. various groups of conquering tribesmen from the North gradually pushed the Aegeans from the mainland of the Greek Peninsula, and on to the islands of the Aegean Sea and the western coast of present day Turkey. The invaders were known as the Achaeans, and the blending of their assertiveness with Aegean sensitivity is said to have produced the finest cultural balance found in the ancient world. These were the people who produced classic Athens.

Dorian (Achaean) towns of the preclassic age tended to be irregular in layout, as Ionian (Aegean) towns tended to be regular. Athens turned out to be a mixture—empirical in the shape of its public open space and arrangement of streets, rational in architectural form and structural relationships.

The location for most towns, including Athens, was based on two important but contradictory factors: protection and commerce. The *protective* qualities of the location of Athens derive from the Acropolis, the steep sided mesa standing high above the present city. This flat topped mountain served as the original site of the city, due to its natural defenses. Most preclassic (archaic) Greek cities were similarly situated, and later, in times when man-made walls would serve for protection, they looked to the Acropolis for religious inspiration—as the home of the gods, so to speak. In classic Athens the Acropolis thus became the site for religious ceremony, the important temples and shrines being located there, while social, political, and economic activities shifted to the *agora*—the public open space that developed in empirical fashion at the foot of the Acropolis.

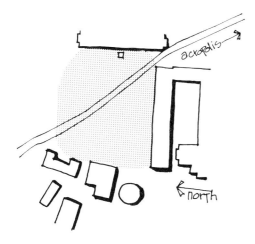

The Athenian *agora* evolved, through long usage, into the form shown here. *Size, shape, internal organization* as well as *location* resulted from adjustments to function, and for this reason the classic *agora* was probably able to satisfy a broader degree of practical need than those that followed. Here there was only the one major open space, about the *size* of two football fields side by side. It was large enough for most any activity, and its *location* was central and easily attainable by foot in the tightly compacted city where blocks measured only a fourth the size of today. Its *shape* resulted from the placement of major structures (enclosing agents), but as you can see from the plans, growth and development was empirical, with gradual changes resulting

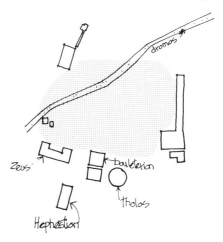

from overall changes in the city. Note the building which frame the space—the enclosing agents. They include the basic behavioral functions discussed earlier. The *bouleterion* and *tholos* are governmental structures. The *Stoa of Zeus* and the long structure which forms the southern edge of the space are commercial, while the *Hephestion* and other lesser temples serve religious purposes. The social function is implied in the agora itself.

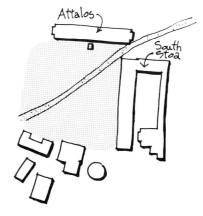

During the Hellenistic period a concern for regularity of form is noted by the introduction of the *Stoa of Attalos* (now completely rebuilt), and the South Stoa. In plan the logic of 90° order is obvious, but where topography is a factor we discover that direct geometric order is not always the best answer. In the case of the Athenian *agora*, the ground rises toward the Southeast, gradually at first, then more sharply, up to about 7 percent at the intersection of the two stoa, where the *dromos* passes between them. In the classic *agora* we see the original south stoa opening away—towards the pathway to the *Acropolis,* allowing the circulation route to take precedence. This is an important point. The *dromos* (pathway) is the primary, ancient route from the *Acropolis* to the harbor. It passes through the *dipylon* gates, bisecting the *agora* itself. It is therefore, the lifeline of the square, connecting it to the essential commercial and governmental elements of the city. Further, the *dromos* (later called the Pan-Athenaic Way) becomes the link to the *Acropolis*—the ancient hilltop city, by this time a shrine to the gods. And another kind of balance emerges in the open, spatial, inviting volume of the *agora*, opposed to the aloof, resistent, solid mass of the *Acropolis*. One is horizontal, feminine, the other vertical, masculine—a timeless linkage.

Hellenistic times (4th century B.C. and later). This is certainly true of the *Acropolis*, where buildings are arranged singularly and from the standpoint of perspective angle, but in the *agora* at Athens the case against classic Greek spatial awareness is hard to make. Although organic in placement, there is nonetheless a rational sense of scale and enclosure at work here. It is no mere accident that the *agora* at Athens succeeds. Its dimensions are correct for the planned uses. Men came here to purchase supplies and food, to get the news, to socialize. The unpaved surface allowed for trees and grass, making it a central park as well as a square. Athletes trained here before introduction of *gymnasia*, and of course, Socrates taught in a corner of the *agora*. Certainly much of Plato's inspiration generated from these teachings—and from the marvel of democracy in action, all about him in the square.

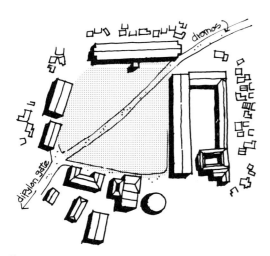

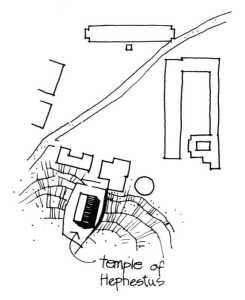

Some historians argue that the apparent formlessness of the Classic Athenian *agora* suggests either a lack of understanding or interest in the organization of external space, and that a conscious application of scale and order did not occur until

The *Hephestion* is situated on the little hill above the *agora*, and because it is a temple, it maintains the proper advantage of height afforded to religious structures. In this fashion it becomes a visual and spiritual halfway point—between the earthly *agora* below, and the mystic *Acropolis* still higher above.

In point of orientation the placement is even more logical, for the participant entering the square by way of the main gate will have the distant rise of the *acropolis*, capped by the gleaming white Parthenon on his left, and the smaller *Kolonos Agoraios* with the *Hephestion*, on his right. The temple's alignment is planned to coincide with the spatial thrust of the agora, so that a line of sight drawn from it will intersect the Pan-Athenaic Way at mid-point through the square. This is not accidental, or the result

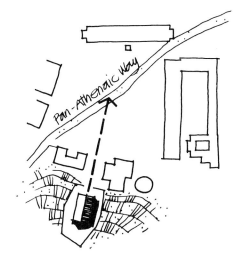

of organic trial-and-error, but is the result of a conscious effort to generate scale and direction in space by visual management. Making square corners in plan is straightforward and fairly obvious. Working three-dimensionally, with eye-level sight lines, uneven topography and varied building forms requires a good deal more sensitivity and spatial acumen. You can observe the intricacies of external form easily by first studying a complex of buildings in plan view (a). It may look very good that way. Then, if possible, check what occurs three-dimensionally, by studying the model (b). Close one eye and squint at the spaces from as low an angle as possible. Finally, visit the complex on foot, looking up this time, into the variety of forms and heights which make up the spatial enclosure. Now the wall planes take control visu-

ally, and the real significance of spatial order unfolds. Errors as well as strengths of the composition are easy to pick out. It was at this level that classic Greek planning was performed.

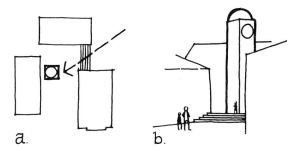

a.   b.

In denying the direct axiality of rectilinear organization, Classic architects and planners were exhibiting a preference for natural order as well as an understanding and appreciation for order in the environment totally. None of their critics considers it accidental that they faced buildings in respect to view, or that they located towns and organized them from the standpoint of their relationship to natural elements. Nor was the aesthetic relationship of external space beyond the grasp of Classic planners. Arbitrary axiality is a product of their followers.

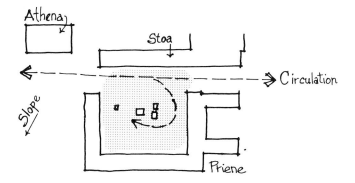

Compare the empirical form of Classic external space with the later Hellenistic examples. At Priene and Miletus, two Ionian cities on the coast of Turkey, we have clear examples of progress towards a rectilinear order which became the hallmark of rational urban space in the Roman era.

At first glance we are aware of certain basic differences between Hellenistic and Classic *agoras*. The space is not only clearly rectangular, but also more regular—the individual buildings surrounding and enclosing the square having given way to a rigid colonnade, with closed corners. The spaces are also much smaller and generally made level, sometimes requiring considerable grading and attendant retaining walls to do so. Such a powerful form was in danger of being subjected to an overpowering static force, and in order to prevent such a deadening effect the builders of Hellenistic squares regularly left one side open, as in Priene.

Priene

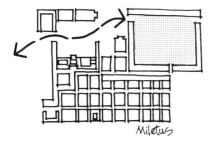

Miletus

In Miletus we see the development of a progression of small market squares, opening eventually to the major square which embraces the harbor, in typical C-shaped form. It was normal for coastal cities to have their squares face the harbor in this way. Priene was built above the coastal plain, for protective as well as practical purposes, on a rounded hillside overlooking the sea. In order to keep the main square relatively flat on this sloping terrain it was necessary to cut the upper side, along the face of the sacred stoa, and fill the lower side. The main circulation runs parallel to the contours, through the *agora*.

Like Athens, there is a dynamic spatial balance here, due to the C- shape, the overlapping transition at the entry to the square, and the diagonal placement of the temple of Athena, which, with its prominent site, provides a sexual balance of mass

and void along the same idea as witnessed in classic Athens, but on a much smaller scale.

The *agora* at Corinth, like Priene produces a sense of dynamic spatial order as a result of the location of the *propylaea* (gateway), and the rather nonspecific shape of the square itself.

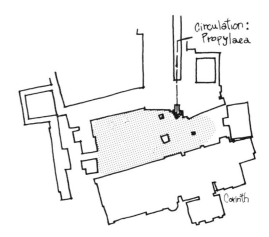

Circulation: Propylaea

Corinth

We can assume from the restoration the existence of a logic to the space, which rests between the practicality of empirical development (in consideration for topography and prevailing custom) and the appeal of rational aesthetics. There is clearly an affinity for rectilinear order present from the Fourth Century B.C. on, and in the *agora* at Magnesia it has been carried out rather directly. Here again we note the Hellenistic preference for the

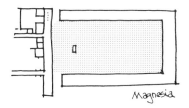

Magnesia

three-sided enclosing stoa—a prevalent characteristic of *agora* design in the period.

Hellenistic urban designers, the best known of which was Hippodamus of Miletus, can be credited with the following accomplishments respective of urban space:

1. attempting to accomplish rectilinear order,
2. evolving the C-shaped or three-sided *agora*, which prevented the deadening static quality inherent to closed spaces,
3. organizing circulation—primarily major and secondary ingress—again by means of the C-shaped plan,
4. creating balance between mass and void by the placement of structures (Priene),
5. developing continuity of enclosure, by emphasizing the stoa, subordinating other enclosing structures,
6. maintaining a sense of human scale (Hellenistic urban space was normally smaller than either the preceeding Classic space or the following Roman space),
7. developing scale and rhythm by use of colonnade and overall balance of proportions (not found in empirical spaces of the Classic period).

Greek towns began, for the most part, in an empirical manner and the location and shape of their *agoras* were highly dependent upon conditions of urban growth and form. Roman towns began with a basic plan and thereafter varied from it as little as possible. This is the ultimate in rational town planning, and it served Rome well—creating a sense of familiarity and presence of order throughout the far-flung empire. Based on a scheme for organizing semi-permanent military encampments, the plan called for a fortified rectilinear pallisade or wall at its boundries, with major entrances intersecting at a central point. There are many examples of this simple rectilinear plan, called a *castrum*, with Timgad, in North Africa, being one of the best preserved.

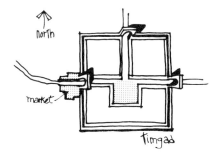

North

market

Timgad

The major street bisecting the town from east to west is called the *decumanus maximus*. This is main street, and is marked at either end by triumphal arches at the entrance to the town. The other major street, called the *cardo maximus*, bisects the town on a north-south axis, and terminates at the intersection where the central forum develops.

Colonial towns, like Timgad, normally followed this plan of development because they began their existences as camps, but certain empirical variations crept in nonetheless. In this case, for example, the main market place developed just outside the walls (at the western entrance), allowing the central space (forum) to retain a more formal status in the town's activities, while the external market place developed independently (a precursor of medieval town growth).

A central space at the intersection of 90° streets tended towards rectilinear and axial formality, as we see at Timgad. Not all towns which evolved from *castri* are this regular in plan, with the forum located directly behind the terminus of the *cardo maximus*, but regularity was commonplace and the forum reflected it. The open space in the center of a castrum, from which the forum evolved, was probably used for military assembly, in this way resembling the parade ground discussed earlier, but as fortified camp became colonial town the function of that space adjusted to civilian activity, and direct axiality remained to become the common form of most Roman *fora* to follow.

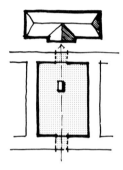

As the plan suggests, Roman space is *formal, axial,* and *dominated,* the main sight line terminating at the face of the primary enclosing structure. Any sculptural elements, fountains, or such are likely to be in line with this axis. The space is symmetrical and usually monumental—that is, larger than human scale. The Romans understood the means by which to order external space and they set about it in a very direct way. Compared to Hellenistic achievement the following differences are noted:

1. Roman space is closed or appears to be closed at all the corners, entrance usually occurring in the center of a side.
2. Roman space is static in the sense that symmetrical balance, rigid axiality, centric placement of elements, and monumentality of scale are emphasized.

Roman planning began with certain preconceived conventions, regardless of the nature of a town's location, available

building materials or its proposed functions. For this reason there is a sense of regularity repeated throughout the towns of the em-

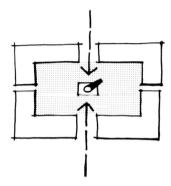

pire (1st to 5th century A.D.). Roman architecture and town planning of this period can be referred to as the first "international style," and the rationale for its continued use is the creed of rational method in design. Change, remember, is the primary challenge to rational urban design; but the Romans, for five hundred years, managed to make time stand still.

Eventually, Roman space became subject to clutter—the antithesis of public open space. The use of the *Forum Romanum* and other such spaces, as repository for temples, tributes, war memorials, rostrums, and such is indicative of the imperial authority's disregard for public need. The Romans were capable of conceiving space **physically,** but probably never grasped the meaning of, or at least the many facets and potential opportunities afforded to a free society by public open space. In Athens they filled the old agora with monumental structures, crowding and limiting activities, and eventually negating all sense of spatial enclosure.

For example, the *Odeion,* a theatre greatly out of scale with its surroundings, was placed in the center of the north-south axis, destroying the carefully developed volumetrics of the square in a single stroke. The *temple of Ares* and the scattering of smaller structures and rostrums completes the destruction, reminding us

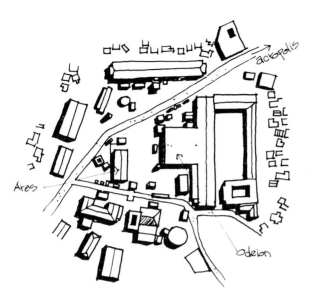

again of imperial Rome's apparent contempt for open public activity.

The negative aspects which flaw Rome's comprehension of urban space derive from political sources. Not only was there a tendency to clutter open space with all kinds of public oriented structures—a not uncommon practice in our own urban culture—but an overshadowing precept of governmental authority dictated form and function in the forum. It is not, therefore, by accident that the basic plan of the square is symmetrically axial, directing a sight line to its termination at the focal point—the central arch of the primary structure.

The best of Roman *fora* are perhaps the smaller squares and market places, where more practical, day-to-day needs prevailed. The forum at Pompeii, for example, tends to be less pompous and theatrical, and more *empirical* than we are led to expect from Roman planning concepts. That is, axiality and symmetrical balance give way to practical function. Pompeii was a busy agricultural center, and the central forum must have been used in a variety of ways. The adjacent granaries suggest an

ongoing trade in farm produce—the forum no doubt acting as depository for such goods during trading sessions.

Where practical considerations had to be taken into account, the Romans would often set aside special *fora,* so as not to cause interference with the more formal or ceremonial functions of their major urban spaces. In this way we see separate market squares for butchers, grocers, cloth merchants, precious metals, and the like. Where possible, and certainly in the larger cities and in Rome, there was a clear separation between economic and political functions in terms of open space.

But regardless of the degree of importance played by political factors the Roman world was geometric, and nowhere is that more obvious than in the shaping of urban space. The Romans clearly understood the elements involved in the volumetrics of external space, and sought to control it totally. But nothing is so elusive to a designer as space— particularly external urban space, where the enclosing agents normally play a double role, and the spatial result is usually accidental and unpredictable. The control of urban space is easiest, for example, when the area (volume) is small; but when we begin to stretch a rigid, geometric fabric—as the Romans did—over a broad urban area, disregarding topographic factors as well as the natural dialectics of city growth, we may be confronted by serious complications. Two examples of Roman intransigence in the face of natural order are shown here. On the following page (a) we see the checkerboard of spaces and monumental buildings in the complex of the imperial *fora,* Rome, all of which have been shoehorned into a rectilinear regimen, which, in respect to natural precedent, results in a very arbitrary arrangement bearing little relationship to the various functional requirements of the squares. At Hadrian's Villa, Tivoli (b), we encounter another example of forced regularity, again requiring massive retaining walls and great amounts of excavation in order to carry out a rectilinear theme which does not correspond very well to the existing topography. Continued growth of the project over twenty

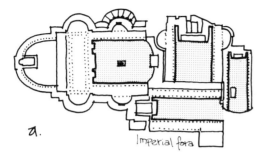

a.

Imperial fora

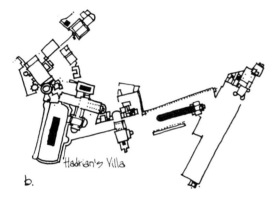

Hadrian's Villa

b.

years or so tends to reveal further the brittle nature of rectilinear formality in civic design—and an irrefutable law of physical planning:

> The smaller the scale of the project the better it is suited to rectilinear form; the larger the project the better it is suited to organic form—and the natural affinity between the order of nature and the works of man.

In the end, Roman success in the design of external space results from a strictly volumetric approach—a limitation of space, carefully articulated by enclosing agents, pivotal/axial points and a major structure acting as dominant element, enclosing agent and axial focus. Limitation and articulation was sought arbitrarily, as an absolute purpose in itself, irrespective of common usage or the prospect of change of any kind. Planners sought absolute solutions because their design criteria were based on absolute dogma: the universality of imperial order. The results are at best

static, monumental, and self-contained (that is, inwardly successful in their articulation and limitation of space). They are at worst unresponsive to change as well as to the activities and uses for which they were planned, and the human need for a comfortable scale relationship. But we cannot fault Roman planners, or the environmental designers of any age, for their failure to live up to our requirements for civic design. For that matter, we won't be far wrong in most instances simply to assume that their solutions to spatial design were precise and correct—that they got exactly what they wanted. It is probably a safer course than trying to evaluate their solutions by our standards. Admittedly, this leads us into making judgments of their political structure rather than their artistic and creative talents—something we might prefer to avoid. It is, nevertheless, a better and fairer way to analyze people's work from a great distance in time. What they built was what *they* thought to be the best they could do. In judging the quality of that space—on both artistic and functional terms—we are really judging the culture that produced it rather than the work itself.

The contrast between Greek and Roman concepts of external space offers us our first opportunity to compare empirical and rational approaches to design. The Greek temple, primary model for later Roman architecture, varied from one example to the next, the designers continually seeking to heighten or lessen certain visual phenomena. The Romans never bothered. Likewise, the Greeks struggled with the great variety of natural factors affecting external space and architecture—the quality of light at different times of day and season, the potential advantages offered by topographic variation, changes in usage and circulation. The Greeks faced major buildings and temples into the setting sun, for aesthetic as well as religious reasons. The Romans organized inwardly, to retain geometric relationship of parts to the whole—regardless of topography or orientation. They disregarded natural factors, or abstracted them in order to employ absolute, self-contained concepts of spatial limitation. Beginning with the town plan, the *crossing* of main thoroughfares, the *placement* of the square, the *enclosing* and articulating of volume by means of peristyles, the *formalizing* and ordering of direction by axial arrangement, the Romans succeeded in achieving a well ordered sense of urban space and a regularity and repetition of rational form.

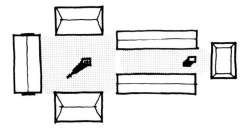

Our own familiarity with geometric space serves as a reminder of the limitations imposed by regular ordering of the enclosing agents. In (a), which could be an arrangement of barracks, school buildings, apartment complexes, or the like, we are reminded of static enclosure, monotonous views from the windows, uninteresting spaces. In the second example (b), there is probably a greater opportunity for a variety of activities and design organization in the external space, and even more importantly, the views from the enclosing structures are not directed into one another.

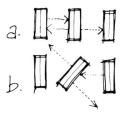

Changes in the wall, ceiling, and ground planes heighten interest and alter the viewpoint of the participator. The heavy hand of rectilinear order sometimes limits the potential for variety—as seen in the classic Greek *agora*—and replaces it with more precise, if restrictive, conditions for spatial organization. The

chart below summarizes Greek and Roman achievements in defining concepts of urban space.

Spatial Concepts	Greek	Roman
process	empirical	rational
form	amorphous	geometric (rectilinear)
orientation	outward/westward	inward
enclosing agents	individual	arcaded, colonnaded
topographic	adaptive	reductive
function	multiple	limited
circulation	variable	axial
scale	human	self-contained
volumetrics	dynamic/organic	mechanical/static

In the Classic age, when the foundations were laid for urban space in Western society, we observe some striking differences. Process, or design method tended to be empirical in Greek hands, rational and unbending as applied by Roman builders. The form of the Greek Classic square tended to be formless, due to influences of topography, orientation, and external criteria. The Romans turned their spaces inward, organized them geometrically, with carefully modulated systems or arcaded logia and closed corners. The classic Greeks used stoa (the long stalls) for partial enclosure, but also depended on individual structures to act as enclosing agents. The Roman penchant for axial formality in urban space helped to create a strongly delineated sense of external order, but limited the potential use and activity by so doing. For this reason the Romans developed a series of spaces with singular designated uses, while the Greeks depended generally on the one central *agora*. Roman circulation was directed along major and secondary axes which crossed at right angles in the center (usually marked). Circulation was rarely directed from the corners, as was common to Greek and Hellenistic squares, but usually penetrated at the center of the enclosing structure, and terminated at the façade of the dominant basilica enclosing the space. Although large by today's standards and compared to surrounding structures, Classic Greek squares maintained human scale. This results largely from the variety and size of the enclosing structures, the uses of topography, internal circulation and the day-to-day functioning of the space. Roman space, external and internal, is said to be "self-contained," which means generally that its spatial proportions—size, shape, structural members, fenestration, detailing, and the like are more tuned to one another than to any human activity or need. Circulation as well, is often "dual," meaning divided equally—with no suggestion of any major direction, or thrown at right angles across a strong axial spine. Such formal structure can be precise and clear in a rational way, but confusing nonetheless to the imperfect, emotional, organic, everyday *human* way. Roman external volumetrics are obvious and straight forward, the limitation and direction of space clearly delineated in the rhythm of an enclosing arcade, even the corners of which were more logically resolved than the Renaissance copiers would be able to do for the most part. Greek volumetrics didn't exist— except in the course of daily activity, and that could only be ascertained momentarily and from eye level, in consort with the changing scene before one's view, and of course from a viewpoint which was itself in movement. Nothing in urban space is completely dynamic or static. It is the *tendency* of one or the other which is implied by the manner in which form and direction have been organized. And it is a test of space we can continue to make through history.

FIVE

Order Evolved: Medieval Metamorphosis

A review of man's accomplishments in environmental design during the Classic Age reveals both a striving for disciplined order and logical volumetric rhythm on the one hand, together with a need for sponteneity, flexibility, and change on the other. Order builds static quality into the fabric of the city. Change is the result of dynamic determinants, and the empirical processes of life. In the Roman world, order was established and maintained, change resisted. But change is inevitable, and historians today lay much of the cause for the empire's decline on its reluctance to accept adjustment to their ways of doing things. The age that followed Rome reversed that policy, and change became the only constant factor in urban life. This is particularly reflected in the development of the square.

The period of concern is the Middle Ages, familiar to us because as school children we were taught to recognize three major divisions of history, by which to sort out the vast regions of time: ancient, middle, and modern. These are European divisions, of course, and they are marked by the fall of Rome (ancient to middle) and the advent of the Renaissance (middle to modern). The beginning of the ancient world as well as the end of the modern world are, of course, open ended.

This concept of dividing time in the western world is arbitrary at best, and even erroneous in its suggestion that there were sudden, world shaking activities which ended one era and introduced another; and it is even more unlikely, that the middle era, was one long, thousand years of social stagnation, between periods of progress and enlightenment.

The originators of this theory were the sixteenth century humanists themselves. They believed that the life line of European civilization had been interrupted for the extent of the Middle Ages, to commence again in the fifteenth century. They believed that the cause of the rebirth of civilization at that time was the rediscovery of the Classic world, and they called the Middle Ages "gothic," associating everything therein with the destructive, barbaric efforts of the Goths. But they were wrong. The cause of the Renaissance was not primarily cultural or aesthetic, but economic. And there would have been no Renaissance at all—as we know it—were it not for the Middle Ages. The relics of the classic world had lain about, we are told—apparent but unappreciated—for all of the Middle Ages, awaiting discovery by a higher level of social awareness, of an expanded aesthetic consciousness which came to be known as the Renaissance. But the Renaissance was not born out of the ashes of the Classic world, nor for that matter from a stagnant medieval society, but was instead the result of a rapidly developing one.

We can chart the Middle Ages as follows:

5-6th Cent.	7-8th Cent.	9-11th Cent.	12-14th Cent.
Early Christian	*Dark Age*	*Romanesque*	*Gothic*
Initial development of Christian order, church architecture. Division of empire and development of Byzantine world. Conversion of Classic to Christian works.	In West, anarchy, local order only. Cultural and artistic progress shifts to Eastern (Byzantine) world. Flight from urban centers. Nomadic life. Protected settlement.	Settlement and growth of economic centers. Organization of empire (Charlemagne) and national order under royal rule. Population explosion and movement.	Growth and development of trade. Structuring of medieval society. Peak of western artistic accomplishment, particularly in cathedrals, secular architecture. Cities hardening into form (walls, roads, squares, major structures).

From the seventh to the fourteenth century there was a gradual but continuing upward movement in the structure of European society, which turned irrevocably on economic progress. In short, it was a process of conversion from a *protective* to a *productive* society. From fortified eyries to growing towns, it was a long period of movement which had begun with a dispersal and ended with a concentration of people.

In the archaic life of the seventh and eighth centuries—the dark ages—life in Western Europe continued only in hideaways or sheltered places—in craggy mountain fortresses, monastic retreats, the walled up shells of classic cities and palaces, off shore islands, river bends, and the like. But life was never at a standstill, and even in these protective enclaves new ways of doing things were set in motion. The process of change—inherent to the Middle Ages—was itself dependent upon various kinds of technical achievement, which in turn brought about economic advantage, such as:

Settlement (*protection*)——▸division of labor——▸achievement of skills——▸superiority of products——▸accumulation of surplus (*production*)——▸trade.

People needed things which others could produce better and cheaper, and barter became a way of life in the Middle Ages.

The village which developed skilled craftsmen in leather working or weaving, or produced surpluses in foodstuffs became a marketplace. Good locations, along reawakening Roman roads, at crossroads, river and sea ports, and in areas of grain productions, developed from primitive villages to market towns, and eventually into powerful, independent cities, with highly organized political and social structures. In fact, many Italian city-states of the thirteenth and fourteenth centuries had freely elected governments, similar to standards of today.

Locations which had originally been selected for their protective features eventually became the great trade centers of Europe. Craggy mountain fortresses became medieval cities like Edinburgh and Salzburg. The bend in the river became a Luxembourg, and out of the protected features of the river isle came Paris. Two things were necessary in order to convert protected enclaves into open, productive towns: proximity to trade and the willingness to take nominal risks—to climb down from the mountain or bridge the river. In a great many examples we can still discover the traces of this movement. Edinburgh, Salzburg, Luxembourg, and Paris became successful medieval cities in spite of their fortified origins because they were blessed with opportunity for economic development; but many a citadel remained aloof to changing times and opportunities, and withered away. Their ruins can still be seen on precipice or promontory, overlooking a life below that long ago passed them by.

The medieval town protected itself by building walls. It left the castle on the hill. But in moving down the slopes to a more

accessible location, it did not abandon precaution altogether. It would be several centuries more before cities could exist without physical protection, and walls offered the ideal solution for the burgeoning market town, providing that measure of protection without denying ease of access or development around a market square. Early Carolingian towns had suffered devastating attack by marauding Norsemen and others, and by the tenth century high, thick walls had become an absolute necessity for towns on the open plain. Many medieval towns, like Angoulime and Perigueux in south central France, were built on low rising hills—a compromise between the old protectiveness and the new accessibility—and then surrounded by turreted walls. Since towns were primarily a result of trade, their development was dependent upon continued commercial success. The key to that success resided in the market square.

A medieval town, growing and changing in accordance with dialectic empiricism, had a morphosis somewhat like the following:

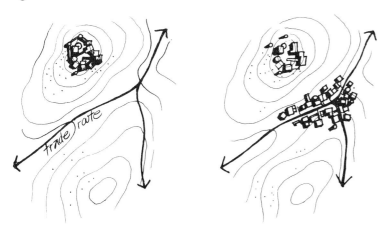

A town which had abandoned its protected location in order to straddle developing trade routes eventually developed a kind of bottleneck congestion, similar to that which a driver experiences when the highway on which he is travelling narrows and slows as it passes through a small town. Merchants hoping to attract the passersby press forward, calling out for attention.

Local traffic, operating at a slower pace, and with a different purpose, adds to the congestion. The logical solution would be to redirect the through traffic which forms the economic base of the town. Routing around the town could prove disastrous—until the town reaches sufficient size and attains internal economic muscle sufficient to exist without the main highway. So it was for medieval towns.

The first step required in accommodating the dual purpose traffic through the town center was simply the widening and distinguishing of the trade route as it passed through the area of heaviest trading (a). Eventually this widened area was more precisely identified, as in our example, by locating structures of some kind at either end which acted as terminals marking the trading area. This precursor to the market square is called a

A.

largo, and can still be found in vestigial form in towns which have retained their medieval identity—or more importantly, in towns which have never developed spatially beyond this form. Many "Main Streets" in the United States or "High Streets" in Great Britain are roughly comparable.

Locations along the *largo* were actively sought by local tradesmen, and when the structures housing their enterprises were on occasion destroyed by fire or other cause they were usually replaced in the same spot—until the pressures for greater street space became intense. At that point in the history of a market-town's growth, destroyed or burned out buildings were no longer replaced—or they were rebuilt further back from the road, in order to allow for the expanding spatial needs of the common trading area. Empirical growth and development of a typical market square is noted by the amorphous external form that evolved (b), leading to the organization of a true market

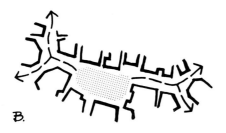

B.

square. The penchant for order—as urgent and natural to medieval life as the need for change—led to a logical organization of function in the square which included the introduction of major buildings like the city hall, guild hall, church and, more than likely, a tower (*campanile*) of some sort. By this point in the evolution of the square (c), *through* traffic could be expected to have been rerouted. Sometimes, however, the opposite appears

c

to have occurred. In the typical example of a "T" crossing following the Roman *castrum* plan, building and development around the square frequently distorted travel ways, causing traffic to bend and jog in order to get through the central area. This was again a kind of crowding and jockeying by local tradesmen determined to gain advantage or improve their locations. In the plans below Roman order (a) is seen to collapse in the face of this medieval empiricism (b). Over the centuries the original Roman form at the town center has been largely obliterated by the layers of succeeding ages, but we can still recognize Roman origin by *name*—in Great Britain, for example, any town with the suffix *-chester* or *-cester* (corruption of *castrum*).

The streets leading into the market square narrowed under similar economic pressure; and the entire central part of the medieval town tended to grow more crowded and unsanitary—as structures grew upward and even over the street, shutting out most of the sun, while the streets themselves were expected to handle runoff and serve as open sanitary sewers. (It would be a while before the sewage systems of the Classic world were rediscovered.) But the crowding, unsanitary conditions and even chaotic growth of the market town was in reality a sign of success—a busy and profitable trade.

Craftsmen and farmers were obliged to come into town to sell their wares, and locations nearest the center were, as we know, considered to be best. Craftsmen who lived and worked in a particular town (and gave it a reputation based on their skills) sought permanent locations facing the square, where the chance for sales was likely to be best. The resulting shape of the market place was *organic, empirical,* and wholly *practical.* Two contrasting forces determined the shape and size of the market square, on the one hand a *competitive* struggle to push inward and even penetrate the square in an effort to secure the best possible location, opposed by a *cooperative* force, supported generally by all townsmen, to push out and back from the center in order to provide a greater amount of common space—and an opportunity for including more merchants and a larger variety of goods. These two forces, competitive (inward) and cooperative (outward), mark the development of central space planning in towns throughout the Middle Ages.

With the market square at the center, and commercial development occurring on its perimeters and along the major thoroughfares which penetrated the center or crossed at the square, a diagram of a typical medieval town might look like this:

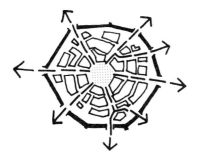

The encircling walls usually followed the topography, along the lines of least resistance, and for that reason were rarely as regular as the diagram used here. The topography was often quite rugged—a compromise, you will remember, between the mountain top and the open plain—which created problems in construction and street design.

The walls were the town's major structural undertaking, and once completed were not likely to be altered frequently. This was because of the great difficulties and cost involved, as well as the temporary exposure to danger. If possible a town would never pull down its old walls until the new sections were complete, but seams had to be made between the two, and even the slightest degree of exposure caused during construction could make the townsfolk apprehensive, and unwilling to undergo changes in the system of outer fortifications unless absolutely necessary.

The main thoroughfares passed through gates in the walls, leading generally toward the center, while the secondary system of circular streets carried traffic around the town, giving it the appearance of a spider web. The worst location for a merchant would have been somewhere between the major radiating streets and towards the wall—the furthest place from any kind of activity. For this reason these spaces inside the walls were the last to be developed. Development along the major thoroughfares and at the center created a "starfish" pattern of growth, with a secondary concentration just outside the walls. This resulted from the requiring of craftsmen to wait outside the gates before being given permission to enter the town, a period of time lasting occa-

sionally for days. Impatient with delays and anxious to make a sale, merchants and craftsmen set up outside the walls at the main gates, a habit which led to the growth of the first medieval suburbs, called *faubourgs* (false-burg).

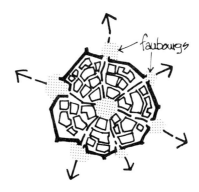

After a period of time the developments outside the walls were usually incorporated into the town, and the walls were extended to accommodate them. This became the typical pattern of growth for medieval market towns.

The village with any kind of marketable commodity in an age of population growth, grew rapidly larger—and denser. The tendency towards increased density resulted from several causes: (1) *Conditions* of *topography.*—A rugged landscape or a village hemmed in by its natural advantages or protective waterways had little opportunity to sprawl (compare Los Angeles with San Francisco); (2) *Walls.*—The physical limitations to growth imposed on the town by its system of walls tended to retard outward expansion; (3) *Centric nature.*—The market itself was implosive, with pressure constantly being applied inward, toward the central market square, where the action could be found. For these reasons the medieval city, like New York today, looked upward for growth. The merchants escaped the noise and odor of the marketplace by building over their places of trade—four, five, eight stories up! Towers were erected by wealthy families, as a means of respite from the din below perhaps, and also as a means of supplying a warning of approaching danger (the bells

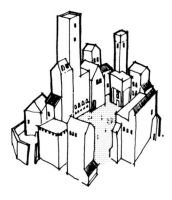

clanged to bring the tillers of the fields inside the protection of the walls), and medieval towns gained a decided vertical appearance. Streets grew narrower, under the encroachment of taller structures, twisting to accommodate terrain and increasing densities. On flat sites street layout tended to be regular—rarely rectilinear, but following the practical logic of the "shortest distance" ideal. Medieval streets appear confused and irregular in plan, but a knowledge of existent topographic conditions as well as the directness of empirical planning practices, reveals an organic order which served circulation needs, in the Middle Ages and on down to our own times. In many European cities today the organic street systems of their medieval period are still largely intact.

In Chapter Two the three basic street systems were briefly mentioned. These are shown in diagrammatic form below:

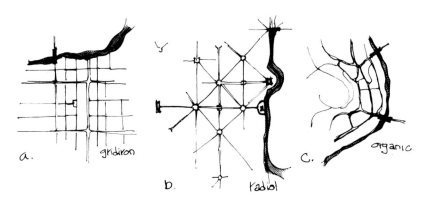

a. gridiron

b. radial

c. organic

The first (gridiron) was in evidence as early as the archaic Greek period (800 B.C.) and is certainly even older. It represents man's forthright efforts to overcome natural form so as to impose a methodical manmade concept of order on the urban landscape. It lends itself to orderly growth, regulates methods of building, and simplifies circulation needs. It has been the overwhelming choice in American city planning.

The second (radial) is somewhat more sophisticated, requiring an entirely different approach to spatial organization, structural design, and circulation. It deserves special attention and therefore is treated separately in a later chapter.

The third (organic) grew out of primitive village life. It is the only true empirical system, and in simplest terms can be said to have developed without regard for any sense of overall planning, or future growth. A street was built over an existing pathway, with paving, curbs, and drainage ditches added only as they proved necessary. Topography dictated street alignment, which usually followed the most direct or easiest access, and at the same time provided a ready means for drainage.

The "starfish" diagram suggestive of typical medieval town development is remarkably similar to the later idealized planned cities of the sixteenth and seventeenth centuries. The similarity is not an accident. Trial an error planning in the Middle Ages followed a natural pattern of nuclear growth: radiating primary streets aimed at the center, the walls closing about to form the boundaries, all points of which are more or less equidistant from the center. Sixteenth century planners simply understood the natural order apparent in this pattern of growth and attempted to regularize it. (We know this from Alberti, who describes the functional and aesthetic uses of streets in the Middle Ages, as a basis for his own fifteenth century treatise on ideal planning). While the concepts may have been similar, the methods of development were, of course, very different indeed.

By the thirteenth century the central square had developed into more durable form. This was a result of financial successes primarily, which brought about the establishment of major civic structures facing the square. The *economic* factor is represented by the establishment of a guildhall. This structure, not unlike modern union halls, housed the offices, and sometimes products of the local craftsmen. The guild, a major medieval economic institution, protected the rights of craftsmen, maintained prices and controlled quality. Nearly every craft imaginable was represented, including leather working, cloth, gold and silversmithing, painting, sculpture, architecture, glassblowing, etc. The skill of a town's craftsmen was its economic strength and political power.

The town hall (*hotel de ville, radhaus*, prior's palace) usually occupied a second face of the central square. As a town's wealth continued to increase, so also did its political strength, and that mark of success is clearly and graphically described by the grandeur of the town hall. Political structure varied considerably in the independent market towns of the Middle Ages, some having been controlled by single rulers, others by elected bodies. The town hall suggests a more democratic or representative rule, with its various chambers where the elected delegates sat in legislative session—not unlike their counterparts today. But in cases where the ruler's palace faces the square, and a quality of guarded force emanates from that structure, it is unlikely that a very democratic form of government held power. But be careful in making a judgment. *Palazzo Pubblico* is just another term for city hall.

After accommodating dignitaries and officials the remaining frontage on the square was, of course, left to tradesmen and craftsmen—the triangular wedge between the square and adjoining streets being considered a prime location for business.

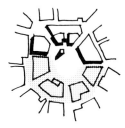

The location of the church varied in medieval town development. On flat terrain it is likely to be found in the central square, along with the town hall, guild hall and palace, but never without

some sign of deference to its difference in status. The church was invariably the most important structure in the life of the town, and when it is located in close proximity to other civic functions in the square we note that its floor elevation is often raised above the common ground plane—with an accompanying flight of stairs. The church was usually faced west, despite the disruption which might result, and not infrequently a space evolved in front of the church—separate but connected to the central square. Zucker refers to this arrangement as "grouped squares," the church square and the market square sharing the town's central area.

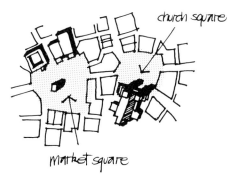

church square

market square

More often, the principal location for the church was a hill overlooking town and square. Like the Acropolis and its Parthenon the medieval church on the hill above bears a *yin/yang* relationship to the town below—the "male/female" or "mass/space" syndrome which we encounter throughout the history of urban evolution. In some cases the hilltop location may have resulted from the town's having grown out of a monastery or other religious enclave, or the church might be a remnant of an earlier citadel—the original fortress dating from perhaps the seventh or eighth century and standing on a pinnacle above and away from potential dangers. But the church's location on high ground also resulted from purely spiritual reasoning—to elevate and thereby dignify and set aside the town's most significant edifice. Chartres Cathedral, like many lesser examples, stands on the crest of a hill above the town—a truly dramatic sight to travelers, today even as in the thirteenth century.

chartres cathedral

Palazzo Pubblico

It is not difficult to determine from available evidence, and in some cases from existing records, the true reason behind the location of any medieval church and *parvis;* and like the central market place, they, too, evolved through the morphosis of organic empiricism. The Gothic cathedral is a marvelous example of the fusion of organic and mechanistic genius. And it is a genius born of native ingenuity, spiritual fervor, and civic pride. The church, the marketplace, the city structure belonged to the town—and the people.

By the end of the thirteenth century that pride had resulted in the beginning of *planned* squares. The *Piazza del Campo* in Siena, for centuries an unpaved open field, was laid out in an approximate semicircular plan, the ribs of the stone pavement design fanning out from the newly planned (1298) *Palazzo Pubblico.*

More commonly, the open space which was to become the market square was eventually paved, usually out of simple necessity, considering the problems that must certainly have arisen in a busy marketplace following a rain. In most instances the paved surface is uncluttered by any form or structure, aesthetic or not, which might restrict the flexibility of the square's purpose. This was a marketplace, and the broad, unintegrated expanse of gravel or stones does not accurately convey its purpose to us until we see it in operation—crowded with the colorful stalls, mobs of people, noise, and activity.

Form follows function—the creed of the modern organic school of design was never more accurate than in defining the medieval square—and the form of the typical square was aesthetically accidental, if practically useful. In truth the essential difference between the empirical approach and the rational design process which followed is found in the emphasis on opposing values—function vs. form. We may have read frequently that the one logically follows upon the other, but in the medieval marketplace function ruled, often to the detriment of aesthetic form—just as the carefully modulated Renaissance square, in the opposite way, suffered from inflexibility and functional austerity. Any design analysis of the medieval square depends, therefore, on *functional* results, observed at ground level. In plan it may appear ill-formed and even arbitrary, until we take the time to walk through it.

The *Piazza del Popolo* in Todi (Umbria) is an attenuated square, formed from an earlier *largo*, the *duomo* and prior's palace anchoring either end like dams to create the widened form of the piazza. The *duomo* (cathedral) is raised above the common level of the square and flanked by a grand staircase,

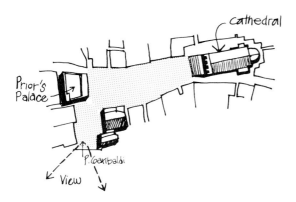

giving it a position of dominance. A secondary square (*Piazza Garibaldi*) intersects at the opposite end causing the prior's palace (city hall) to act as terminus and enclosing agent for both interlocking spaces. A tower adds to the significance of this relationship, and gives vertical balance to the composition. The smaller square overlooks the surrounding countryside, providing an additional visual linkage, this time between town and place.

Perugia represents a classic example of medieval dialectics, the ancient *largo* being terminated by the façade of the *duomo* which thrusts itself across the wide street like a boulder in a stream, thus forming the *Piazza 4 de Novembre*, the central marketplace, the opposite side of which is anchored by the prior's palace. The form of the square tends to create a funneling effect, introducing traffic from three sides, and the precise placement of the Great Fountain, midway between approaches to the two major structures, exemplifies the typical nuclear square. The opposite end of the *largo*, is terminated by the *Piazza Italia*,

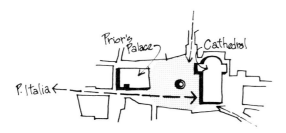

redesigned in the nineteenth century. Halfway between these polar spaces is a smaller, pivotal square (*Piazza della Repubblica*), which completes a grand scheme of empirical order. The widened street itself, called the *Corso Vannuci*, is the key to the entire complex of spaces, and is itself a primary urban space once again—the automobile traffic having been removed in 1972 to allow the return of pedestrian oriented activities.

In all, the variety of spatial uses which derive from medieval planning continue to provide examples for study today: the *surprise* which derives from entering a square along a narrow, jagged walkway; the placement of the *well*—a pivotal agent of the square, rarely located symmetrically but always spatially functional; the half hidden *terminus* which looks accidental but always succeeds in exciting our curiosity, drawing us on; the uneven *floor plane*, often requiring steps and emphasizing spatial effect; offsets in the consistency of the *wall plane*, creating secondary termini, interlocking spatial units—places for our eye to rest for a moment; the *acute angles* acting as funnels, closing or opening spaces to accommodate particular needs; the *verticality*, closing in which enhances *spatial modeling* and *human* scale; the variety of *materials, colors, textures*.

While the medieval market square continues to absorb change, even to the present, it retains its original purpose in most regards. Despite the advances of technology and modern ways it remains oriented to pedestrian exchange, the nature of its form acting as a limiting factor to modern traffic and parking requirements. During the period of the Renaissance we see the medieval square infused with classic metrics and stylized spatial concepts, but confusing as this may be for students who insist on a ready means of classification, the medieval square is otherwise untroubled by the intrusion. It is, after all only another form of *change*.

In Arezzo, for example, the *Piazza Grande* is formed half by medieval and Gothic structures, which march down the sloping square, and half by Renaissance structures of much grander dimension. On the negative side, external space here, as in the Middle Ages generally, is happenstance. Little thought went into the planning, which often produced an unbalanced, dispropor-tionate relationship between wall and floor planes, and unrelated enclosing agents. Renaissance architects, imbued with a desire for order, often left the square a mixture of architectural as well as spatial values, as in Arezzo. The *Piazza San Marco* in Venice carries the question further. It would appear to be a Renaissance square, but its history suggests otherwise. It was never a "planned" square, having evolved in empirical fashion from about 800 A.D. to Napoleonic times. There are no square cor-ners, except in the paving pattern, and there is the accident of in-terlocking squares. In fact, the typically medieval characteristic of wall plane off-sets tends to create a series of interwoven spaces, aided by the placement of the flagpoles, columns, and the pivotal *campanile*.

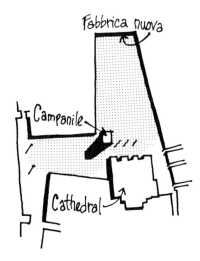

Finally, while four of the major enclosing agents date from the Renaissance, they were planned and built independently of one another, and except for the *Fabbrica Nuova*, without regard

for the total spatial effect they were creating—in other words, empirically in the tradition of the Middle Ages.

Art historians have long praised the artistic qualities of *San Marco*—its spatial proportions, its enclosing agents, its location and relationship to the surrounding city, its physical connections and entrances, the aesthetic merit of its vistas and *termini*. All of these qualities were obtained gradually, empirically, and like the *agora* of ancient Athens, *San Marco* has always functioned in consort with the city as an integral part of its pattern of growth through the centuries. It is truly the heart of Venice. Now, frozen by law since the nineteenth century, the *Piazza San Marco*, as well as many other empirically formed squares, is denied the essential quality of its history. Ironically, the planners of modern new towns seem to have recognized a value in change and are attempting to build it into their plans for new urban spaces, while other planners devise laws to prevent change—even in those places where change proved to be their primary means of ex-istence.

The medieval town badly needed its central open space. With its narrow, twisting streets and structures crowding together on hillsides like gulls on a rock, the town grew and changed without building code, ordinance, sanitation technology, or traf-fic control. It was often a raw, unhealthy place. It was also a suc-cess, insofar as it was a place where people wanted to be. When the wealthy merchants assigned manufacture to others, quit their apartments above their shops facing the square and began mov-ing to "suburban" palaces outside the walls, the unique quality of medieval town life came to a close. Classes separated, social stratification, and sprawl began: and though the alarms are now sounded by planners about more recent flights to suburbs, the pattern of modern urban growth began as early as the fourteenth century, and marked the end of the medieval town.

SIX

Order Imposed: Renaissance Volumetrics

The traditional time given for the beginning of the Renaissance is the early fifteenth century, where, in Northern Italian cities like Florence, the works of Brunelleschi, Alberti, Michelozzo, and others are seen as early attempts to alter medieval empiricism in architecture and urban design.

Actually, the transition began much earlier. There is no precise point, of course, when the medieval world came to a close and the Renaissance started, and in the limited view that sees the Renaissance as little more than a re-creation of Classic precepts there was no absolute break between Imperial Rome of the fifth century and Christian Rome of the fifteenth. But this would mean a rejection of the Middle Ages entirely, and today we see the Renaissance as a combination of Classic form and late medieval socioeconomic progress.

Further, the Renaissance was more an ideal than a reality, and Renaissance cities did not exist factually, in the same way as did medieval cities. This can be confusing to students visiting Florence for the first time, knowing it to be "the cradle of Humanism" but finding it to be a very medieval place. It had, after all, evolved over a thousand year period of empirical and organic order—a long series of day-to-day physical changes. Renaissance ideals, thoughts, and design concepts made but a slight dent in its medieval fabric.

The era we call the Renaissance was nonetheless a powerful force in the development of a spatial design vocabulary, its mark remaining in architecture and urban design to this day—particularly through a sequence of classic revivals in Europe and the new world.

There are many reasons given for the onset of the Renaissance at the beginning of the fifteenth century—the flight of the Greek scholars following the fall of Constantinople, the discovery of classic works, the writings of Dante and Petrarch, the great population increase in the cities of northern Italy, the rise of a wealthy and independent middle class. These may well be related pieces, but the total picture, including all of the cultural, economic and strategic factors, can only emerge from a conscientious and exhaustive sifting of the complexities of medieval life. We shall find it simpler to concern ourselves with the Renaissance for what it came to be—particularly in respect to urban design. With this kind of approach we can recognize and categorize the following developmental criteria.

Socio-economic Factors

The medieval city made slow but steady progress from the eleventh to the fifteenth century—from the formidable citadel to the expanding market town. This growth in size and awareness is the key to Renaissance development. The "discovery" of the classics could have occurred, after all, at any time during that 400 years. It occurred in the fifteenth century because socio-

71

economic factors had paved the way throughout the Middle Ages. Society had reached a point in time when it was ready to deal with new ideas. Long before the advent of humanism the social and economic machinery of medieval life had ground out the formula described in the previous chapter: the division of labor led to the development of *skill,* which produced *surplus,* which in turn produced *trade,* which in its turn led to quality and variety of goods, competition for markets and eventually leisure and wealth—both of which were necessary ingredients in the nurturing of humanism. Markets were created for goods not previously available or thought to be necessary, and a new division of labor began to grow. Ornament in precious metals, jewelry, silk and other rich cloth, finer tableware, woodcarving, and newly devised leather goods came into demand. The old artisan guilds of the middle ages, which had not distinguished between craftsman, owner and salesman, split into two camps—craftsman (worker) and merchant (boss). This distinction, together with the flight of the merchants from market square to palace and suburban villa, marked the end of the medieval market town and the beginning of the modern merchandising process.

Medieval social structure had been based forthrightly on a simple three-tiered anthropomorphic system: the feet and body of the society being the peasant class, the arms being the nobility and the head, of course, the clergy.

Peasant society was protected and controlled by the clergy, while serving the nobility. In the division of artisans into workers and merchants, we see the old medieval structure collapsing and a new order emerging, with peasants and urban laborers at the bottom, a growing middle class of merchants, bankers and other groups in control of wealth—and the shrinking in strength of church and nobility alike. The basis of power shifted to money, and a new ruling class of the Renaissance emerged in the fifteenth century which was more dependent upon bankers than bishops and kings.

Political-religious Factors

There were other significant changes which mark the termination of one era and the beginning of another. Politically, the internal structure of government in many northern Italian city-states began to change from a predominantly republican form, or representative government, towards rule by family, hired strongman or prince (over a largely impotent local assembly). Externally, the city-state concept of the middle ages gave way to the nation-state, as rulers combined wealth and power to extend their spheres of domination over the adjacent landscape and previously independent neighbors. In France and England the nation-state had been in existence for some time, and in Central Europe there was Charlemagne's empire (800 A.D.). But in Italy we see it as part of the changing political structure which marks the Renaissance: from a medieval city-state system comparable to classic Greece—to a capital city/nation-state. Thus, the Republic of Venice, the Duchy of Milan, the Republic of Florence, and the Papal States, among others, became the powerful new nations of fifteenth century Italy, with relatively clear boundaries, capital cities, and offensive military strength. By the same token the planning of streets, squares and new civic architecture, including churches, became a conscious political activity—not unlike Imperial Rome.

Likewise, the shifting political structure affected the character of Christianity, and the church began losing a measure of its spiritual force, at the same time taking on the trappings of Roman classicism. It was a decision made consciously by a papacy caught up in the struggle to retain authority over Christianity in Europe, amidst the growing worldliness of Humanism on the one hand and the threat of the rival Avignon papacy on the other (The Great Schism, 1378–1417). Thus the worldly church of the early fifteenth century abandoned the fervent mysticism of the Gothic cathedral in favor of neoclassic monumentality. Westward orientation gave way to regularization within the limitations of a doctrinaire planning concept—as had also occurred in Imperial Rome. Chartres gave way to the basilica of St. Peter's, where size and volumetrics reflected political creed more than Christian zeal.

Humanism

The spirit and guiding force of the Renaissance was found in the awakening interest in classical Rome, and though the term has a somewhat broader meaning to us today, in the fifteenth and sixteenth centuries it was limited simply to the study of Classic works—particularly literature, drama, music, sculpture, and architecture. For the early humanists that meant the works which literally lay about them. Their only contact with Classic Greece came from Vitruvius and references in Roman relics, and for that reason Alberti's and Palladio's views of Greek architecture and public spaces are quite inaccurate.

The pursuit of classical study was made possible only by the economic advances discussed earlier, which led to the acquisition of wealth, and more importantly to leisure. Alberti's family, for example, were of sufficient means to provide him with the opportunities and the encouragement to pursue music, architecture—and particularly classic history. Humanists believed literally in the infallibility of the Romans and labored tirelessly to bring to light once more the beauty and purity of their artistic wisdom. Alberti, one of the foremost architects of the fifteenth century, built only half a dozen major structures, and these primarily as a means of establishing in fact the principles he espoused in theory. His life's work was in truth his book, *De re Aedificatoria* (Ten Books of Architecture).

Humanists calculated proportions, reconstructed Classic design theory and wrote books in order to guide the thought processes of their peers in the ways of Classicism. They were more interested in the struggle of ideas than in wrestling with the day-to-day means of practical form. They rarely tore down cities to build new ones, except to plan new fortifications, streets and monuments. In fact, cities changed during the fifteenth and sixteenth centuries mainly by the addition of monumental civic buildings and the palaces of the wealthy, which in turn affected the character of adjacent streets and squares. There were exceptions, of course, in the way of totally planned market and civic squares, and rules governing their proportions, which we will deal with shortly.

Rational Design Philosophy

The study of ideal proportion in classic form led the humanists into development of a rational approach to design. The writings of Alberti and Palladio, along with Sebastiano Serlio, Filarete, and Giacomo da Vignola are absolutely filled with rules, laws, and measures. The meaning of design rationalism has been explained earlier, and through their words and works we shall see how it was formulated by the architectural humanists of the fifteenth and sixteenth centuries.

What motivated Renaissance form givers? To assume that their study of antiquities constitutes the only source of inspiration to peer architects is to relegate the whole of Renaissance spatial art to that of eclecticism or neoclassicism, without any originality or spirit of its own.

The Renaissance spirit, which embodies the art forms emerging in the fifteenth century, was actually the result of a blending of Classicism with a fresh, individualistic approach to design, not witnessed in the Middle Ages. The "backward look" engaged the imagination of Alberti and humanist thinkers for generations to come, but it is the "look forward" which gives the Renaissance its spirit of independence from medieval practice. It is on the shoulders of artists and thinkers of individual genius that the Renaissance was truly carried forward—from the early efforts of Filippo Brunelleschi to the culminating triumphs of Michelangelo. For those who used classicism as inspiration, rather than in slavish adulation, the art of the Renaissance flourished. In this regard we associate the "forward look" of the age with its most advanced thinker, Leonardo da Vinci. His work involved the search for truth in natural order, and its pursuit made him a careful and patient observer of all things. He knew that the answers to questions which mankind had rarely dared to ask lay before him, requiring only his eyes and mind to understand their meaning.

Leonardo's search for the truths enbodied in nature coincided with the search for natural form determinants, undertaken by him and other creative minds of the Renaissance. Classic form was not enough for them. They sought more basic, absolute criteria upon which to lay a design rationale, a search which led them in three directions: toward *nature, man,* and *music.*

Nature. In their efforts to understand some logic or purpose in form and structure the Renaissance scholars turned to plant and animal life, as well as to the stars and planets—greatly aided in both directions by the inventions of microscope and telescope. There, on the threshold of modern science, they made awesome discoveries, which they related abstractly to mathematical form. The structure of a peach blossom or bean pod provided Renaissance architects, for example, with natural proof for the logic of centric organization as well as structural engineering.

Man. More significant, however, to Renaissance scholars and architects was the relationship between physical human form and the universality of centric structure in design. Their studies of anatomy were intensified, because they believed that the secrets of organization in architecture and urban design could be revealed to them through the human body—as God's greatest gift to mankind. In this way, the circle and the sphere—the most basic forms found in nature—were juxtaposed over the figure of man, by countless architectural theorists, in an effort to convince

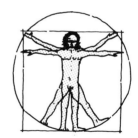

themselves of the magnitude of this "discovery." Leonardo and the others were sometimes hard pressed in their efforts to prove man's place at the center of nature—the substance of which was itself reduceable to simple geometric form. Man became thereby the center of life, elevated by fifteenth century scholars to a place on the right hand of God. In truth, God was himself recreated in the image of *man*—a discovery by which the humanists saw themselves greatly benefited. Whether *God* or *man* came first mattered very little—as long as in the end they were the same.

Man was elevated thus by Renaissance scholars to a place of dominance over nature, rather than simply a part of it. Proportions for architectural works, cities, squares, and nearly everything in art could be reduced to geometric form—the basis for which was, in theory, human form.

Music. The architects of the fifteenth and sixteenth centuries found in musical harmony their best means of establishing criteria for artistic proportion.

From early Greek musical notation and the studies of classical thinkers like Pythagoras and Plato, Renaissance scholars were able to formulate a basis for harmonic proportions in architecture and civic planning. For example, Greek musical theorists had long before discovered and recorded that when a vibrating string (as in a *magadis*) was divided by 2/3 of its length it vibrated in two octaves; that is, when the length of the string is halved it will vibrate a full octave higher.

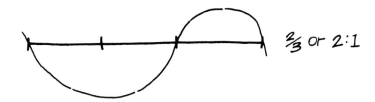

$\frac{2}{3}$ or 2:1

In this simple illustration we see the cornerstone of musical ratio, which led the humanists into an abiding faith in the integral relationship between musical and physical form.

But doubling a proportion, or a vibrating string, produces no harmony. The basis of harmonic proportion in the age of Humanism rests on those intervals which produce pleasing combinations in pitch—primarily the interval of the *fifth*, shown as:

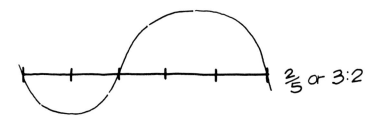

$\frac{2}{5}$ or 3:2

The musical interval of the *fifth* produces the most melodious relationship between two notes—a fact as true today as when recorded by Classic scholars—and is represented on the diatonic scale (8 notes) by *do* and *so* in any key. Count these out for yourself and hum the two notes aloud. You will know immediately that the interval is correct.

The next interval of significance in musical notation is the *fourth*, or 4:3. This is an interval of four, and is represented by

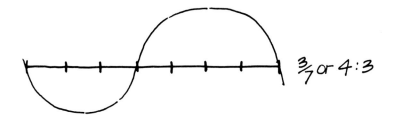

$\frac{3}{7}$ or 4:3

do and *fa*. The Greeks discovered that these basic musical harmonies had a ratio of vibrating string lengths as:

Octave	fifth	fourth	or,
1:2	2:3	3:4	

$$1 : 2 : 3 : 4$$

Humanists, like Leone Alberti, thereby evolved a series of proportions which were pleasing by "law of nature" and not by whim or individual taste, for logic, as a basis of proportion, was the cornerstone of humanists' thought. Palladio in the sixteenth century recorded these proportions as being proper for the length and width of rooms, as:

a square and one-third	(3:4)
a square and one half	(2:3)
two squares	(1:2)

Further analysis of musical notation reveals that each note, (including their sharps and flats,) vibrates at specific number per second, and that these vibrations form ratios which are comparable to measurable dimensions.

To successfully *generate* height, or the volume dimension, Palladio used arithmetic and geometric formula to produce the mean dimension. For example, a space measuring 60 × 120 would have a mean dimension (height or width) of 90. The first term is to the second as the second is to the third. His formula for generating the mean dimension by harmonic proportion is more complicated. According to Palladio three measurements are in harmony when the distance of the two extremes from the mean is the same fraction of their own quantity. Eighty is the mean in this case, as:

$$\frac{80 - 60}{60} = \frac{120 - 80}{120} = \frac{1}{3}$$

80 exceeds 60 by 1/3 of 60, as 120 exceeds 80 by 1/3 of 120.

The dependence upon accepted formula in the practice of architecture and civic design became the habit of all Renaissance architects, and harmonic proportions was unquestionably the leading influence, as Alberti states:

> We shall therefore borrow all our rules for harmonic relations from the musicians, to whom this sort of numbers is extremely well known, and from those particular things wherein nature shows herself most excellent and complete.[1]

Nature, man, musical harmony were the keys to the Renaissance scholars' search for form, and combined with Classicism became the basis of architecture and civic design for some time to come. With this in mind we can better understand the restrictive, calculated nature of the *principles* which governed their work, as follows:

(1) *Spatial unity.* The overall guiding spirit of rational design, and particularly Renaissance design order, guarding against empirical change, whimsy or any aspect of form unrelated to the concepts governing the whole.

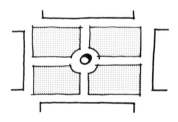

(2) *Limitation of space.* A major characteristic of Renaissance space is its finite nature. The volumetrics developed by Filippo Brunelleschi and other fifteenth century architects were precisely calculated and visually apparent, giving the participant a clear idea of the structure and an awareness of the spatial rhythm occurring around him. The Church of Santo Spirito in Florence illustrates this quality of spatial modulation. External space was similarly treated, whether it be in the matter of garden, street or piazza; the scheme was conceived in total, the enclosing agents carefully planned. When vistas were to be extended they were likewise terminated in a rhythmically controlled manner, as in the Uffizi Palace gallery, Florence, which connects the *Piazza* with the River Arno.

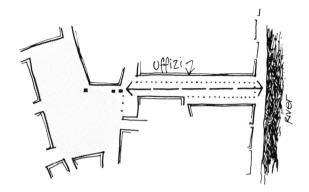

(3) *Measured order.* Renaissance space is geometric, measured, and proportioned. Rhythm results from a repetition of geometric device or form—arcade, colonnade, bay, window detailing, or paving pattern. It strives for symmetry, regularity, and axial organization. The structures acting as enclosing agents are employed to establish the volumetrics of the square, resulting in a strongly articulated statement, defying alteration or addition.

(4) *Absolute standards.* The architecture of the fifteenth and sixteenth centuries, like its imperial predecessor, depended upon a self-contained system of harmony, balance, rhythm, and proportion. This is to say that Renaissance architects, working from

1. Wittkower, *Architectural Principles*, p. 97.

drawings, scaled plans, and orthographic projection, developed building designs which carried out their concepts of artistic form without respect for human functions or sense of scale. This was almost exactly opposite to the organic nature of the medieval square, where human needs and usage took precedence over form or any pretence of aesthetic purpose. Absolute standards were abstracted for use in architecture and urban design from the humanists' studies of harmonic proportion and natural form.

(5) *Advances in military technology.* The use of gunpowder, leading to the development of the cannon as a leading siege weapon in the fifteenth century, brought about a need for revolutionizing of walls and structural defenses. Several architects of the time, including Leonardo da Vinci and Antonio da Sangailo (the elder), were employed as designers of cannon-proof fortifications. Successful solutions included the introduction of low, thick walls, battered to withstand cannon fire, and often including a long, sloping *glacis* and counterscarp for the purpose of preventing the use of siege machinery as well as improving the defenders' view.

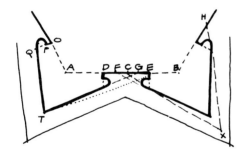

The result of these greatly altered methods of defense, which often included a series of walls, ditches, and arrow point bastions, was to seriously affect growth and change of any kind in a city's physical form. This led to the wholesale replanning of existing cities and gave stimulus to the designing of new cities from scratch. Alberti, a designer of "ideal cities" himself, makes this observation relevant to the problems inherent in monumental defenses; mainly, how far out beyond present limits should walls be constructed in order to allow for future growth:

I think there is a great deal of wisdom in the old proverb which tells us that we ought in all things to avoid excess; though if I were to commit an error on either side I should rather choose that proportion which would allow of an increase of citizens than that which is hardly sufficient to contain the present inhabitants. Add to this that a city is not built wholly for the sake of shelter, but ought to be so contrived, that besides mere civil conveniences there may be handsome spaces left for squares, courses for chariots, gardens, places to take the air in, swimming and the like, both for ornament and recreation.[2]

Alberti's farsightedness is often amazing, particularly his anticipation of the need for the profession of landscape architecture!

(6) *Conditions of health.* The medieval town, you will remember, was subject to crowded, unhealthy conditions which limited sunlight and the passage of air, and led to problems of sewage disposal and other sanitary shortcomings. Both Alberti and Palladio observed these conditions and made plans for their correction. Here is Palladio's advice:

The more the city is therefore in a cold place, and hath subtle air, and where edifices are made very high, so much the wider the streets ought to be made that they may in each of their parts be visited by the sun!

Palladio adds that in cases of hot climates the streets should be narrower, but continues:

. . . . however, for the greater ornament and convenience of the city, the streets most frequented by the principle arts, and by passengers, ought to be made spacious, and adorned with magnificent and sumptuous fabricks, that foreigners who pass through it may easily be inclined to believe, that to the beauty and largeness of this, the other streets of the city may also correspond.[3]

These principles, which in general governed the form of Renaissance external space, led to the following tangible results, which

2. Leone Alberti, *Ten Books of Architecture;* Book IV, p. 71.
3. A. Palladio, *Four Books of Architecture;* Book III, Ch. 2, p. 59.

we can observe in extant squares of the fifteenth and sixteenth centuries.

(1) *Total Planning*, aided by the discovery of *orthographic projection*, became an accomplished fact in the Renaissance. It is the first time since Imperial Rome that external space was resolved in plan, three dimensionally. This includes, of course, a predetermination of the function of the square and its enclosing structures.

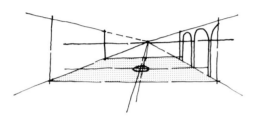

(2) The *use of arcades* to unify, limit, and organize planned urban spaces. The arcade, according to Alberti, was the only acceptable form for a free standing, open wall. The colonnade, in his opinion, was meant to be used only as engaged decoration on a solid wall or structural façade. (Bernini obviously took exception to Alberti with the colonnade at St. Peter's Square.)

(3) The *subordination of enclosing architecture* in order to maintain the significance of the whole. Standards of proportion were fixed by both Alberti and Palladio so as to assure an aesthetic balance of form, as well as a healthy space—open to the passage of air and sunlight. According to Palladio:

> All the edifices made round a piazza ought not to be higher than the third part of the breadth of the piazza, nor lower than the sixth.[4]

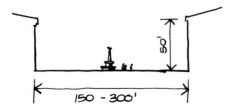

(4) *Specific organizing elements*, such as fountain, obelisk, or sculpture, were used to punctuate the planned volumetrics of the square and its axial organization. The *centric square*, you will recall, depended upon these devices to generate a sense of visual dynamics. The centric placement of fountains, obelisks

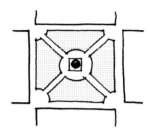

and the like had become, therefore, a conscious act of design, altogether different from the seemingly arbitrary placement of medieval focal points. It is another aspect of total planning and the rational basis of Renaissance form.

(5) The advent of *monumental scale* in Renaissance space was a result of self-contained proportions as well as an augmentation of political strength, similar to the manner of Imperial Rome. But the city-states of fifteenth century Italy bore no other resemblance to empire, and the copying of Classic monumentality often appears as haughty posturing—especially in view of adjacent medieval structures of humble, human scale. In urban spaces of the Renaissance we are aware of such examples of monumentality as the *Loggia dei Lanzi*, which partially encloses the *Piazza della Signoria* in Florence. To visually project this monumental arcade around the entire square, completing the Renaissance theme of measured order, is to envisage a grand, self-contained spatial scheme, out of touch with the status of human relationship that now exists in that place.

(6) *Domination over nature*. The humanist philosophy of the fifteenth and sixteenth century caused the extension of geometric form over the natural landscape and greatly influenced garden planning. This had a very lasting effect on

4. *Ibid.*, (Also Alberti, L. B., p. 173).

garden design and particularly on urban planning. It was the garden of this period that served as forerunner of later urban design schemes, including the radiating avenues and nodal traffic coordinators which became so popular in the seventeenth and eighteenth centuries. In the sixteenth century garden the basic elements of nature were exploited: stone, water, plants, earth. Walls were formed from evergreen plants, clipped into rigid, architectonic form. Stone was laid in flat planes of geometric pattern, always maintaining a level line, or forming into steps and retaining walls when it became necessary to resolve grade change. A hillside, cut into a series of cubistic facets of horizontal and vertical planes stood apart in sharp contrast to its surroundings. Water was diverted from natural courses to flow into the intricate piping system of the garden, in order to create the cascades, fountains, and mirrorlike pools, as if by command. This seeking of supremacy over nature offers perhaps the most revealing glimpse into the rationale of the humanists' design philosophy.

Villa Lante

In summary, the geometric theme which overshadows garden and urban design in this age was a result of the following:

1. The study of *classic* form.
2. The study of *nature*, from which geometric abstractions were made.
3. A renewed interest in *mathematics*, and the objectivity resulting from a dependence on rules and methods based on precision.
4. The rediscovery of *harmonic* principles in musical consonances.
5. The study of *human* form, resulting in man becoming physically as well as intellectually central to the design process. (In *Le Modulor*, Le Corbusier brings this process into a contemporary focus.)

The change from an organic socioeconomic structure to a rational political theme was responsible for much of the change that occurred in urban design from the Middle Ages to the Renaissance. The conversion from market town to capital city assisted the humanists in their efforts to convince the growing establishment of middle class bankers that urban order suited their prestigious needs.

But the city of the fifteenth century had not come into being overnight, nor could it be changed that easily. Despite the spate of ideal plans emanating from urban designers, the real work had to be done in the existing urban structure, and the Renaissance architects set about the task of converting market and church squares into the formalized *piazze* advocated by Alberti, Palladio, and Serlio.

Many of these appear half-hearted or incomplete, like the *Piazza Grande* in Arezzo or the *Piazza della Signoria* in Florence, but some proved to be absolute triumphs of rational will over organic dissonance.

The *Piazza Annunziata* in Florence depended upon the efforts of several men, over more than a century, before its axial symmetry

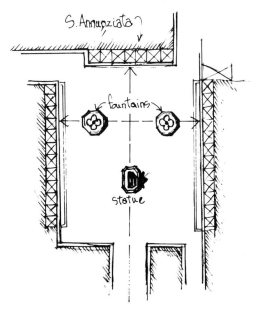

and volumetric rhythm was realized. Filippo Brunelleschi's Foundling Hospital (1421–45) established the rectilinear theme and rhythm by its placement to the side of the old church and its classic proportioned arcade. The form was eventually repeated on the opposite side, and the addition of a repetitious colonnade all about the square, together with the central statue and flanking fountains, completed the composition in strict axial form.

In Pienza a few years later Bernardo Rossellino was presented with the prospect of designing a square in front of the cathedral, the form of which had already been determined by the acute angle of the flanking structures.

Rossellino's success, and the sense of exaggerated perspective achieved by the opposing colonnades and paving pattern was repeated and greatly improved upon by Michelangelo's treatment of the *Campidoglio* in Rome. Again, the existing acute angle, made by the *Palazzo dei Senatori* and the *Palazzo dei Conservatori,* was

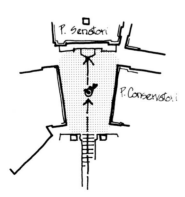

balanced symmetrically by the addition of an opposite structure canted at the same acute angle.

The sense of forced perspective was thus assured, and like Rosselino before him, Michelangelo had made the most of an empirical relationship, but unlike Rossellino, Michelangelo demonstrated a superior sense of volumetric order by the further addition of both a strong axial development and a masterful centric order. The first evolves from the arrangement of in-line visual termini. The tower over the Senate building, the flight of stairs, the flanking equestrian figures, the statue of Marcus Aurelius, and the sculptured niche at the base of the stairs flanked by the Neptune figures. As one approaches the square from below each of these elements in axial alignment punctuates the experience of movement upward, into, and through the square.

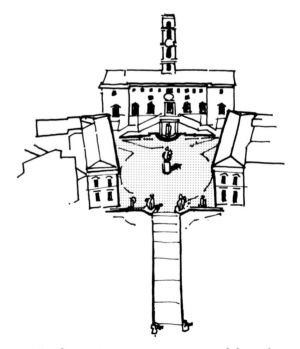

The centric theme is even more successful, and results from the placement of the classic figure of the emperor Marcus Aurelius, at the center of an elliptical shape which is literally carved into the square—the edge of which is curbed and stepped down, and then, rising from all sides towards the center. More than a mere paving pattern, the elliptical design is truly a three-dimensional form, to which the three flanking structures play a subordinate but wholly supportive role.

By comparison the *Piazza San Marco,* Venice, although Renaissance in many respects, remains empirical in its historic evolution. This does not result from the enclosing buildings themselves, several of which are clearly Renaissance, but the overall lack of coordinated volumetric organization in the resulting spaces (see page 70). There is order and rhythm in their individual facades, and rational logic in the arrangement of visual termini, but the resulting space is more a matter of happy accident than planned achievement, the final empirical note being the connection of the *Fabbrica nuova* with the *Procuratie vecchie* made at the beginning of the nineteenth century.

The *Piazza San Marco* remains nonetheless one of the exceptional examples of successful urban space in the western world. It is actually a series of interrelated spaces, each subtly overlapping the other, the one leading inevitably to the next by a sense of curiosity and spatial manipulation which is both oriental and medieval. In the drawing the movement patterns and overlapping spaces are illustrated.

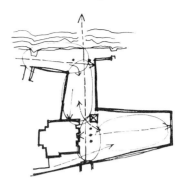

The primary concern, however, of Renaissance urban designers was the creation of entirely new spaces, based on the same rational formulae governing architectural volumetrics. The fifteenth century was still a little early for massive urban restructure, and Renaissance squares designed and built from scratch are precious few. One noteworthy example, the *Piazza Ducale* in Vigevano, is sufficient for our purposes as it serves very well to illustrate the spatial criteria of the age. Here we see spatial unity, limitation of space, measured order and absolute standards in the rectilinear form, its enclosing structures subordinate to the whole, while generating rhythmic movement along the arcaded facades. Its axial plan is dominated by a directional force terminating at the church facade, which is further emphasized by carefully placed sculptural form and paving patterns. Vigevano,

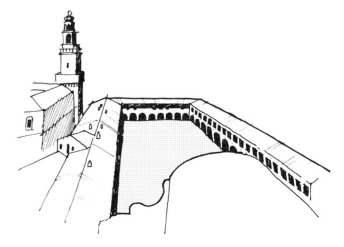

more than Florence, Rome or Venice, offers the textbook example of Renaissance spatial concepts (pp. 112-113).

These concepts, derived intellectually rather than emotionally—from objective logic rather than any intuitive sense of beauty—became the doctrine of urban form for a long period of time following the sixteenth century. As coldly formal as many of these followers tended to be, the Renaissance itself was not wholly without emotion or intuitive form. Michelangelo's superiority as a designer is not based on a better understanding of mathematics and musical harmony, nor was he totally subservient to the proportions dictated by Alberti. He used his eye as the final arbiter of form—a clearly intuitive device! And he embellished his work with curves, volutes, and garlands of decorative floral brocade. Absolutism in rational design was thereby rendered palatable by the intuitive instincts of the designers themselves. Even Alberti refused to accept the dictates of his own writings when, in the design of *Sant' Andrea* in Mantua, he discovered the proportions previously determined to be unpleasing to his own eye! It is unfortunate that so many lesser followers placed a greater faith in rules than their own visual acumen. It is the only explanation for the long, dreary line of neoclassic works which have succeeded even to the present. It,

therefore, becomes a test of the design student's own sensitivity in differentiating between the classic and the classless in rational art.

Large scale rational concepts were rarely achieved by the builders of Renaissance towns, but in declaring their principles of design and form the humanists of the fifteenth and sixteenth centuries provided the impetus for succeeding generations of visionary planners. And there were some physical successes nonetheless. Palma Nuova was completed in the sixteenth century, and Granmichele, although it follows a century later, is without doubt the definitive example of Renaissance rationalism in urban space. In fact, it seems a casebook study of ideal planning, with its hexagonal plan, centric square, radiating streets, and equidistant subordinate squares representing neighborhood centers (p. 115).

Granmichele is unique in this respect, owing its existence perhaps to a location in Sicily, where the Renaissance was only just arriving in the seventeenth century, and where opportunity for such an undertaking was certainly apparent in that forgotten land of medieval and foreign design. It is the final statement of an age of ideal principles, which had itself already passed into history.

SEVEN

Order Expanded: Radial and Neoclassic Form

Despite the considerable achievements in art and science during the Renaissance, the greater part of the sixteenth century was marred by religious warfare raging across the face of Europe.

The Protestant Reformation, caused in part no doubt by Papal excesses, resulted in major political realignment and a broad reassessment of standards in respect to matters of faith, which in turn led to major changes in the architectural form of the seventeenth and eighteenth centuries. The centric, self-contained volumetrics of Renaissance space did not suit Protestant requirements for a simpler spiritual interpretation of aesthetic values. The counter-Reformation, which we define as the primarily militant reaction against Protestant reform carried out by Spain and her allies, offered no aesthetic alternatives—only massacre and inquisition.

The Catholic Reformation, on the other hand, sought a positive reinforcement for Church stability by reexamining and then redirecting the old spiritual values. The Catholic Reformation was in part a reaching back to medieval Christian spirituality, while restructuring the static tenets of classic metrics into a dynamic, positive artistic force. The art and architecture resulting from this spiritual redirection is called Baroque—a term which in the seventeenth century came to represent the reawakening of church principles.

We should not, however, confuse "Baroque" with "baroque"—a term often used by art critics to mean the embellish-ment, even ornamentation, of an otherwise unchanged style or motive (see page 28). As the principal artistic tool of Catholic reform, Baroque architecture is noted by its dynamic qualities, its restless movement, bright interiors and elaborate organic modulation of form and detail. A Baroque interior is a gold and white crescendo of expanding volumes, punctuated by cherubic and floral forms captured at the prime of their essence.

While church architecture remains the definitive form of Baroque art, there was nonetheless considerable expansion in the art of urban design at this time. In fact, the seventeenth and eighteenth centuries are represented by the greatest achievements and richest variety produced by the western world, in the broad area of civic development.

In view of this great variety in form and purpose it will be necessary for us to define the terminology we expect to use, and categorize types.

Baroque, as we are using it, refers to the dynamic, theatrical volumetrics of seventeenth century church architecture—particularly from Italy. The eighteenth century form—often called *Rococo*—refers more specifically to the advanced dynamics developed in the Roman Catholic Church architecture of southern Germany. In urban design, Baroque identifies the primarily *radial* street systems developed first in Rome and later in many other European cities, featuring an interconnecting network of hub and spoke pattern (see page 117).

Neoclassic generally refers to a return in the eighteenth century to the classic, self-contained tenets of urban form developed during the Renaissance. We will apply it specifically to rectilinear urban spaces, as developed primarily in the eighteenth century.

The functions carried out by urban spaces of the Baroque and Neoclassic periods had by this time evolved in complexity. In addition to the traditional needs served, as marketplace, parvis, government square, the seventeenth and eighteenth century squares fulfilled the following important roles as well:

1. overall traffic coordinator
   a. as central hub in a radial network
   b. to facilitate approach and departure
2. as central element to the general urban structure
3. as a means of defining and structuring secondary urban centers and residential complexes
4. as a means of providing visual relief through
   a. open space
   b. variation in form and materials

The physical structure for all the above Baroque and Neoclassic squares is geometric—largely a result of Renaissance influence, including the external restraints of increasing regularity in urban form. Organic street patterns were being rapidly eradicated by Baroque planners. As such, we find two primary forms evolving:

Radial
Rectilinear

The Radial Square

If one can accept this contradiction in terms, the radial square epitomizes the first function listed above—that of *overall traffic coordinator*. It is the hub, or node of the Baroque street system, receiving and dispersing the traffic flowing through it. Normally circular, hence the name, it is by definition an *open square*—so much so that it loses much of its usefulness as *place*. And it has been further reduced in that respect in today's high speed automotive city, retaining little of its earlier pedestrian function.

The radial square is nearly always *centric*, particularly when serving as a traffic coordinator. We will usually find some form of traffic pylon in its center, the only safe place for a pedestrian to linger. In Rome, where the radial street system was first envisioned by Sixtus V (1590) as a means of relating the various disparate urban elements into a structured system, the central fulcrum was usually an obelisk (taken from Egypt). The value of the obelisk as a choice should be obvious. It punctuates the open space, giving meaning to its circular form by acting as a radius point, and three-dimensionally as a traffic directing pylon around which autos soar, peel off, or gather. It provides aesthetic balance as the singular vertical theme (as well as sexual balance, with obelisk as male symbol, circular open space as female). But most importantly, it provides the necessary dynamic punch to the score, by its arresting visability. From one radial square, accented by its central obelisk, our eye is led down the various diverging avenues to other nodal points, accepted by their own obelisks or other similar devices.

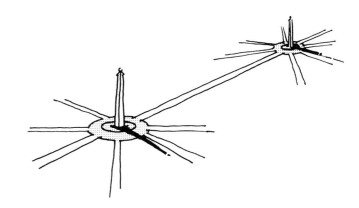

It is the *tension*, created visually between two such squares, which gives Baroque urban space its dynamic quality. This visual attraction tends to make it *centripetal* (see page 21).

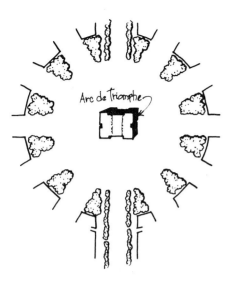

The *Place de l'Etoile*, Paris, (above) is an example of the radial square as a traffic coordinator, and in this case the *Arc de Triomphe* replaces the obelisk. The visual effect is to arrest the eye, as expected, while allowing the sight line to pass cleanly through, and along the *Champs Elysees*. It was not the original purpose, perhaps, but it serves to illustrate an advantage over the solid obelisk which, by placement on axis interrupts sight line continuity.

Paris, like Rome, is primarily a radial city, after the monumental street system restructuring by Baron Georges Haussmann, although it belongs to the nineteenth rather than the seventeenth century. It nevertheless abounds in examples of radial squares, like the *Place Bastille,* with its great column at the center and the *Place des Victoires* with its statue of Louis XIV.

In Rome, the old *Piazza Esedra* (in front of Diocletian's Baths) was redeveloped in the nineteenth century into the Neptune fountain, but its older function as traffic coordinator remains unchanged (p. 116).

The radial square has also functioned as a means of providing an *approach* or *departure* point, as the obelisks placed before St. Peter's basilica and the Church of Sta. Maria Maggiore in Rome serve to illustrate. It is of course the obelisk which first receives our attention, completing the visual connection which leads us to the square, along the several converging avenues. Should the prime structure facing the square not benefit from its location then the square itself may accomplish the purpose, serving as visual recipient to the radiating sight lines, which, of course, focus inevitably on the vertical shaft at the center. This concept was the basis of Sixtus V's plan for Rome.

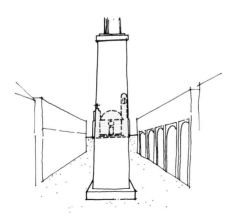

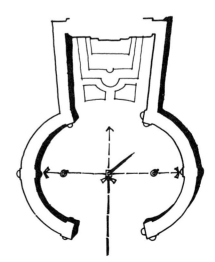

In respect to St. Peter's, the obelisk was placed on axis directly in front of the facade, at a distance of 275 meters (900 feet). Using this as fulcrum for both primary and secondary axial sight lines, Gianlorenzo Bernini enscribed his great elliptiical colonnade, like the arms of the church reaching out to offer its comfort. He chose this form partly no doubt out of respect for Michelangelo's handling of the *Campidoglio*, but by laying it out *across* the main axis (The *Via Conciliazione*) he achieved the opposite effect. Michelangelo's elliptical space—in line with the main axis—serves to heighten and accelerate movement along the single sight line (page 80), while at St. Peter's a slowing down occurs. Here the axis of the ellipse opposes the main sight line, creating a visual pause in the directional impetus, slowing and eddying the traffic—much like the flow of water is effected by a wide place in the stream. A rectangle on cross-axis would bring about a similar result; but the ellipse, like a circle, maintains the potential for radial movement, as the paving pattern here suggests. The ellipse is therefore unique in maintaining the properties of both circle and rectangle.

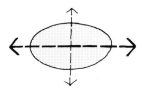

We can observe the marvelous properties of circle and ellipse in funneling radial traffic patterns, but the dome is equally successful for much the same reason—that of visual terminus—in that it always looks the same, no matter the angle from which it is viewed.

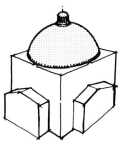

The radial approach was commonly used in garden design in the seventeenth century, illustrated by Versailles and Hampton Court—the great palaces of the French and English kings of the time. Again, its function as a receiver of converging avenues makes the radial square a useful design tool, in pedestrian as well as vehicular traffic patterns.

The *Piazza del Popolo*, Rome, illustrates the same theme in reverse. The diverging avenues which lead away from the elliptical *piazza* were intended to distribute to the various parts of the city those arriving at the *Porto del Popolo*.

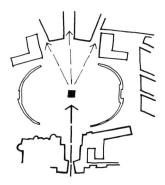

In any event the radial square, acting as hub to the overall Baroque street system, performed its function of traffic coordinator very well in the seventeenth century and for the two centuries that followed. In today's traffic however, one need only imagine the anguish which results from the convergence of six, eight, even ten avenues of autos maneuvering for position on the pole, or struggling to reach the outside lane—for to pass your point of exit means to stay on this nerve jangling merry-go-round another revolution.

The Neoclassic Square

For our purposes, remember, we will use the term *Neoclassic* to identify the post-Renaissance rectilinear spaces of the eighteenth century. In terms of their grandeur of scale, their haughty splendor and formal disposition, their carefully delineated volumetrics and their position of significance in location, these squares represent a successful conclusion to the experiments in urban space conducted by Brunelleschi and others in the fifteenth century market towns of northern Italy. If those early attempts at regularity in external volumetrics presaged a change in the purpose of urban space—a shift from economic to political purpose, then the grand formal open space compositions of the age of Louis XV were infinitely well suited to their function. Like the gardens of Versailles and Vaux-le-Vicomte, the grand *places royales* depicted precisely the character of France at the height of its royal power and glory. They also represent a significant shift of design leadership from Italy to France, and in time the idea of the large, formal *place* was recognized throughout Europe (except in Great Britain, where the same kind of formal emphasis in landscape design produced instead the country estate).

Although the Neoclassic *place royale* owes its conception to the form and purpose of the Italian sixteenth century *piazza*, there are a number of significant differences between them. First of all, the Neoclassic square was rarely if ever considered incidental to the urban whole. It was from inception intended as the heart of the city, and the core of its physical structure. In short, whole sections might be razed if necessary and rebuilt around the central space so as to effect its physical integration into the area and its sense of unity with the city as a whole. This idea, above all other differences, is the most significant aspect of the *places royales*. With this broader, all encompassing view of urban space design, the Neoclassic square could hardly miss. Add to that its second most significant attribute—spatial sequence, and the major differences from basic Renaissance form are revealed.

By spatial sequence we refer to the continuity of visual or spatial experience beyond the square itself. This was accomplished in several ways. First, the street systems continued through the square, along predetermined sight lines, with specified termini. In this way the square appeared to bond itself to the central urban scheme, its open form and axial avenues in balance with the enclosing mass. Secondly, by addition of other

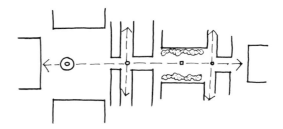

aligned squares, a series of urban spaces emerged. When carried throughout the urban structure, this device became a method of overall urban design much the same as the radial system first envisioned by Pope Sixtus V in Rome.

The best example of the first type is perhaps the *Place de la Concorde*, Paris. Designed primarily by Jacques Ange Gabriel in 1763, this square is the principal form in a structure of streets and spaces stretching over a mile in two directions. From the center of the square we can follow a grand system of sight lines, the

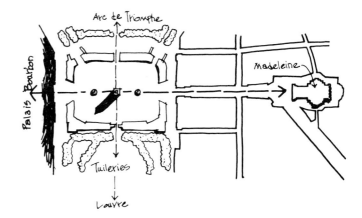

north-south axis terminated by the Madeleine Church at one end and, across the Seine River, by the *Palais Bourbon* at the other (which actually faces the opposite direction, but was given a classic portico on its rear in order to match the Madeleine and thereby complete the grand visual scheme pp. 118–119).

This monumental cross axis is marked at the crossing of the two sight lines by an obelisk (originally a mounted figure of Louis

XV), the short north-south axis reinforced by two fountains Flanking the obelisk, and emphasizing the cross-axial function of the *place* itself—much in the same way as the elliptical *Piazza San Pietro,* Rome, stands across the primary axis leading to the cathedral.

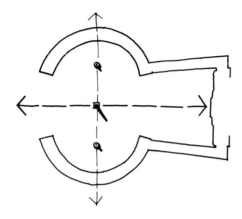

At *Concorde* the sight lines leading away, down the *Champs Elysees* toward the *Arc de Triomphe,* or through the *Tuileries* to the *Arc du Carousel* and the *Palais de Louvre,* as well as those of the short axis, give the scheme a centrifugal dynamic force from the central point at the obelisk. But looking towards the obelisk from any direction, the opposite dynamic quality is expressed. The scheme is thereby balanced but not static.

The sculptural moats which gave the great rectangle a sense of form no longer exist, and the automobiles whizzing down the Champs wheel to the right in the manner of the radial system, scattering tourists who have come to see the spot where Louis XVI lost his head, then turning sharply the traffic swings left, rounding off the corners of the *place* in a battle for pole position and the dash toward the Madeleine. Subjected to the brutality of modern traffic, the Neoclassic squares with their hard angularity and stodgy formality have proven less adaptive than have radial squares.

One of the finest, however, remains very much in tact at Nancy, in eastern France. Here a series of carefully articulated

spaces unfolds along a single sight line, each separate but dependent upon the total spatial progression. The series begins with a government square (*Place Stanislas*), framed by the city hall, shops, and other government buildings. It is cleary centric, the statue of Prince Stanislas marking the intersection of the primary sight line. Here the rhythm narrows (where it once bridged the moat), passes through an archway and into a grand tree-lined mall (*Place Carrière*). With its elaborate gardens and clipped *allées* this square acts as a connector to the final space (The Hemicycle), terminated in grand formality by the Ducal Palace. A diagram of the system of spaces illustrates their functions relative to the total complex. *Place Stanislas* maintains two axes,

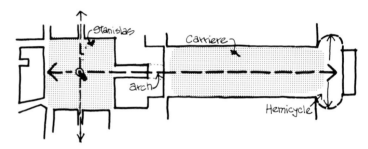

is centripetal and becomes the primary means of developing movement—along either axis. *Place Carrière* is the connector, and like the *Campidoglio* is aligned *with* the axis in order to keep the system in movement. The Hemicycle, like St. Peter's Square, is placed on cross axis to terminate the system. The two major buildings act to enclose the primary sight line. Archways, elaborate gates, and steps insure the sense of separation each space needs for its own identity, while providing the necessary scale relationships.

The overall purpose of the system of squares at Nancy, apart from connecting political and economic functions, was to bridge the historic and cultural charm that had existed between the old and new sections of the city, and to unify those parts which had literally developed as two cities, due to the restraints of ancient moats, walls, and unrelated street systems (p. 120).

A similar example is found in Lisbon. Here the city center (*Cidade Baixa*) was rebuilt following an earthquake, in the form

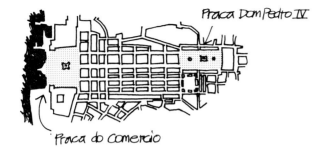

Praca Dom Pedro IV

Praca do Comercio

of two major squares—at the center and at port side. The *Praca Dom Pedro IV* is the heart of the city, enclosed by shops, hotels, and restaurants, while the *Praca do Comercio,* overlooking the River Tagus, is enclosed by government structures. The means of connection is a single axis from the elaborate Baroque pier to the centric statue and through the grand archway of the *Praca do Comercio,* along the colonnaded avenue which connects the squares to the *Praca Dom Pedro IV.* The series is terminated on a classic facade. Again, the diagram illustrates the spatial organization at work. Like the sqaures at Nancy, the *Cidade Baixa* acquires a pedestrian scale through its detailing—particularly in the *Praca Dom Pedro IV,* made pleasant by its enclosure of street trees, arcaded enclosing structures with bright colored awnings overhead, and the unique, fascinating sidewalk mosaics of black and white marble. The sedate *Praca do Comercio,* enclosed by its ponderous neoclassic facades, reflects the stern grandeur of the majority of the eighteenth century order.

The *Amalienborg Square,* Copenhagen, also demonstrates the Neoclassic development of urban spaces linked together

along an axial line. The church dome with its exaggerated drum provides a striking vertical contrast while acting as terminus to the entire spatial complex.

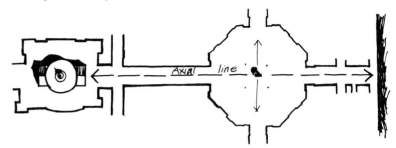

Axial line

The most significant difference between radial and rectilinear, or neoclassic squares is perhaps the variety of functions potential in the latter. Radial squares are little more than traffic hubs but the neoclassic spaces of the eighteenth century were intended for a greater variety of purpose. All of the behavioral factors—social, political, economic, religious—could be accounted for in their planning. It is the automobile, as we know, which has proven so destructive—turning *Concorde* into a race track and other squares into parking lots. In many cases, as in *Praca Dom Pedro IV,* the encircling auto roadway has separated the square from its enclosing agents. The effect is to isolate them from the main stream of pedestrian fairways—now pinioned to the walls, along narrow sidewalks. One does not idly pass through the square of this design, but must make a conscious effort to reach it, seeking the pedestrian crossings —which exist like bridges over moats filled with high speed steel alligators. Whether the square has been converted to a parking lot or re-

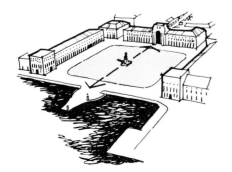

mains a lovely formal garden, the encircling speedway has done more to destroy the spatial quality than any other single factor. Of course, in the eighteenth century traffic conditions were altogether different, and the insidious qualities of the encircling drive were not apparent.

It is mainly for this reason that the major shopping centers have proven so successful, for once we have left our cars behind— in the parking areas beyond the shops—we can enjoy the quiet, pleasant open spaces of the inner courtyards—not unlike the auto-free squares of the *Piazza del Campo* and *Piazza San Marco*. Here the basic factor of spatial success lies in the fact of continuity— between space and enclosure.

Residential Square

Radial and Neoclassic squares were representative of the city's primary traffic systems for government and commercial areas. At the same time there were secondary spatial systems developing— outside the city's heart—enclosed by housing rather than banks, city halls, and libraries. These were the residential squares, which by the eighteenth century had come to play a major role in the design of western cities.

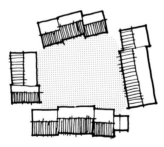

Amongst the earliest of residential squares was the *Place des Vosges*, Paris. The design concept was simple and straightforward—a three-story housing block enclosing a gravelled open square, whose primary function was one of service to the residents. It was, in fact, a common backyard for storage, and various domestic uses, having for embellishment only the centrally located statue of King Louis XIII.

Later in the century, when the formal garden style of Andre Le Notre had come into popularity, the grounds were redesigned to include planting beds, fountains, and a border of trees—without disturbing the equestrian statue of Louis XIII. It was in effect a conversion of service yard to entry garden, the apartments facing inward onto the square.

The transition of *Place des Vosges* from service courtyard to formal garden was typical of development throughout Europe during the second half of the seventeenth century, as the French Formal landscape style, with its ornately embroidered *parterres*, disciplined plant beds, and clipped trees, continued to gain favor. It was to be

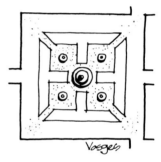

Vosges

the design form of most enclosed spaces for the next century, and even today we find that it remains in favor in many parts of the world (p. 122).

The Place des Vosges was originally named Place Royale, and is the first of a series of formal squares developed throughout the 17th century in most French cities. For the most part these 'royal squares' were planned as straightforward open spaces, gravel covered, accented at their centers by statues of the current king (Louis XIII to XV), and in their original form devoid of plant material. Not all of these were considered to be residential squares. Place Vendome (p. 37) was mixed commercial and residential (Both the central royal statue and the name were changed following the revolution of 1789-91). Like Vosges, many of the royal squares were redesigned in the late 17th and 18th centuries to include grass, trees and water in the manner of the Tuileries gardens and the French Formal garden style, but for the most part they retain their geometrically regular design schemes.

During the seventeenth and eighteenth centuries a great number of similar residential squares were built—in Europe and the United States. In London St. James's Square, Grosvenor Square, Leicester Square, and Bedford Square were laid out in the latter half of the seventeenth century. They were all planned in the manner of the French formal garden—a distinct departure from the earlier Covent Garden square by Inigo Jones, which had been done in the older Italian style—entirely hardsurfaced and enclosed by classic colonnades, with no trees or plant beds to soften the hard edged Renaissance proportions.

These, like *Vosges,* were individual open spaces, related only to their immediate enclosing structures. Shortly thereafter, however, we see the beginnings of a more complex relationship between residential space and surroundings, starting with the efforts to relate the squares of the Bloomsbury section, London, and continuing in the latter part of the eighteenth century with the careful articulation of mass and space in the development of the residential additions to Bath and Edinburgh.

Shown here is the general chronological progression of the individual residential square, from the unadorned gravel courtyard (centric) (a), to the French Formal (centric) (b), to the English open center (c), to the pseudo-Romantic or Natural of the nineteenth century (d). Russell Square, shown in its original form (below), is a combination of b and c, having a centric element as well as an encircling walkway.

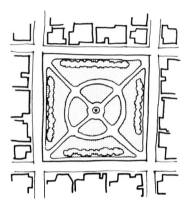

The following diagrams illustrate early attempts to relate individual residential squares to the larger framework of the city: the Bloomsbury squares (a), showing Bloomsbury, Russell, Bedford, and the grounds of the nineteenth century British Museum; St. George Street, Edinburgh, terminated at either end by Charlotte and St. Andrews Squares (b); and colonial Philadelphia, as planned by William Penn (c).

Perhaps the most significant aspect of these modest complexes is the placement of squares over the crossing of streets. In this way

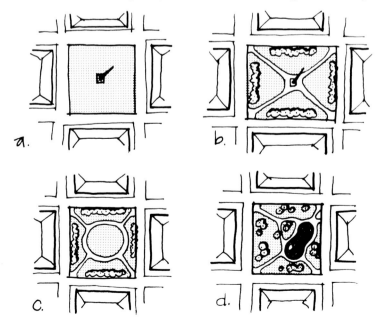

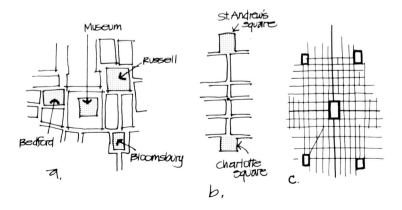

the open green space becomes the terminus of the street vista, much in the same way as the Baroque fountain or obelisk in the radial square. The same visual connection or sense of tension between parts is effected, as seen in the Bloomsbury and Bath examples. In Philadelphia, Penn achieved these sight line connections with the placement of four green squares, while also establishing the basic residential neighborhoods of the city and its early boundaries. The location of the fifth square at the center is based on the *quinconce* of French formal garden design.

Although planned in the manner of the typical English residential square, the addition of large trees and informal usage have largely transformed the squares into small neighborhood parks. One has become a radial hub (Logan Circle).

In 1733 James Oglethorpe devised a similar plan for Savannah, Georgia, using small squares laid over the intersections of alternate blocks to create a systemized balance of open space on a regular gridiron plan (p. 124).

There was little variation in the design of any of these squares, stretching from the *Place des Vosges* to the beginning of the nineteenth century. They were symmetrical, square, circular, or rect-

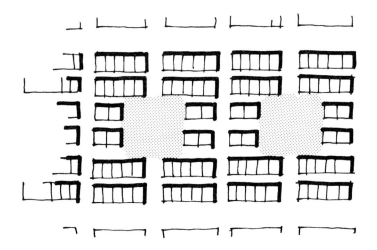

angular as determined by the external street pattern, and laid out in geometric pattern after the French *parterre* (although the English

squares made much greater use of grass and trees by the eighteenth century). The chronological progression (page 91) marks four separate stages of development, particularly relevant to the English and Scottish examples. Russell Square, from the Bloomsbury group, has now entered a fifth stage—post-war contemporary.

Many of the London squares were converted to the Romantic style in the mid-nineteenth century—a result of the urban park movement which carried the English natural landscape from country estate to city center. Grosvenor Square is an outstanding example of this conversion which, in effect, introduces the small park to the residential complex—a forerunner of super block residential developments like Baldwin Hills Village, Los Angeles, and the cluster condominiums that followed.

The natural design is suited to Grosvenor, and preferable to the original scheme, which was stiffly formal. The very unfortunate addition of the Roosevelt Memorial, added after World War II, effectively destroys that concept.

The "British flag" pattern, common to the two block square, was the natural result of a particular function—walking. The cir-

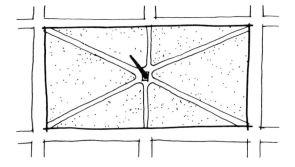

cular and oval variations resulted from a desire to vary the form without significant alteration to the function. Passive recreation and simple exercise—sitting and walking—along paths of straight forward geometric layout assumed a formal character in the usage of these spaces, particularly in view of their orientation to the fronts of houses and the quality of isolation given the square by the encircling roadway.

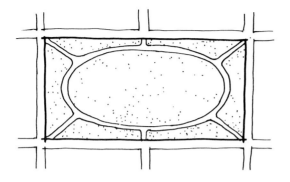

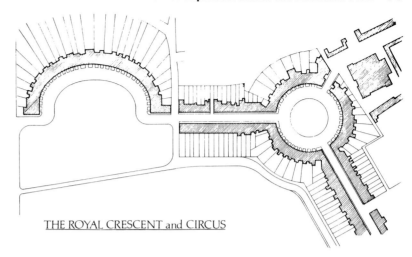

THE ROYAL CRESCENT and CIRCUS

Some English green squares borrow their shape from the radial design of Baroque Rome, but the similarity is one of form only. The Royal Circus in Bath and Moray Circus, Edinburgh, as well as countless crescents (half ovals) from the same period, are mostly the result of a penchant for curvilinear variation in street layout. John Wood is the best known designer of circus and crescent, from his work in both cities (carried on by his son, John Wood, the younger). The crescent proved most useful in varying the monotony of the gridiron, as well as providing open space in the streetscape which could be utilized as park area for adjacent neighborhoods. A circle

is, however, a powerful organizing form, quickly seized upon when gridiron planning fails, and unlike the *Place de l'Etoile*, the Royal Circus is spatial in the true sense of the word, having an immediate enclosing framework of apartments and an open center of trees and grass.

The green squares of English residential complexes began to accept an increasing variety of recreational use during the early nineteenth century, as expanding industrial development extended and intensified urban pressures. The formal *parterre* of a more leisurely era was fenced or walled and the residents, by means of private key, took possession. Shrubbery planted along the edges completed the transformation from public square to private park. Eventually the "key park" became the primary form of open space in urban Great Britain, the best example perhaps being Edinburgh, which abounds in semiprivate green spaces, available only to the surrounding residents. Known as *subscription gardens* due to the use fees charged to surrounding town houses, these small, fenced semi-private parks continue to be managed in this same manner today, Bedford Square itself being an example. These small, residential parks, designed for the limited use of the surrounding populace, may appear to be the forerunners of the modern neighborhood park which is so common to most American cities. Such is not the case. Although similar in function, size and design, our neighborhood park—indeed, the city park movement in general—derives from the social and sanitary conditions of mid-19th century industrial growth, in Britain as well as the United States. This subject is dealt with in the following chapter.

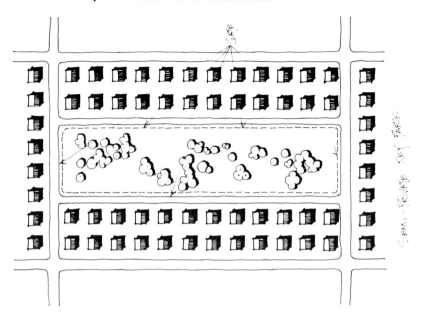

In colonial America urban space had not progressed so far as this. The village green, not unlike the *agora* of classic Greece, performed as residential square, marketplace, government square, meeting place, and parade ground—all in one. Its form was generally determined by empirical method, anchored by a simple Georgian church with its whitewashed wooden steeple serving as vertical accent, the necessary storage buildings, an official structure, and houses of the leading citizens.

The green owed its shape, as in medieval European cities, to the town's growth and change, and to the topography of its location, and like its empirical predecessors it developed primarily from economic determinants, along the route of trade.

Colonial settlements sprang up along these routes wherever it was propitious—at a stream crossing or inlet, a highway crossing or the like. The green evolved from a formless central space used for market activities, or was staked out according to measurements and proportions established by a colony's mother country. In Spanish settlements for example, the shape and size of the plaza, the setbacks, architectural form, and surrounding building heights were precisely calculated in accordance with predetermined criteria. In

New England greater variety prevailed and the unpaved floor of the square, unlike the hardpan earth of the South and Southwest, was a refreshing grassy plain.

Many of these have disappeared or undergone extensive change, but the resurrection of colonial towns like Williamsburg, Virginia, and Deerfield, Massachusetts, make it possible for us to know these early American spaces again.

While most colonial greens were empirical in nature, the Renaissance rationale for harmonic proportions, which had been passed on to England via Inigo Jones, appeared in the colonies by way of Neo-Palladian architects like Thomas Jefferson, whose plan for the University of Virginia seems a far cry from the Williamsburg green. Jefferson selected a hilltop site for his principle building—the Rotunda (a copy of the Roman Pantheon), behind which the open stretch of lawn steps down the gentle incline, in a series of terraces bringing to mind the *parterres* of the Italian Renaissance garden. The open green space is neatly enclosed by long, matching colonnades, behind which are located the students' apartments, along with the pavilions of the scholars which punctuate the enclosing form with a rich, visual cadence. Here, in colonial America, we find

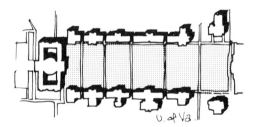

U. of Va.

one of the finest examples of abiding Palladian rule: axial symmetry, vertical/horizontal ratios, limitation of space, terminus, measured and rhythmic enclosure, and domination over natural form.

Open space in urban America during colonial times was for the most part simple, functional, and unpaved. A row of trees was often employed to delineate its form, and where street systems had been laid out on a grid the space enclosed was usually a tree-lined square or rectangle.

The tree eventually came into its present usage as an enclosing agent for streets and squares during the early eighteenth century, particularly in Paris (after the concepts of André Le Notre), and later on a much grander scale as used by Baron Georges Haussmann and Adolphe Alphand in the nineteenth century reconstruction of the city. Here the tree is used in double rows or more—eight deep on either side of the *Champs Élysées*—in order to provide the proper sense of scale and solidity of enclosure required. At this point the tree replaces architectural facade as the primary means of enclosing streets and squares—and at the same time providing scale and the long needed relief of contrast.

This was indeed the great era of urban space—beginning with the visionary plans of Sixtus V and ending with the onset of industry. There were exceptions like Paris, but for the most part the western world experienced a decline in the splendor, beauty and even functional requisites of the city and city spaces, as the Agrarian Era came to a close. The changes in the structure of society were rapid and shattering, in respect to the structure of the city. Factories and tenement housing sprang up slapdash, side-by-side, making a mockery of the civil standards of architectural form and proper spacing, overloading the capacity of streets, and filling the air with din and smoke—toward an urbanscape we readily recognize today.

The city can eventually absorb the economic-caused changes in its structure, but it is still far too early to say that it has even begun to do so. The battle lines which have been drawn and the general struggle to preserve the city is, in the main, a fight to preserve nineteenth century industrial standards—quite apart from any effort to restore the eighteenth century concept of urbanism. This smacks of nostalgia and takes the form of reincarnating details of the past, hitching posts, gas lights, wooden railings, leaded glass and a host of architectural artifacts which have nothing to do with regaining urbanity, and instead represent only a forlorn recognition of something lost.

Perhaps, the rapid pace of change prevents urban design from ever catching up with the cutting edge of progress and the economic values which tend to give form to the city. The railroad, for example, changed not only the method of travel, but restructured the time-honored means of collection and dispersal of goods—and in doing so changed the physical character of the city as well. Manufacture became the *raison d'etre* of towns, involving the movement of people as well as goods, and as a result the railroad station with its warehousing and industrial spurs replaced the market square.

Manufacture and the movement of goods and people became the way of life in the western world. England, determined to lead and thereby, in the ways of Adam Smith, capture a headstart over others, probably sacrificed more of the eighteenth century to progress than did any other European nation. A little later the United States followed their Anglo-Saxon leaders.

Throughout the seventeenth and eighteenth centuries the design base for both radial and Neoclassic urban space had emphasized circulation over place. In the nineteenth century with increased emphasis on transportation, this imbalance deepened. Later, when automobiles came to replace much of the public transportation in cities, the square was often pressed into service as a parking lot. With this step we no doubt reach the abyss in the history of public open space; and unless this trend can be reversed the future of public open space remains uncertain.

In *summary,* the seventeenth and eighteenth centuries produced open space systems which, unlike their Renaissance predecessors, were fully *integrated* into the fabric of the city, and were likewise more closely associated with *movement* than place. The *radial square,* more of a nodal point in the traffic system than an urban space, represents the idea of the open square in its ultimate form—neither *closed* to movement of any kind nor *enclosed* in the sense of spatial sensation. As a traffic coordinator it makes use of strong visual connections which tend to create *tensile* relationships. This visual attraction, usually centripetal, works towards accomplishing an overall interrelationship of diverse parts—a homogeneity based on movement systems, visual and actual.

Neoclassic squares derive from the gridiron street plan, or a combination of gridiron and radial streets, and are themselves generally rectilinear. They also tend to be traffic organizers, but more significantly perform the function of defining the central urban structure. In this way they become the heart of the city, as illustrated by Lisbon and Nancy. We also find here a system of movement, as organized through a series of interrelated spaces developed along an axial sight line and symmetrical balance. Secondary axes are regularly employed and accented at the crossings by statuary and the like, in much the same manner as seen in *centric* Renaissance planning. The Neoclassic square of the eighteenth century exemplifies the urbane spirit of the times—perhaps the finest hour of western cities.

The *residential* square, which first appeared in France in the early seventeenth century, received its major impetus in Great Britain during the eighteenth and early nineteenth centuries. It differs from the previous types primarily in *function,* and for that reason tends to be *smaller, less formal* in organization, *carefully defined* spatially, and *restrictive* in use. It began as a gravel courtyard, obtained the quality of the French Formal garden, advanced to the informality of the Romantic Age, and eventually to other stylistic forms which have followed—demonstrating once again the force of *change* in urban structure.

The residential square, because it became the collective garden or recreation space for surrounding apartments, steadily increased in use of plant material, giving rise to the employment of trees as spatial modulators and visual relief.

The colonial *green,* which may physically resemble the residential square from the standpoint of its green walls and grassy floor, is more closely associated with the Classic Greek *agora,* where in simpler times each was capable of responding to the multitude of public needs—political, social, economic, religious. The colonial village green, with few exceptions, is not distinguished in form but in the multi-faceted spirit of its functions. The planned squares of the seventeenth and eighteenth centuries, like those in Savannah and Philadelphia, followed the pattern of the English Palladian form, or the stricter dictates of Spain, depending, of course, on the colonizing nation. The use of cast iron and iron filigree in the late nineteenth century, particularly in France, had a profound influence on Mexico, where today we can still find in the *plaza central* of many small towns the opulent wrought iron work of the circular

bandstand—always in the center of the square. And here we can find the Sunday concert and *paseo,* performed and enjoyed by townspeople who seem happily unaware of the twentieth century and its urban problems.

The chart on page 97 compares the major urban spaces of this chapter:

The various forms of rationally conceived urban space emanating from sixteenth and seventeenth century Europe established the major thrust of city planning in America to the present time. And further, it was during the Italian Renaissance, particularly the sixteenth century—that our concept of modern city planning came into being. From the fifteenth century plans of Alberti and Filarete, the sixteenth century humanist planners developed their rationale of universality and idealism for cities of the future. But in many ways it was already too late for Europe, her ancient cities and towns clogged by a thousand years of medieval patchwork.

A few "new towns" were built, like Palma Nuova—mostly associated with military or economic strategies, much the same as the *bastides* and *villes neuves* of the fourteenth century, but by and large Europe was no longer ripe for wholesale new town building, and city planners soon began looking to the new world.

The sixteenth century was Europe's greatest era of expansion, following immediately on the heels of those intrepid explorers, Columbus, Cortez, Magellan, DeSoto, Hudson, Raleigh. And with a speed that belies the technology of the age, Spain, England, France, and the Netherlands were carving up unknown lands of such prodigious scope and magnitude as to defy all but the most arrogant of men.

A newly conquered land, thirty times the size of their own homeland neither awed nor befuddled these conquerors, who saw their discoveries not as exotic lands with culture, climate, and animal life different from their own and worthy of their respect, but as treasures to be reaped.

The new world was from the beginning discerned as an extension of Europe, and the colonizers, giving little notice to either human culture or ecosystem, commenced the "Eurofication" of America. It was ripe ground indeed for the planning and building of ideal cities. Spain, having only recently won her independence

	Radial	Neo-classic	Residential
Form	circular, elliptical nuclear, centric	rectilinear, centric/open	circular/elliptical/rectilinear
Enclosing Agents	minimal	political/religious	housing blocks
Volume/Scale	flat, monumental	classic volumetrics, varied monumental	regular, human
Function/Purpose	traffic coordination, movement	principal space, urban center	semi-public open space
Circulation	radial, centripetal open	lineal, along major axis and cross axes	diagonal, circular, pedestrian use
Internal Use/Place	minimal	formal, group related, gathering	informal outdoor use, domestic, singular, recreation
Entry	along radial avenues, centripetal, tensile	along major or secondary axis	corners
Street System	radial, Baroque	gridiron	radial/gridiron

from seven hundred years of Moorish dominance, was anxious to try out a new found Renaissance architecture—both at home and in her growing colonial empire. Palladian law thus entered the building of Lima, laid out in 1532 by Pizarro, and Mexico City, by Cortez in 1520. In fact, the organization of Spanish towns throughout the Americas was based on detailed specifications calling for the location of various primary government structures, and the determination of horizontal/vertical ratios, as had been specified by Palladio and Alberti.

The same was true of French, British, and Dutch settlement, where newly conceived towns reflected stylized architecture and planning methods derived from or specified by parent cultures. It was merely an extension of the "dominance over nature" theme which characterized the sixteenth century, but it indelibly marked the future of a vast, pristine landscape and smoothed the way for conquerors and despoilers yet to come. The land—its material riches,

the wealth from its soil, and its animal hides—was seen only in its capacity to serve mankind. It was the legacy of sixteenth century arrogance.

If Pompeii had been discovered in the nineteenth century rather than the eighteenth, at a time when scientific knowledge and a greater respect for antiquities prevailed, the terrible plunder of that unique discovery might have been avoided, and today a far richer and more useful picture of the first century might have survived. Perhaps the same could be said for America. "Discovered" in the seventeenth or even the eighteenth century—gentler times in some ways—perhaps our beginnings as new world nations would have reflected stronger influence from indigenous cultures (as well as a mellower European conquest). China and Japan might have played a greater part in the shaping of new world cultures, a role which could have resulted in a different balance in spatial harmony (as suggested in the following chapters), and the emerging American nations might have experienced a more sedate period of growth—instead of the endless bloody conquests which marked the progress of most of them.

The sixteenth century conquest of America by the nations of Western Europe assured the continuance of occupation by violence, including the War of Independence, the Civil War, and the ruthless conquest of the West. America—as it is today—North, South, and Central—is largely a result of European hegemony. It is important to understand this, and the nature of our culture, before we can begin to develop a society and a physical urban form that is respective of all cultures represented here. Token Africanism won't do it, nor the superficialities borrowed from the Orient—an occasional Thai restaurant, a transplanted Japanese garden, or the widespread popularity of Navajo and Zuni jewelry. It isn't a style or a passing vogue we're concerned about here.

When you look at the downtown of an American city what do you *feel?* After your first reaction try being academic—what do you *think?* Some of the lessons of the first seven chapters may come to mind; and finally, with a fresh historic perspective, you should be able to peel off the layers of the years—the decades or even centuries. What does all the masonry of urban form tell you? Growth and change are apparent. They have always been there, as you know, and something is always being destroyed in order to make way for something new. But what? Is it better than what it replaces? How do you judge?

And as the pace of change in the city grows more rapid so apparently grows the need for respite—a kind of relief found in nostalgia. We love Williamsburg, I believe, for its scale, its quiet, comfortable pace, and opportunity for human contact as much as for its nostalgia or its history lessons, yet we often fail to capture those qualities in newly planned spaces. And we may consider brick to be a pleasanter surface than concrete—harking back to simpler times and hand crafted construction, but brick is ageless, belonging to the future as much as to the past, its qualities deriving from color, texture, and the sense of scale determined from patterns of installation and the awareness of individuality expressed by each

unit—aspects perhaps not fully grasped by designers who continue to specify amorphous concrete.

Arcades, their sense of rhythm, scale, and direction offer fantastic opportunity and variety in the articulation of space, but they don't become *Classic* until we make them so by adding capitols, fluting and such. We don't have to render everything old or European, or Oriental to make it work. And neither did Cortez when he ignored the Aztec culture in laying out Mexico City. Cuzco and Machu Picchu were close at hand when Pizarro built Lima, but he chose not to see them. He had Palladio.

The Romans invoked internationalism of urban form throughout their far reaching empire. The Renaissance imposed a widespread rationalism of even greater breadth. British Imperial/Classic architecture may seem a bit foolish in the nineteenth century India, but is Le Corbusier's Chandigargh a more ethnic contribution? And for that matter is twentieth century Modernism, with its soaring cubes of glass and shiny metal, that much different in principle from any other period of imposed rational form?

Easterners brought their Victorian mansions of brick and clapboard to a Southern California climate made livable by a strict adherence to thick adobe walls and small windows. Native foliage, tolerant to heat and alkaline soils was passed over in favor of the beloved hydrangea, boxwood, and lilac—and lawns of course. Like Cortez and all those that followed, settlers in a new land have preferred cultural familiarity to indigenous practicality. The wave of "Spanish" architecture which hit Southern California after World War I was initiated by the pseudo-Baroque buildings of the San Diego World's Fair, and not by any late blooming recognition of indigenous heritage.

Shopping malls, in order to escape heat, smog, ice, and snow, have sought enclosure—and an unvarying 70° temperature, the cost of which is tremendous in view of rapidly diminishing sources of energy. Heritage of the sixteenth century? Not altogether of course, but you will often notice that when concern for these diminishing energy sources is expressed at all, it is in terms of "alternate sources of energy," rarely "adjusted life styles." Dominance over nature? I believe that it remains a part of our heritage—along with the pioneer ethic which we probably inherited from the seventeenth century English pilgrims fleeing religious persecution. But whatever the cause, we Americans continue to exhibit anti-urban tendencies—expressed by our infatuation with the single family residence, private ownership of land, and individualized transportation in preference to public spaces and collective effort. By the same measure, the blackbirds of eastern Kentucky farmland may be a functioning part of nature's cycle but when, by their sheer numbers, they interfere with the plan of man—? Well, we know the answer.

And knowing is the key to successful future cities. Rene Dubos, the modern ecologist, expressed this in hard, practical terms. Nature for its own sake, he believed, is not the issue, nor has it ever been. It continues a matter of man's ability to shepherd existing resources and discover new ones in order that nature and man might remain in harmony.

Empirical urban form of the Middle Ages derives from basic economic functions—the competitive urge to locate at the center of the market place and the cooperative effort to maintain an open center with equal frontage for all. The growth of trade directed urban development inward during this period, creating high densities and forcing vertical expansion.

Regensburg (Stadtbiltstille)

Natural defenses played a major part in site selection in the early middle ages—the fortified hill town was difficult to approach, and once breached more difficult to defeat due to steep and narrow twisting streets which were easy to defend from adjacent houses (opposite page).

Rothenburg-ob-der-Tauber
Germany. (Wolff & Tritschler)

Edinburgh. The Castle.

Regensburg. Nächtliche Kramgarse.
(Stegerer)

Locations on river bends or islands offered natural defense, as long as the opposite shore could be bridged and controlled. Later, the river provided the means for trade advantage—and economic prosperity.

Regensburg (Ernst Tremel)

Rothenburg ob-der Tauber (Wolff & Tritschler)

The narrow streets resulting from hilltop locations, defensive walls and empirical growth often became steep sided urban ravines, but towers and steeples rising high above the town's roofline provide points of orientation for pedestrian movement.

Regensburg (Gertrud Herbrick)

The morphosis from street to square in the empirical development of the medieval town includes a transitional widening of the main commercial thoroughfare, called in Italian—'largo' (wide street), as illustrated in these two carefully preserved Bavarian towns. Note (below) the largo's termini—church and town gate, each clearly visible.

Dinkelsbuhl (Derkehrsamt)

Rothenburg ob-der-Tauber (Wolff & Tritschler)

Arezzo. Piazza Grande. The central market square of this Umbrian hill town. Note the well at lower end (foreground) has been replaced by a modest fountain (ENIT).

Todi. The enlongated square is terminated at one end by the cathedral, the raised floor level and flight of stairs giving it a position of prominence over other buildings facing the square (ENIT).

Siena. Piazza del Campo (ENIT). The Palazzo Pubblico faces the Campo and separates it from the old
market square (opposite side). Note visual balance
provided by the Tower (Torre del Mangia).

San Gimignano. Piazza della Cisterna. One of the best preserved squares of the Umbrian hill towns.
Note the centric function of the well in this amorphous square. The openness of the medieval piazza is
still intact here, allowing for the free passage of all traffic (ENIT).

Walls protected towns from attack, but greatly limited expansion. Medieval walls (below) were relatively easy to dismantle or build around, but the walls of sixteenth century cities were very thick and rigid in design layout (right), resisting charge of alignment. The medieval walls of York have been restored after long having been breached by urban growth, but the Renaissance fortifications of Lucca still hold the city in (right).

York

Lucca

Steps were discovered by Renaissance and Baroque architects as a means of connecting spaces and buildings on different levels. An entire hillside could be architectonically stepped and thus controlled by this device (above), in triumphant scale.

Rome—Villa Borghese

The contemporary example (below) uses stairs in a similar manner, and by utilizing the convex shape channels traffic upward, while dispersing it downward.

Los Angles. Security—Pacific plaza.

Transitional squares in the process of development from medieval dynamics to Renaissance volumetrics. The Piazza della Signoria, Florence (left), is enclosed by the dominant Palazzo Vecchio (late 13th C.), and the arcaded Loggia dei Lanzi, an early Renaissance attempt at regularizing urban space. Later Renaissance structures enclosed the square, but the Loggia remains incomplete (ENIT).

The Palazzo Comunale in Bologna (below), a partially arcaded structure with pointed windows, artificial parapets and classic portals and niches, suggests the transition in urban space occurring in the fifteenth century (ENIT).

Piazza San Marco, Venice, for all its variations in architectural form and alignment retains a fragile balance of diverse parts and an overall harmony in scale, volumetrics and spatial form.

Venice. Piazza San Marco (ENIT)

The Piazza dei Signori, Vicenza (below), is not as successful in this balancing of extraneous parts. The square is too narrow, and too small for the 'basilica' a late medieval civic structure made larger and more imposing by the addition of Palladio's heavily classic double arcade. Note the vertical balance and emphasis provided in each case by the Campanile.

Vicenza. Piazza dei Signori (ENIT)

The Piazza Ducale in Vigevano represents the epitome of rational order in fifteenth century urban volumetrics, and unlike most squares, was carried to completion as a single concept of unified form; and it is likewise disassociated from the surrounding medieval street system.

Vigevano, Italy. Piazza Ducale (Giuliano Carraro).

Vigevano. Piazza Ducale. From the Cathedral (note shadow). (Giuliano Carraro)

Michelangelo's magnificent achievement in total control of external space, all parts of the composition—enclosing agents, centric statue, nodal points, paving pattern are in harmony. But the trucks and taxis seem quite out of place. (ENIT)

The ideal Renaissance city, in reality.

Sicily. Granmichele (Quilici).

Paris.

The radial system emphasizes circulation over place. The Piazza Esedra (left) is a classic example of the radial square, in which the enclosing architecture acts to receive and give volume to the nodal point (fountain). The tree lined Parisian street (above) was primarily the work of Haussmann and Alphand in mid-nineteenth century development. The Arc de Triumphe (right) stands astride the Place de l'Etoile with its ten radiating exits, in this view towards the Place de la Concorde (French National Tourist Office).

Rome. Piazza Esedra.

The 'vie de la triomphe,' the spine of Paris street system, is coordinated through the place de la Concorde (left). In this view the Place de l'Etoile lies to the right and the Tuileries/Louvre to the right. Behind is the Chamber of Deputies (Palais Bourbon).

Paris. Place de la Concorde. (French National Tourist Office).

The 1846 drawing (left) shows activity in the square prior to automotive traffic, and also prior to the final development of the Champs by Haussmann. Compare with upper left, opposite page.

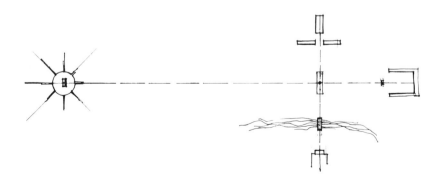

These photos of the Place de la Concorde were taken at the centric point, the obelisk. Above and below (left) are the long axis views (E-W), Arc de Triomphe and Tuileries (Louvre). Above and below (right) are the cross axis views (N-S), to the Madeleine and the Palais Bourbon.

The series of squares at Nancy, looking from the Place Stanislaus to termination at the Ducal Palace. The Place de la Carriere is just visable in the center, behind the arch.

Nancy. Place Stanislas. (French National Tourist Office)

Below: A view of Place Stanislas during the Crimean War, 1855. (Ill. London News).

Washington, D.C. the Mall. First conceived by Pierre L'Enfant, two hundred years ago, the neo-classic plan of the city continues to stumble in that direction.

(Smithsonian Institute. Photo by James H. Wallace, Jr.)

(D.C. Office of Planning and Development)

(Skidmore, Owings & Merrill)

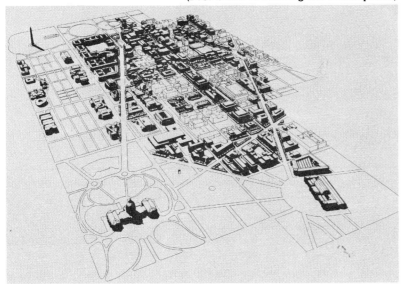

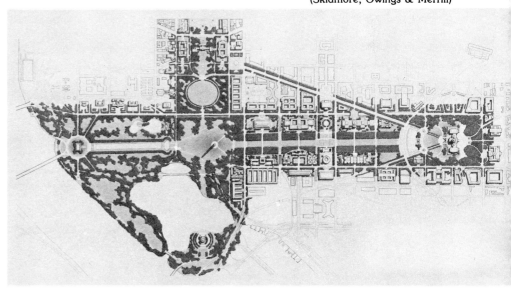

Paris. Place des Vosges. The beginning of the concept of neighborhood (residential) squares. (French National Tourist Office)

Illustrated London News

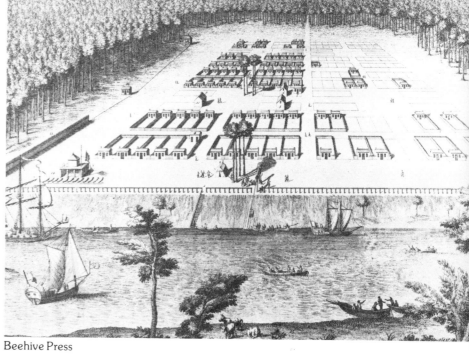

Beehive Press

Village green/residential square in the new world. Above left the green at Bassiterre, Guadaloupe about 1800. Above right, Savannah as it looked in 1734 (P. Gordon), and (below) as it looked a century later (J. Hill) facing page, Wright Square, Savannah, 1867 (Frank Leslie's Illustrated Newspaper 1867).

Beehive Press

EIGHT

Order Diversified: The City Park

There is understandably a great deal of overlap between park and square. Many urban pursuits and enterprises are followed in both, and today we may have some real difficulty discerning between the two. They both serve as *place.* Unlike streets, sidewalks, malls, promenades and the like, parks and squares are places to be, in order to gather, relax, pause before beginning anew.

But there are also many significant differences between them, and environmental designers must take into account the factors that separate them, making the park a new kind of place from the spaces we have studied up to this point. But don't look for physical differences alone. A square with trees and flowers is still a square. A park of geometric concept and axial symmetry is still a park. The differences will always lie primarily in *purpose,* as we suggested in Chapter Two. If we consider then that the park, first of all, should serve as a kind of green oasis, a retreat from the congestion ad active nature of urban life, we are at once close to understanding its purpose, and likewise its heritage.

In order to futher understand purpose, and to separate park and square conceptually, the following may help:

Things that we like to do in

THE SQUARE	THE PARK
Gather	Disperse
Watch	Do
Get into	Get away from
Be seen	Hide out
Buy things	Make things
Get the news	Forget the news
Shop, meet, demonstrate	Read, relax, play

We may plan an entire afternoon's activities around the park's facilities, while the square is more likely to be visited fleetingly, by shoppers and passersby. At any rate watching people in each gives us a better clue as to their function and value in urban society.

Things we see in

THE SQUARE	THE PARK
Dressed up people	Barely dressed people
Dogs on leash	Squirrels, rabbits
Pigeons	Robins
Statues	Trees
Elaborate fountains	Brooks and ponds
Waiters and tables	Picnics on the grass
Elegant enclosing architecture	Contrast, leafy enclosure

In most American and European cities the park concept is readily understood, but rarely achieved, and in Oriental cities it is perceived like so many Western customs as something to emulate without clearly knowing why, as we can judge from the stiffly formal style which began to appear in Tokyo and other industrial Japanese cities following World War I.

Most Western city parks were originally something else anyway—estates, fairgrounds, quarry pits. The general rule in urban park development has been one of inheritance rather than sound planning, and a park system resulting primarily from donated, inexpensive and useless sites hasn't much of a chance for success.

There have been exceptions of course. Jackson Park in Chicago and Forest Park in St. Louis are the sites of The World's

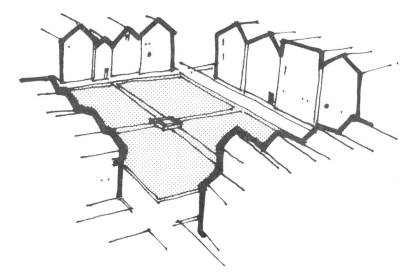

THE SQUARE

THE PARK

Columbian Exposition of 1892–3 and The Louisiana Purchase Exposition of 1904 respectively. Parc Buttes-Chaumont, one of Paris' most exciting public places, was a gravel quarry. The famous commons of London—Wimbledon and Hampstead Heath—were simply left undeveloped through the city's long history because of poor drainage.

But more often than not a city is expected to accept donated properties to be developed into parks, regardless of location, size, shape or present status. This may require putting up with existing buildings, gardens and other structures unrelated to park usage and subject to remain intact for one reason or another. A park which is little more than a setting for a great house is unlikely to be successful, and when the house serves a singular annual function such as the election of the Rose Bowl Queen (Wrigley Park, Pasadena), a broader range of park facilities and functions may be discouraged if not quashed.

How did this idea of parks as green retreats from urban congestion, ever come into being? Surely, the park seen as such, had a far different origin in urban life than the traditional market square. A gathering place in the village center is, as we have noted, basic to urban structure and as old as the idea of the city itself. But throughout the long history of urban development we have briefly traced, there has been little or no need for the introduction of greenery and natural form to the city. True, Leone Alberti called for the planting of trees to provide shade over city streets and even foresaw the need for recreation:

> A city is not built wholly for the sake of shelter, but ought to be so contrived, that besides their civic conveniences there may be handsome spaces left for squares, courses for chariots, gardens, places to take the air in, for swimming and the like, both for ornament and recreation.[1]

1. Alberti, L. B.; The Ten Books of Architecture. p. 71

But for the most part Pre-Industrial European cities provided no parks or park-like spaces; indeed, there was as yet no compelling reason for them. Nature was always close at hand, even too close at times, as history frequently recalls to us.

For the purpose of tracing the history of the city park as it developed in the western world, we must look again at the fabric of cities before the era of industry changed everything, from Classic times through the 18th century, in order to establish the roots of the park—as a separate but parallel relation to the public square.

Classic Green Space

The Athenian agora and those open spaces in Classic Greek city-states of the Fifth Century B.C. may well have been the first and last of their kind. Large, unpaved and for the most part lacking the geometry of enclosure or grading, they were more park-like in appearance than the Roman spaces that succeed them. The activities that took place in the Classic agora also suggest *park,* as we have just defined it. There was plenty of opportunity in such large, unrestricted spaces for any kind of active or passive recreational pursuit, like athletic exercise, studying and conversing with Socrates himself, contemplation no doubt, and all the other uses one can imagine, now as well as then. In time the *gymnasion,* the school

and the church took some of the many and varied activities out of the agora, but throughout Classic times, or until the conquest by Rome, the Greek agora was both park and square—a phenomenon which reoccurs in history only occasionally.

In Roman times the Greek agora became cluttered with structures and all sorts of heraldric bric-a-brac, while its softly integrated dimensions became enclosed in a hard geometric frame—the form all of Europe was to inherit, and the park-like quality of the agora disappeared forever. Nor did the original Roman spaces, the fora, offer much in the way of park-like activity. The ruins of these spaces today reveal a quality of informal human scale, softened by wildflowers, grasses and weedy shrubbery pushing up through broken stones, while flowering vines wind their way over tumbled marble cornices. But the quality of such romantic softness is inherent to the ruins alone, and not the original concept. Imperial Rome, unlike Classic Greece, put little faith in democratic institutions, so necessary to the evolution of the public park. The gathering spaces of Rome, as we recall, were intended more for imperial display, ritual and marketing—not idle contemplation, exercise and the like.

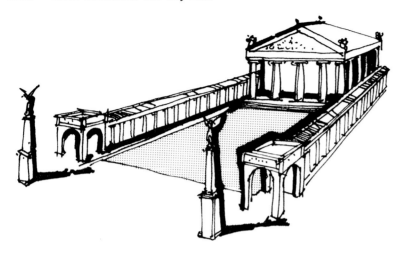

Green Vestiges

In contrast to the contributions to open space from Greece and Rome, it is not so much the philosophy of spatial use but the physical remains of a harsh life which form the basis of park heritage from medieval towns and cities. The protective nature in the choice of citadel location often resulted in towns which clung to hillsides and elaborate systems of defensive wall enclosures. In later, safer times when considerations of defense were no longer paramount, the steep hillsides and walls became vestigial relics of the past. Such an example is found in Edinburgh, where a lofty natural rise above the Firth of Forth gave early settlers of the region both a port and a natural stronghold. And while the heights upon which the castle was built were sufficiently steep to deter enemies, inconvenience and discomfort made it a disagreeable place to live, and later, as the emphasis of life swung from *protection* to *production,* development shifted to the foot of the hill and to the harbor. The castle on top the hill remains as a museum and military functionary but the hill itself, useless for building yet centrally located, became in later more democratic times, a park.

The accident of nature such as a steep rise in the landscape, had once been a primary factor in site selection and settlement, and remained as an unnecessary curiosity in countless cities and towns across Europe. As at Edinburgh, the hillsides were often too steep for development and the citadel on top remained isolated and forgotten, although central to the developing city below. Eventually after a sufficient passage of time to render them historic, the old fortresses were restored and thus became commercially successful as tourist attractions, set in a nice park-like environment.

Water was also a means of defense in the early Middle Ages, leading to the location of several cities we may recall, situated on islands (Paris, Mont St. Michel), promontories (Lisbon), river bends (Luxembourg) and the like. Where such sites were found to be commercially valuable, especially in the development of trade routes, the same urban morphosis occurs, leading eventually to park usage. Luxembourg is nearly surrounded by its river gorge, a natural and very successful means of defense. Today the gorge acts as a belt park, lending charm and scale to the old, inner city.

In some instances, where natural defenses were not sufficient, defenders were forced to rely on their own resources to a greater extent, leading to considerable variation and refinement of the wall, in combination with earthworks, wards, moats, ramparts and revetments. Attacking armies laying siege to a medieval town, used trees very effectively for protection, and in the era before the development of gunpowder, as ramming devices. As a result of this, citadels of the time caused the land outside the walls to be cleared of all vegetation which could be useful to an attacker for up to 300 yards beyond the walls. This cleared land was itself often graded and fitted out with a system of pallisaded trenches cut into a sloping esplanade, and further reinforced by raised earthwork ramparts, the whole encircling the outer walls as a formidable arrangement of defense. This method was greatly expanded during the 16th Century, when gunpowder rendered the old stone walls obsolete, but some form of peripheral defense, together with broad bands of shaped and cleared land, continued to form the edges of cities until the standing armies and national boundaries of the 17th Century made them unnecessary. (p. 108)

But during those centuries which saw nature removed from the proximity of urban life, the need for natural surroundings was seldom expressed. In truth, during the Middle Ages nature was nearly universally viewed as the enemy of man—a force to fear and guard against. Life was torn from a penurious and punitive nature by skill and effort, and long, hard winters often saw man the loser in this constant struggle. Winter and starvation in turn gave way to Plague, the most virulent forms of which reduced the population of Europe by half during the 14th century. Disease and deprivation were harder enemies than spear and sword, and what man could pluck from the ground in order to maintain a meagre diet—mostly tuberous vegetables and some fruit and grain—was not sufficiently satisfying to endear to him the beauty of trees and wildlife that enthrall us today.

Christianity, from the words of the bible to nearly every Protestant pulpit throughout the North American colonies, reproached and feared untamed nature. The Christian church awarded man unquestioned rule of nature in all her forms, setting mankind aside—as the only form of life on earth given divine purpose and the right

of life and death over all other forms. The 18th Century view of nature and its proper uses is summed up by John Adams, second president of the United States, in this fashion: 'the whole continent was one continued dismal wilderness, the haunt of wolves and bears and more savage men. Now the forests are removed, the land covered with fields of corn, orchards bending with fruit, and the magnificent habitations of rational and civilized people.'* This view of nature, as something fearful and unproductive, was commonly held throughout the 18th and 19th centuries. Indeed, it has not altogether disappeared in our own times, and explains in part the late arrival of parks on the urban scene. But people have always appreciated certain aspects of nature, and by the 19th century cities in Germany, France and Gt. Britain were poised to reintroduce wilderness to the urban scene. In the 18th Century gardens of English aristocracy the concept of idealizing and abstracting from natural form had long been in vogue, but a common respect for nature in her original garb of wilderness and wildlife occurred much later. And in consort with this new found admiration for natural beauty came the growth and technological evolution of the 19th Century Industrial city.

It was of course the growth and development of the Industrial city that brought about the need for parks—those green oases of retreat from the noise and congestion of modern times, but the heritage of public open space, as we have seen from the examples of civic defense systems goes back much further in time.

Geometric Green

From the earliest development of palace gardens and suburban villas of wealthy Italian merchants, church officials and aristocrats comes the origin of many of Europe's renowned parks. The Renaissance as we know, drew heavily upon geometric proportion and

*Lopez, Barry H.; *Of Wolves and Men*, p. 142

musical harmony as design determinants. By using nature's materials—water, stone, gravel, plants—in an unnatural, geometric way, the garden architects of the Renaissance clearly demonstrated man's assault on and eventual dominion over nature, and religion as well. Such gardens reflected an extension of man's new freedom of thought, and thus remained passive, visual, and contemplative in use. This is of course completely in line with the rationalistic approach to the design of open space that was discussed in Chapter Six. (see p. 79).

But these precisely made geometric spaces do not adapt well to modern park usage, for fairly obvious reasons. On the whole they are too small, and they are located generally on hillsides above the city, where they are less accessible to the public, and because of the terrain, less adaptable to active play and varied usage. The Villa d'Este is a noteworthy exception, its many fountains, pools, statuary, ballustraded walls and stairways make it a most intriguing playground for any six year old. The secret perhaps is to allow them to decay, gracefully and mystically, into arcane ruins.

Through the years many of the great estates of Europe have come into public ownership—one way or another—and the history of the meticulously created geometric garden of the 16th Century is one of neglect and decay, re-design, or high maintenance and limited usage—after joining the city's park system. Far more adaptable to modern park needs have been the great hunting parks of English and French kings of the 16th Century, like Henry VIII and Francis I. On London's west side, scattered around the king's palace at Hampton Court, Richmond Park, Kew Gardens and Bushy Park in particular and all of the other eight royal parks in general, such spaces form the basis of the sprawling city's vast public park system. As a result the city of Richmond and its surroundings enjoy a ratio of five people per park acre, while the average for most of London, as well as American cities in general, is more like 500 people for every park acre. (Some cities, including Los Angeles, are far worse than this!) When we add the large commons—those areas left undeveloped since antiquity because of poor drainage—we have the basis for an admirable public park system long in advance of the

19th Century park movement. London's major park problem—then as today—is poor distribution within the metropolitan basin.

During the 17th and 18th Centuries the size of the private estate grew enormously—from a few acres to many square miles, encompassing forests, grazing land and entire villages. In England this was the direct result of royal confiscation of church lands by Henry VIII and their re-distribution amongst cronies and loyal supporters. As most of these were far from urban centers they have added little to city park heritage, with certain notable exceptions. Kensington Gardens in London remains a well visited public park while retaining much of its former elegance. This is also true of Rome's Villa Borghese and Villa Doria-Pamphili, and any number of Parisian estates which became public property during the French Revolution, Versailles being the most noteworthy and least altered.

But during the late 18th Century a sweeping change in design taste was to have a significant impact on the future park development, first in British cities and eventually throughout the world. This was the evolution of the landscape gardening school', also referred to as the 'English Natural Style' of garden design, which attempted to abstract and simplify natural form into an assymmetrical style generated by softly curving forms, primarily composed of meadow and water, punctuated by clumps of conifers or oak and romanticized by 'eye catchers' such as Greek temples, oriental bridges and pagodas, and even Gothic ruins.

The new natural style, a clear repudiation of the tiresomely repetitive 'straight line' gardens of the past century, developed sporadically through the latter decades of the 18th Century, finally reaching a maturity of balance with the past in the hands of Humphrey Repton. By this time English Natural estates had replaced most of the formal gardens in Britain and Northern Europe. Repton and his partner, John Nash were employed to design Regent's Park in London, which was to be a semi-private retreat for the future George IV, and after Repton's death in 1818 Nash was given the responsibility for redesigning St. James's Park in the natural style. Although they were royal parks, enclosed and unavailable to use by the masses, these two parks, located centrally in London's fashionable west end, became hallmarks of the English Natural Style, as translated into park usage. Installed in 1825, St. James's Park in particular, because of its central location, accessibility, and the quality of its design, can be recognized as the bridge between the 18th Century 'improved' estate and the romantic 19th Century city parks to follow.

The Urban Park Movement

The Machine Age came to England gradually during the last quarter of the 18th Century, but with the conclusion of the Napoleonic Wars on the continent the tempo increased with a roar that shattered the tranquility of the countryside and plunged the quiescent towns into agonies of activity previously unknown to them. There was seemingly a rush to succeed, almost as if the long war period, which had interrupted normal commercial growth, had to be made up for in double time. The age of steam had been waiting for 50 years to be harnessed, and at last the energies of the nation's economic strength seemed ready for the challenge.

While the Industrial Revolution is so named because of the emphasis on machine rather than hand-made goods, it would be innaccurate to describe it in only such terms, for the period includes broad change throughout the nation's economic structure over a long period of time. Agriculture, for example, underwent considerable technical adjustment. The primary agricultural industries were of course wool and cotton, but food production was also greatly improved through the application of science to fertilizers, plowing methods, drainage and hybridization. The textile industry advanced

rapidly through the development of spinning machines, power driven looms and eventually textile mills. Like the rapidly expanding developments in iron and ceramics, the textile mills had in common the necessity of centralizing the entire manufacturing process under a single roof. Such an endeavor was in part accomplished by new structural techniques which made use of iron columns and trussed ceilings which were able to span greater distances, allowing for high ceilings for better smoke dispersal and unencumbered space to house the large and bulky machinery. Because they were steam driven, a source of fuel as well as raw material was vital in determining locations for the new mills. And of course the entire industry had to be centralized due to these circumstances. The one essential ingredient which had to be completely re-adjusted, in order for the new methods to succeed, was labor.

In the villages throughout Britain a kind of cottage industry had existed for centuries, which depended upon hand woven goods and hand driven machinery. The skills of local craftsmen were recognized, giving a particular village a distinction for excellence in weaving, dying, pottery or flatware. The new machine age decimated village industry and drained off the labor force as well. The steam looms produced finished cloth quicker and cheaper, the cloth buyers no longer visited the villages to make their purchases, and those who had made their living in the textile crafts as well as other cottage industries, found their way to the mill towns of Manchester, Sheffield, Birmingham and Leeds, where work in the mills was available to them.

The economics are easy enough to follow. The myriad of social change, upheaval and chaos which industrial centralization brought to these cities was unexpected and overwhelming. Crowding, pollution of every kind—human and industrial followed, while village life with its organic economy and cottage industry, crumbled back into the 18th Century. People came to the cities for jobs, and they came in such numbers as to nearly double the urban population of mill towns in two decades. Other than the building of the mills themselves however, the cities were unprepared to take on this additional population of poor country folk. Housing was quickly thrown together in order to house the newly arrived factory workers, but it was frequently lacking in heat, ventilation and sanitary needs. There were no medical facilities available to the 'laboring poor'. Police and fire protection did not exist, except by private charter for the wealthy. Sanitation and sewers were primitive or non-existant. The need for a centralized labor force in the industrial cities completely rent the fabric of social structure in Britain. It emptied the villages and filled the mills. Open space was quickly grabbed up for shoddy new housing, usually alongside the mills themselves, and tenement life became even more crowded, uncomfortable and hazardous.

In the town centers open space was also lost to agricultural development as a result of the Enclosure Acts which had been revived at the time of the Industrial Revolution, depriving peasant and laboring classes from the time honored use of commons which provided them with both food and winter fuel on a more or less individual basis. New agricultural practices increased yields, but the foodstuffs, as well as the profits, found their way to other markets— and other pockets. Enclosure, as a means of protecting one's growing and grazing lands, had been an institution in Britain since established by a feudal society in the Middle Ages. Enclosure during the Industrial Revolution however meant the end of peasant society and its freedom to use public lands for general benefit. Peasants were usually offered a monetary settlement, as required by law, after which their ability to survive became even more restricted.

And of course, many of them found their way to the mill towns in hope of work. Enclosure, combined with steam-driven machinery, produced some very real negative effects on both urban and rural working classes:

through enclosure: loss of income or livelihood
                    loss of open space for recreation
                    destruction of peasant class
                    loss of village society

through industrialization: uprooting of rural society
                            loss of cottage industry
                            crowding, lack of health and safety
                            loss of urban open space

The uprooting of Britain's peasant class, by appropriating their lands and their livelihood and leaving them little recourse but the mills, left the country with a large and virtually helpless laboring class, with no bargaining position and rather at the mercy of their times. There is little doubt but that the major opposition posed by working people was built along lines of economic privation, at least in the beginning of their travail. Moral, aesthetic, sanitary, safety and spiritual deprivation would be discovered later, while at the same time the middle class was becoming wealthy and powerful from the products of agriculture and the new machine-made goods. In the rush to speed cheaply made goods to European markets, along the new high speed railroads and in power driven freight boats, the plight of the urban poor was all but overlooked. Under

Queen Victoria's heavy handed moral conservatism Gt. Britain gained an economic and then political edge over the rest of Europe, setting the stage for her greatest period of imperial glory, at high cost to those who bore the brunt of industry's success.

The problems resulting from rapid, generally unplanned growth in the industrial cities of Britain's midlands began to attract the attention of various reformers representing a rather wide range of interests and occupations. Edwin Chadwick, a social reformer and associate of Jeremy Bentham, devoted his life to the improvement of health and sanitation in cities. Charles Dickens, in *Hard Times* and other works, exposed the plight of the laboring poor to Britain's reading public. John C. Loudon, writer and landscape gardener, proposed public walks, as an early form of working class parks, to provide healthful exercise on Sunday, and Joseph Paxton, architect and horticulturist, successfully argued the need for public parks on behalf of the industrial cities' working poor. Parliament eventually considered the matter, and established a committee to investigate the need for open space in working class neighborhoods of the industrial towns, reporting the woeful inadequacies of such in 1833.[1]

Progress was painfully slow however, and conditions in the midlands cities actually worsened between 1830 and 1840, leading to staggering statistics of infant mortality, drunkenness, pulmonary diseases, and continued loss of open space, as factories, rail connections and warehousing sprawled over available land.

In 1841 however, Paxton was successful in convincing land owners and merchants in the ship building city of Birkenhead (across the Mersey River from Liverpool) that a park for the working and middle classes combined was in their best interests. In the same year, against the feelings of the queen, parliament lowered restrictions on entry to the royal parks, and planned two additional parks — Victoria and Battersea — to serve London's working classes. James Pennethorne, the designer of both these new parks, followed the precedent set by Nash and Repton in Regent's and St. James's parks by adapting the romantic English Natural Style in preference to the more formal French and Italian precedents.

Lagging behind in park planning, Paris quickly caught up with Britain following the ascendency of Napoleon III to the presidency of France in 1848 (and to emperor in 1852). With his appointment of Georges Haussmann to direct the massive modernization of the city, the park system of Paris became second to none, particularly in view of the splendid work of park-engineer, Jean-Adolphe Alphand. Including the many existing formal gardens into the system, Alphand added new neighborhood parks in the 'English style', and revamped the huge hunting forests of the Bois de Boulogne and Bois de Vincennes into successful public parks. Inside each of these are found a marvelous variety of gardens, pleasure parks, menageries, playgrounds, race courses, boating lakes, and all the romantic imagery and Beaux Arts grandeur that the Second Empire could produce. Haussmann and Alphand were extremely successful and innovative, converting an old quarry (Parc Buttes-Chaumont), an old Fortress (in Vincennes), hunting grounds and marshes into playfields and lakes (in Boulogne), and adapting old royal gardens into usable public parks (Parc de Tuileries).

The 19th century urban parks, for all their dependence upon design themes developed from a romanticized view of the past, remain a cornerstone in the evolution of the modern urban park concept. Developed as a response to pollution, overcrowding and a need for healthful outdoor recreation in working class neighborhoods, they illustrated the need for open green space in large and

1. Great Britain, Her majesty's Stationary Office. Report of the Select Committee on Public Walks, 1833.

increasingly complex urban centers. At a time when London, Manchester and Paris were building their new parks, American cities were just entering the Industrial Age. Plagued by competition from abroad and political division at home, the 'captains of industry' showed little interest in the amenities of urban growth, and following the great economic and productive set-back of the Civil War, the newly emerging industrial cities of the North swept aside all but industrial expediency in their determination to become competititve with European markets.

A few stalwart individuals however, self-appointed champions in the cause of the urban green, labored diligently on behalf of the park concept—first for New York City, and eventually throughout the growing industrialized cities of the nation.

Frederick Law Olmsted and Andrew Jackson Downing sought parks of the English Natural Style for American cities after visits to Britain, and were eventually successful in the development of Central Park in New York, although Downing did not live to see its realization. Olmsted went on to become the premier city park designer in 19th century America, with representative examples of his work in New York, Brooklyn, Boston, Chicago and New Orleans. Horace Cleveland, and later Jens Jensen, became outspoken city park advocates throughout the Midwest as the American industrial frontier continued to move West.

By the end of the century every American city of any size possessed a park of some prominence, replete with all the trappings of European antecedence. Most of these, like Central Park itself, were funded through public expenditures. Others, like Forest Park in St. Louis and Jackson Park in Chicago developed, as we noted earlier, out of the period's favorite amusement—the exposition. And some parks came into public ownership through outright bequest, like 4000 acre Griffith Park in Los Angeles. Grant Park, Chicago, is the centerpiece of a lakeside park system which stretches out along the coast of Lake Michigan for some twelve miles—nearly half the city's coastline. Over five miles of this system is found in the city's largest park, Lincoln.

Chicago is perhaps the best example of unplanned, unchecked growth in America's industrial era. An early link to the iron ore

fields of the upper lakes, Chicago quickly established itself as a transport center, first by way of canal and later by rail. Between 1830 and 1850 its population multiplied seventeen times (from 30,000 to 500,000), unaccompanied by any form of civic plan or design whatsoever. Following the 1871 fire the city failed to take advantage of a great opportunity to re-build in an orderly way, and the previous slum-tenement housing built adjacent to steel mills and slaughter houses repeated itself with a vengeance. By 1880 Chicago had outstripped every city in the nation in following the dismal example of the British midlands cities of the early 19th century. Lake Michigan supplied all of the city's drinking water, direct and untreated, and in turn received the city's sewage—direct and untreated. But the fire had left the image of hope on some, and when Chicago was successful in acquiring the rights to hold a world's fair in 1892-3, the idea of a new and orderly civic development was born. Chicago is truly a man-made city, planned and developed out of a flattened, windswept lake front plain, having no natural harbor or natural amenities, it became one of America's best planned cities in the 20th century, although the 1909 master plan and physical design plan by Daniel Burnham have not been fully completed. (p. 156)

Likewise, the 1904 world's fair in St. Louis (Louisianna Purchase Exposition) provided the city with a great stimulus for orderly growth, and a healthy appreciation for monumental grandeur. Today the grand staircases, lofty towers, formidable pavilions, fountains and ballustrades seem dated and out of place to us, within their glass and steel surroundings. And many of those architectural oddities—reminiscent of a proud and less sophisticated age, remain in poor repair, with their crumbled cornices and eroded plaster facades—real ruins rather than the artless constructions of 18th century Romanticism. But such living museums—Grant Park, Jackson Park, Forest Park—deserve our attention, if not altogether for the form they took, then for the role they have played in the physical improvement of cities in the Industrial Age, and the evolution of the city park movement these past hundred years.

The city park movement, spawned by ills of urban life in early 19th century Britain, swept across Northern Europe, jumped the Atlantic Ocean, and by the close of the century had implanted the city park concept throughout the western world. The heritage of the 19th century park movement is further noted by its absence, pointedly in Southern and Eastern Europe and Latin America. Following World War I Tokyo has experimented with western styled park design, including the formal symmetry of Parisian influence, without great success. On the other hand, Stockholm has developed the most complete and modern park system, joined by means of an interlocking network of continuous green space which undulates through the city, squeezing under bridges, around commercial centers, and flowing towards the sea along the spiny ridges of the Baltic Coast.

Copenhagen's park system is based on two concentric rings, the remnants of 14th and 18th century fortifications which now lend themselves to waterways and corridors of green. Amsterdam's canals, which radiate from the city's center like ripples in a pool, offer tree lined corridors in the heart of the old city, while a complex greenbelt system maintains its historic urban structure. The Amsterdamse Bos, perhaps the most successfully planned park in Europe, represents the primary element in this system.

In addition to Paris, Amsterdam and London most German and Scandinavian cities enjoy well planned park systems. Even in bad weather—common to Northern Europe any time of the year—the parks are never empty, and on a pleasant Sunday afternoon, Fall, Winter or Spring, they are likely to be jammed with active participants. Such enthusiasm for parks does not exist in America. Given other options city dwellers here appear to prefer avoiding each other. Some describe it as the 'frontier mentality' that has existed since Colonial times. At its worst it creates artificial walls between people in *all* public places—restaurants, buses, sidewalks as well as parks—and renders parks inhospitable, bleak and even dangerous. Park funding is cut, programs and maintenance reduced. An unkempt quality creeps into the greensward, and unsavory elements enter as the public departs. Parks become less important to the city fathers in their distribution of revenues. People learn to get along without them, turning to other forms of escape. Services to parks are further reduced, and in order to justify them to fiscally oriented voters money making proposals are introduced—restaurants, sports arenas, arcade amusements and any variety of presumably non-conforming attractions. No one comes to the park for any purpose that has anything remotely to do with why it's there. In this way a city's park system dies.

The alternatives of course exist, even at the present time, and persistant individuals—urban designers, city administrators, park commissioners, civic minded individuals—persist in the effort needed to restore parks to their proper place in the urban society. For city folks the park is their backyard, encouraging all those activities pictured on page 183—and many more. It is the awareness place, the grand open meadow for running, the cultural retreat, the zoo and arboretum that no backyard could ever hope to match. It may include any number of walks, fountains and statues (including some pleasant departures from the military heroes, as indicated on page 135), along with some museums and other such cultural buildings. But the park should remain, for the greater part, a green space—an escape from hard geometry, a stroll in the woods. At best its shape is reflected in the people who use it, not in the structures that frame it. When Central Park was first opened in New York, a woman visitor was supposed to have inquired, "so where's the park? This just looks like nature". To which Federick Law Olmsted was reported to have remarked, "the best possible praise I could have gotten".

NINE

Order Implied: Oriental Urban Space

Development of this chapter was undertaken by Takeo Uesugi, Associate Professor of Landscape Architecture, California State Polytechnic University, Pomona.

Oriental urban space, particularly as it evolved in Japan, is a study in its own right, and is included here in an abbreviated form to illustrate contrasting thought processes in the evolution of Eastern design principles.

With the exception of the Medieval Period, Western culture has continued to seek conscious, predetermined solutions to civic design and particularly to the physical organization of the square.

As we have seen thus far, there has generally been an alternating emphasis on rational vs. empirical spatial organization, but the truly unplanned, undisciplined evolution of urban order has rarely developed to any degree of sophistication in Western culture, and in fact most scholars of the art dismiss empiricism in urban space as being on the whole primitive—having neither beauty nor efficiency.

There exist far too many good examples to the contrary for us to accept such a dismissal of trial-and-error urban design, but it remains true nonetheless that most solutions of this type depend on *time* and *change* to produce any measure of success, and usually as a consequence suffer from the awkwardness of unrelated form, material, color, and position of enclosing agents.

Oriental, and particularly Japanese urban organization is, like its Medieval counterpart, an evolution of spatial order dependent upon and resulting from day-to-day change; but it succeeds more frequently and to a greater degree of sophistication than the former. The secret to this success is the *conscious* search for order, usually missing in Medieval empiricism or Western trial-and-error design in general.

In this case, a conscious search for order is in no way intended to suggest the Western rational approach, as in Renaissance order with its predetermined scale, proportion, rhythm, and structural enclosure. Conscious organization of urban space in Japan leads to a sensitive and skillful disposition of parts, each of which bears upon the whole. There is a sense of order here, as well as beauty and efficiency, but it is more *implied* than imposed.

The basis upon which this implied order has developed throughout the history of both China and Japan is the worship of nature. This is easy enough for us to comprehend as we look back through centuries of agrarian culture. The people of Japan and China have always lived close to the earth, and the evolution of religion, philosophy, and social structure are imminently involved in the soil. Therefore, the three criteria by which we measure Japanese urban space: the condition under which the space is produced, the function and form of urban space, and the user group for which the space is intended, are all tied to and reflected in the worship of nature. Without dwelling on this point we can refer, for example, to the development of *Jomon* and *Yayoi* earthenware, the sophisticated and natural systems for

137

joining materials in architecture, nature as a basis for poetry, literature and painting, and the art of garden design—a refinement and abstraction of natural order as yet unsurpassed in intuitive and ritualistic order.

Despite the rather heavy influence from China, organization of spatial order evolved quite differently in Japan. The reasons for these differences derive most certainly from nature. Climate, a mountainous terrain, limited space for cultivation, a richer and more varied native plant life and an insular state all contributed to the individuality in Japanese culture and a sensitivity and refinement of spatial order not achieved in China. Throughout their history the people of Japan have been tied to the soil, to nature, and their economic, religious, and social development reflect this marriage to a greater degree than is found in China or other parts of the orient. As a result of these things, Japan remained both agrarian and feudal until the middle of the nineteenth century.

The feudal structure of Medieval Japan retarded progress of any political nature, and for centuries Japan remained divided by military supremacy—fractured like Medieval Europe into tiny warring principalities, without benefit of a Renaissance or Baroque Age, without a classic heritage or need for classic revivals. There was only China—and nature to draw upon for cultural development and aesthetic inspiration. In addition, and again resulting from China and natural influences, Zen-sect Buddhism began to develop as the main stream of Japan's religious philosophy.

Out of this economic, political, social, and religious milieu grew the different classes of Japanese villages, separated as to: temple towns, castle towns, and market towns, not unlike a similar development of Europe's early Middle Ages.

Temple Towns

Buddhist and Shinto temples and shrines were usually placed in lofty locations, on hilltops, or mountainous promonitories. A pilgrimage to such a temple provided spiritual benefit as well as social and recreational satisfaction. As pilgrimages increased, the need for accommodations nearby gave rise to the development of an urban structure surrounding or adjacent to the temple. Kiyomizudera Temple, founded in the seventh century, became one of the most important temple towns in Japan. As shown below, the temple is located on a hill near Kyoto. Two streets lead up the slope to the main gate. Along these streets, leading to the temple proper, a series of spaces has evolved, whose form and organization are dependent upon the degree of slope and the direction toward the temple. Japanese urban space thereby began to develop in attenuated form, along routes of circulation. The sequence of spaces in Kiyomizudera is as follows:

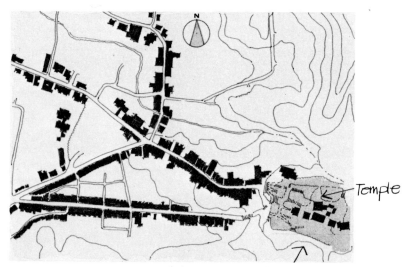

Kiyomizu Temple area

The Castle Town

Similar to development in Europe, the fortress of the Medieval war lord eventually moved from protective hilltop to the more accessible plain. With this change began the evolution from fortress to town. An advancing, open agricultural economy paved the way for this development, but the castle town, like Europe's *ville neuve* and *bastide*, remained primarily an element of political and military strategy—an outpost against potential

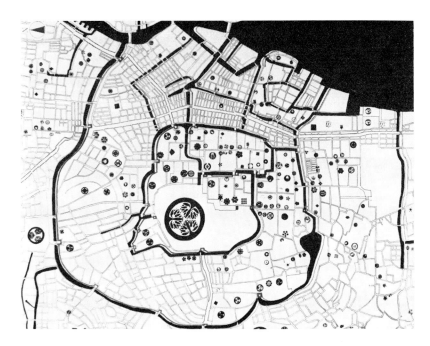

enemies. The irregular pattern of streets connected soldiers' residences, temples and shrines, shops, and finally the agricultural fields beyond the system of walls and moats.

Cities like Kamakura, Kanazawa, and Takayama, which developed as Castle towns retain many aspects of their original

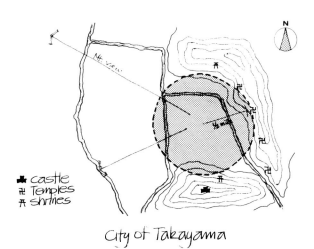

♣ Castle
卍 Temples
卉 Shrines

City of Takayama

form. Takayama, in the center of Japan, illustrates the same degree of human qualities as found in Medieval European towns, whose growth was limited by walls and fortifications.

The Market Town

The market town resulted directly from the exchange of goods. As a result of trade routes, the town evolved in linear form and the exchange of goods took place along this route—as we have observed in western development, along the major thoroughfare from one town to the next, or along the riverfront, where trade occurred.

Kurashiki is an example of a market town, having developed as a center for rice exchange during the eighteenth century. As shown below, the town developed along the riverfront, where were located the rice granaries, merchants' homes, and public spaces for trading.

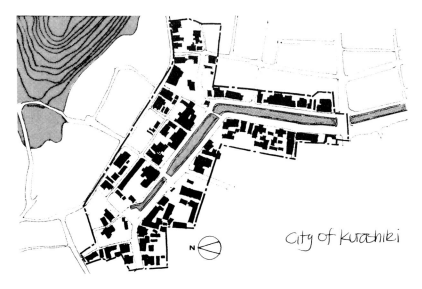

City of Kurashiki

Because the marketplace in such towns remained linear, the shopping malls developed in industrial, post-war Japanese cities continue to reflect this spatial character.

The drawing below illustrates the mixture of shops, restaurants, tea rooms, bars, and residences in downtown Kyoto. The variety of activities, limitation of space, and sense of human scale combine to make this a most exciting and intimate complex of interrelated spaces. For greater contact and urban relief, two rivers adjoin the complex and provide a surrounding of park space.

order was established, never to be relinquished. Buildings, no matter the purpose, usually reflected (in their form and placement) a consideration and respect for natural surroundings. Such surroundings became the essence of the garden, and took on a highly symbolic form, suggestive of Zen-sect views of natural order.

Ise Shrine, Naiku

Primitive   Ancient-times   Middle-ages

Natural setting
Garden
Building

Downtown Kyoto

Vehicular + Ped.   Ped only
P   Parking   mixed Land Uses

0   300'

Concepts of Urban Spatial Organization

One of the most important aspects in the evolution of Japanese urban space is the rather special relationship between a building and its site. In primitive times nature was worshipped as a deity, providing all the needs for life-shelter, food, clothing. Later, nature was symbolized in the form of the Ise shrine, and the beginning of a relationship between man-made and natural

This precise art of building siting, in keeping with Zen and Taoist philosophy and symbolism, is perhaps best captured in the complex of buildings at the Katsura Imperial villa, developed in the seventeenth century. Unlike Chinese urban order with its walled enclosures, North-South orientation and rigid axiality, Japanese planning developed along a human scale concept of external space related to the natural environment and oriented to natural phenomena, without symmetry or formal axiality. There are exceptions of course, as seen in the Buddhist temples in Nara and Osaka, where precise symmetry and North-South orientation prevail.

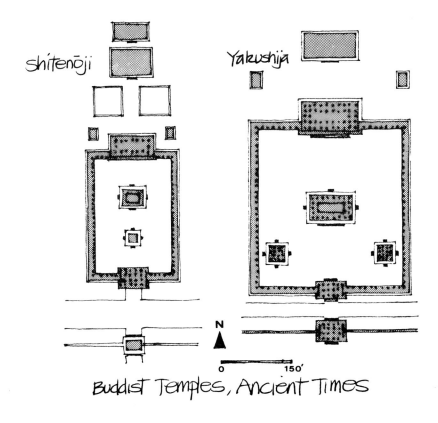

Buddist Temples, Ancient Times

But this kind of Chinese influence was on the wane as early as the ninth century, and assymetry, characteristic of the Japanese love of natural order, was again in ascendency. Furthermore, this sense of natural order depended upon a concept of form *in the process of being completed.* Both Zen and Taoist philosophy teach the principle of dynamic arrest—the suspension of time, by resisting completion. It is the leaving of something undone, the landscape which awaits the viewer, the house just beyond the tree, the wave about to break. In this respect the art of Japanese planning seems virtually opposite to Renaissance theories of external space.

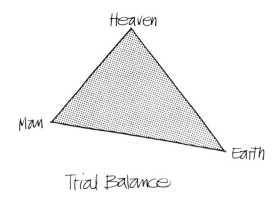

Trial Balance

Symbolism

Chinese and Japanese religious views have always involved symbolism, and in Zen-sect philosophic teachings nature becomes the basis of symbolic meaning. Spring meant flowers, and happiness. Autumn color and the falling leaves was a signal for reflection, and nostalgia. The cheerful songs of insects in summer, as well as winter's blanket of white snow, held meaning for everyone. All things in nature were selected to serve as symbolic lessons in living, through the application of Zen-sect principles. Haiku poetry was developed to express symbolically the profound and intricate discipline of nature's teaching. Noh is a form of drama which depends upon a system of simplified movement for expression. In the garden, stone and sand became representations of more complex natural forms—mountains, islands, the sea. Symbolism of form and representation taken from nature led to philosophic interpretations of space, based on nature and evolved in a time sequence.

Spatial Sequence

The concept of sequential spaces, separate but related, probably began in Zen monasteries and tea gardens of the late Middle Ages. The pilgrimage to a temple, and the evolution of a town along the route, is perhaps the origin of this sequence, since the pilgrims would have been directed through a series of

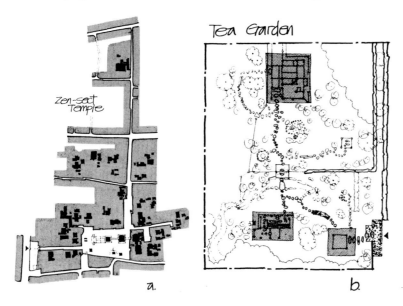

Tea Garden

Zen-sect Temple

a.　　　　　　　　b.

experiences—shops, open markets, housing, eating places—before arriving at the temple. In a smaller way, the tea ceremony repeats this sequence.

The absence of symmetry in Japanese art objects has been often commented on by Western critics. This also is a result of a working out through Zennism of Taoist ideals. Confucianism, with its deep seated idea of dualism, and Northern Buddhism with its worship of a trinity, were in no way opposed to the expression of symmetry. As a matter of fact, if we study the ancient bronzes of China or the religious arts of the T'ang dynasty and the Nara period, we shall recognize a constant striving after symmetry. The decoration of our classical interiors was decidely regular in arrangement. The Taoist and Zen conception of perfection, how-

ever was different. The dynamic nature of their philosophy laid more stress upon the *process* through which perfection was sought than upon perfection itself. True beauty could be discussed only by one who mentally completed the incomplete. The virility of life and art lay in its possibilities for growth. In the tea-room it is left for each guest *in imagination* to complete the total effect, in relation to himself. Since Zennism has become the prevailing mode of thought, the art of the extreme Orient has purposely avoided the symmetrical as expressing not only completion but repetition. *Uniformity of design was considered as fatal to the freshness of imagination.*[1]

Up until the time of the Meiji Restoration in 1867 which ended feudalism in Japan, cities grew and developed slowly, based for the most part on religious, feudal, or agrarian concepts. Industrialization came to Japan late in the nineteenth century, following the intervention of American and European economic interests. As a result of this gradual development the old capitol cities of Nara and Kyoto grew to maturity before the explosion of the Machine Age, and remain today as the best examples of traditional Japanese urban planning.

The drawings at the top of the following page show the layout of the old capitol at Heijokyo (Nara) in diagrammatic plan, based on the form specified for Ch'ang-an, the earlier capitol city. Both cities were planned on a gridiron scheme of about nine square miles in area. The imperial palace was located in the center of the Northern end, and occupied about seven percent of the total area (2/3 of a square mile). The original symmetry soon gave way to emperical usage and activity.

Kyoto as well was laid out on a gridiron plan, its streets occupied by a vast mixture of social, economic, and religious activities—industry mixed with shops, temples, housing. It is a pedestrian oriented city, the streets being narrow and intended for walking. The spaces and activities develop and change at human scale, and at a pedestrian pace. Again, it is primarily a *linear* experience.

1. Kakuzo Okakura, *The Book of Tea*, New York: Dover, 1964; (author's italics).

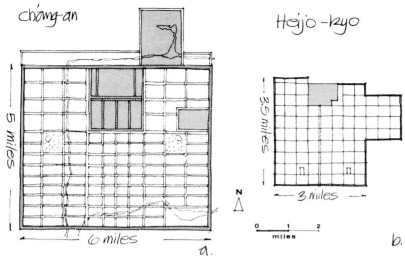

Ch'ang-an

Heijo-kyo

a.

b.

Plan of Ancient Capitol

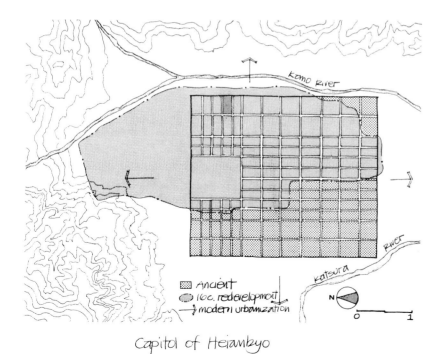

Ancient
16c. redevelopment
modern urbanization

Capitol of Heiankyo

The three plans below illustrate the sequence of pedestrian spatial development from ancient to modern times. An original city block, 360 foot square, changed from small cottage farms into an area of exchange of goods, and the location of merchants' homes during the Middle Ages. The street enclosed by these town houses functioned as the center of social activity and trade, and the common space within the block was used jointly for public vegetable gardens, toilets, storage, and disposal. As in its European counterpart, a well was usually dug here in order to provide for a public water supply.

After the long period of feudal warfare (thirteenth-sixteenth centuries) the town houses developed private courtyards, which largely replaced the traditional common space. During the seventeenth century the size of the courtyards was further increased, eliminating public space altogether—except of course

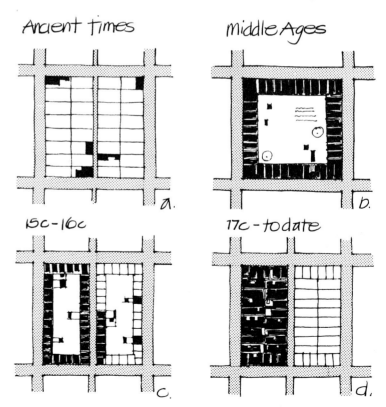

Ancient Times

Middle Ages

a.

b.

15c-16c

17c-todate

c.

d.

for the streets. From that time on the street has remained the major area of public gathering, divided into clusters of about thirty houses. This clustering of units along the street became the basis for neighborhood identity and activity which remains to the present time.

The plans below illustrate the typical street layout for Kyoto. In (a) we see the regular gridiron developing along a major East-West commercial strip. At (b) and (c) we see the irregularities which have developed as a result of residential occupation. These areas have been humanized by empirical usage. Note the "T" intersections and acute angles.

gardens, squares, and parks have since evolved in Kyoto and other cities, but largely as a result of Western influences. The narrower secondary streets, too small for auto traffic, have retained their ancient purpose as neighborhood delineators and public gathering places—the historic urban space of Japan.

The plan below shows the structure of Kyoto in diagrammatic form. The major avenues act as sight lines to distant views of natural beauty—forests and mountains. The temples punctuate the otherwise horizontal roof line, acting as visual points of

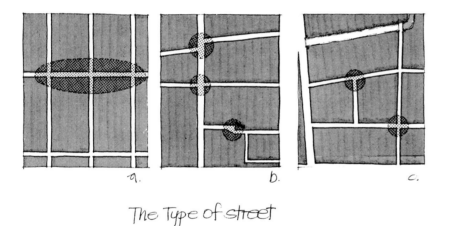

a.   b.   c.

The Type of street

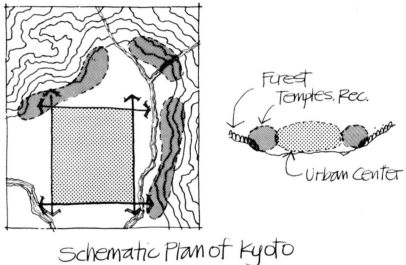

Schematic Plan of Kyoto

Japanese cities did not develop specific squares, similar to those of Europe. What spaces did evolve, as we have seen, were empirical in nature and of purely practical necessity. The street remained the formally designated avenue of public intercourse and exchange—until the advent of the automobile! Public

orientation, or nodes along a sight line, carrying the vista as intended.

Kyoto's series of linear spaces and gridiron sight lines has, unfortunately suffered greatly with the advent of the mechanical age, the factory and most of all, the automobile.

In summary, the following characteristics generally apply to oriental, and particularly Japanese urban space:

1. Space is *empirically derived*, consciously but rarely manipulated by preconceived plan. It depends more upon people, and other temporal qualities, and is therefore *implied* rather than rationally conceived.

2. Because of the historic significance placed upon streets and movement, space in the city, as well as the whole concept of spatial sensation, becomes strongly *linear*.

3. Oriental space, characteristic of Japan as well as the Near East, is seen to be in the *process of unfolding*. It is the state of being incomplete, and therefore dynamic and progressive. Something needs to be added.

4. Urban space in its development, like architecture, garden design and other arts, is largely a product of the religious/philosophic worship of *nature* and natural order.

5. To a large degree, *symbolic* meaning pervades Japanese architecture and the environmental arts in general.

TEN

Order Re-defined: Resolution

The need for varied, efficiently organized public open space in today's highly charged urban atmosphere is probably greater now than at any previous time. Technology and our vast network of dependencies have made us the most urban of societies, and perhaps the least urbane. The bedlam of an industrially successful city results in a large part from the advancement of labor-saving machinery, which permeates every aspect of a modern city's life—manufacture and dispersal of goods, communications, transportation, public services.

The high density of the Middle Ages gave way to the relative low density planning of the seventeenth and eighteenth century radial and neoclassic periods, but since the coming of industry in the nineteenth century higher densities and greater urban populations have resulted. Density offers an obvious clue to spatial needs. Generally, higher density argues in favor of an increased percentage of open space allotment—particularly for recreational purposes. For example, a high density residential complex, usually high-rise apartments or tightly stacked town houses, precludes any possibility for traditional backyard space characteristic of single family residential development. This normally places greater responsibility on the city to provide the needed open space, in the form of parks, malls, tree-lined walkways and recreation places.

High density obligates planners to make use of public open space in other aspects of urban life as well. Commerce brings people together in crowds, the relief from which may be provided in the open space of the modern marketplace—the shopping center. Government spaces continue to function as of old—in the form of the

civic center, a collection of administrative activities housed in structures which enclose some form of open space. Public open space—governmental, commercial, or social—has, of course, changed in many ways, but not in basic purpose. It is important, therefore, to address ourselves again to the basic factors which influence urban form, and the kinds of urban spaces which meet today's needs. In Chapter Two we dealt with them as the *behavioral factors* in determining *form*. This time let's consider them as categories of public activity.

The political factor

civic center

government center

The economic factor

shopping center

shopping mall

the civic mall

refurbished town center

"new town" center

The social factor

green square

city park

recreation spaces

147

The religious factor does not play a major role at present in the organization of urban form and space. For the others, modern development usually occurs as follows:

The Political Factor

The civic center of government center normally includes these basic governmental activities, divided into *administrative, regulatory* and *civic* functions:

Administrative

licensing

maintenance (sewers, streets, parks, trees)

services (utilities, trash)

education (schools)

engineering (codes, ordinances)

planning

transportation

communication

Regulatory

police

fire

emergency services

courts

detention

Civic

education (library, museums)

recreation

entertainment (auditorium, theatre)

To think collectively of the diverse uses associated with the public functions of today's city means also to be able to distinguish and separate nonconforming activities. Certainly, no compatibility exists between jail and library, between theatre and fire house. For such reasons the civic center concept ought to be understood in terms of these three basic components. In most in-

stances the regulatory facilities are compatible and can be combined in one building or complex of buildings. City administrative offices may likewise be combined, even when different levels of government are involved, i.e., post office, water department, county and city offices. It also makes it easier for the citizen who has business to conduct with more than one public office or agency.

Likewise, the library, museum and civic opera share a common bond. They represent the city's amenities, and may be well suited to a common grouping. As our cities continue to grow in complexity the need to consider this kind of separation in function becomes increasingly relevant.

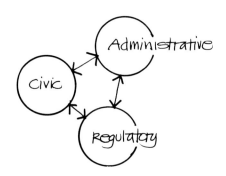

Albany, the capital of New York, in 1977 completed a new administrative complex to house affairs of state government. Its plan, including a row of domino like high-rise buildings, emanates from the same rational design spirit of sixteenth century Italy, projecting at once a mood of sober efficiency, amidst sterile, pretentious architecture.

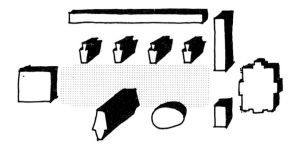

In Phoenix, the new civic center reflects a self-conscious image seeking appeal to the arts, and to visiting delegates with its 120,000 square foot convention center. In much the same way the Music Center in Los Angeles concentrates on the performing arts—housed in three buildings which enclose a square of formal simplicity.

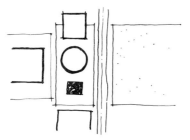

Unfortunately, the civic center complexes at Albany and Phoenix (p. 192-193) lack softening details of any significance, and are subject instead to harsh, repetitive geometry, and blocky architecture of no particular merit.

San Francisco's civic center reflects a neoclassic tradition—a great, domed city hall standing at the terminus of a series of symmetrical spaces strung out along an axial sight line.

San Francisco's sedate civic center, although under attack for years by renovation enthusiasts, retains however an impressive bal-

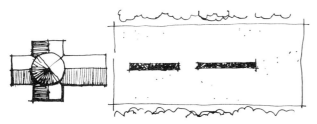

ance in form, space, and detailing not often found in more contemporary governmental centers. Its pleached *allees,* formal fountains, and broad, axial walkways would seem to belie the axiom of change in urban space. Eclectic design is one of the realities of art—particularly architecture, and we continue to encounter it in some urban form as we move back and forth between rational and empirical, symmetrical and asymmetrical, imitation of nature, and dominance

over nature. Eclectic form may appear fresh and imaginative or staid and repetitive—depending upon the skill of the architect, and its timing.

Another eclectic example worth noting is Philadelphia's Independence Mall. Here we have a truly historic building in need of a spatial setting; and much like San Francisco's Civic Center, the major design element hinges on a primary sight line, balanced symmetrically, through a series of geometric spaces which terminate on the cross-axial facade of Independence Hall. The mall, with its series of fountains, steps, walkways, and formal planting is quite contemporary in its detailing, although the design in overall concept rivals Nancy and Paris (pp. 194-195).

The Economic Factor

The modern marketplace does not greatly resemble its medieval counterpart, although basic purposes have not changed much. The changes in both form and function began with industrialization—the coming of transportation centers and mechanized production. These two courses alone were mainly responsible for the termination of the marketplace—as traditionally developed, although the market square continued to function as a secondary place of barter.

Following World War II, with the advent of mass produced suburban housing and two car garages, the *shopping center* came into being as an alternative for the housewife, who would otherwise have shopped in the downtown commercial sections of larger cities. And she would have gotten there and back by bus or streetcar. Grocery shopping would have been accomplished the same way, except that in the older neighborhoods of pre-World War II vintage the market might well have been the ground floor of housing blocks.

Shopping centers therefore answered the growing needs of suburban consumers. They were intended at first to serve the lower levels of economic exchange, while major marketing in industrial goods and agricultural produce was transferred entirely from the scene, behind telephones and cables into distant glass towers. But the departure of commodities from the open marketplace had been anticipated since Christopher Wren's day with the building of the

Royal Exchange and in the 19th century *Les Halles* in Paris. The old market squares of medieval times may still be vital, but the level of exchange is now that of the suburban shopping center in America: restaurants, fashionable boutiques, a gallery, and book store. . . .

The shopping center was initially successful because it provided ample free parking and the variety of stores which could normally be expected to serve a single stop. In time, the major centers dropped the term "shopping" and broadened their economic bases to include professional services. The concept has been so successful that in some twenty-five years it has grown to include just about every commercial use or service, has added a number of recreational and social activities, and has in some instances greatly influenced the economic conditions of the region, affecting the relocation of the civic center and growth patterns generally.

Fashion Island in Newport Beach, California, embraces all behavioral functions of open space (except religion), and because of its powerful economic clout, has caused its encirclement by the general business community: banks, professional offices, and by a

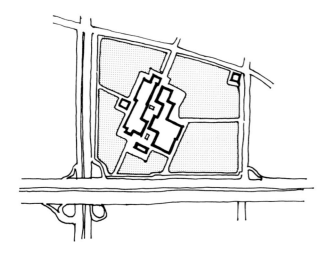

developing residential community. It has, in effect, become a viable city.

The shopping center's success has been phenomenal in post-war United States, and understandably detrimental to traditional commercial areas. *Town centers (centre, centrum, centro)* have been fighting the ebbing commercial tides in various ways, great and small: more parking, better lighting and protection, resting places with benches, trees and other kinds of overhead protection, plant boxes, art displays, canned music.

Limited to the narrow strip of pavement between street and building front, the pedestrian was understandably delighted by the sense of open space projected by the first shopping centers. They are reminders of places like Venice or Dubrovnik, where streets are only for walking (or paddling) and one can concentrate on shop windows without an eye out for autos.

But the shopping center, and its latest offspring, the enclosed mall, does a disservice to the city by reversing the centric tradition of urban development, and creating a kind of centrifugal economic force in the city's growth pattern. After twenty years of shopping centers, that pattern is clearly developed throughout American cities in the form of decaying urban centers with all the attendant economic and social misfortunes, and a general weakening of the traditional urban fabric.

Perhaps economic/social stability can be restructured on the urban fringes, through the developing rings of shopping centers, but no one as yet has done much study along this line. Instead, the following methods have been introduced with the thought towards reversing economic decentralization.

The Shopping Mall. For our purposes we will consider two kinds of shopping malls (and a civic mall as well, which we will deal with later). The first, and older form, involves merely the clearing away of automobile traffic on several blocks of a downtown commercial street, and dedicating it entirely to pedestrian usage. Some planners refer to this process as *pedestrianization*. A certain amount of re-design is called for—often merely cosmetic treatment—and the mall is in business. In some cases a few plant containers are employed, and if any degree of permenance is envisioned, curbs are blended into sidewalk and a few benches appear. These early, tenuous steps have led to more complete pedestrianized schemes in Pomona, Fresno and Riverside, California in the 1960's, and Eugene, Oregon, where attempts were made to interrupt gridiron monotony with the introduction of human scale amenities such as play areas, fountains and waterways, paving changes, sitting areas and plantings.

The Pomona Mall is an exception, lacking this kind of innovative approach. Instead it retains the repetitious lineal alignment of the original grid pattern. Moreover the placement of planters pays no heed to storefronts or entries. It fails therefore, in both practical and aesthetic terms (pp. 198-199). On the other hand, the Fresno Mall fails by perhaps attempting too much. There is a point beyond which curves, angles and patterns are no longer an argument for contrast, but become elaborate extensions of the designer's ego. (pp. 214-215).

No mall can hope to compare spatially with public squares like *Piazza San Marco* or even Newport Beach's Fashion Island Shopping Center, but the limitations imposed by lineal form and a restrictive gridiron regularity are not impossible to overcome. The Mall in Riverside, California which pedestrianizes four blocks of Main Street possesses all the aesthetic requisites necessary for success— variety, contrasting forms and materials, good seating spaces, play opportunity, shade and recreation. An added plus is its proximity to the renowned Mission Inn—a favorite retreat of presidents. Competition from shopping centers has prevented its becoming an economic success unfortunately, but like other downtown malls a change from commercial to professional activity appears to be occurring— empirically of course. (pp. 196-197).

A unique underground mall has been developing since 1975 in the heart of Los Angeles, in association with street level public spaces—Bowron Square and the Los Angeles Mall (pp. 218-219). Almost an afterthought in the city's priorities for re-vitalizing the commercial center, the underground shopping mall developed from a growing awareness that space alone—even when beautified by fountains, landscaping, and a crazy musical tower—was not sufficient attraction to the public. Restaurants were brought in, then gift shops, a book store, some specialty stores and a very special children's museum—a major key to the mall's success, along with the adjacent 2400 car parking structure.

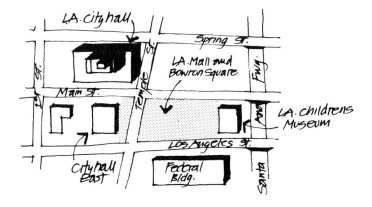

Limited to the width of a single downtown street, malls of this nature play small roles in any city's open space requirements. Many of them have not produced the hoped for re-vitalization of downtown centers, whether owing to design, lack of parking or the competition from nearby shopping centers with their oceans of parking. Europe and Latin America have fared better in experimenting with the conversion of vehicular to pedestrian traffic in crowded downtown areas, for reasons that are probably more a result of social than economic factors. Manchester, England and Guadalajara, Mexico for example, have been in the process of pedestrianizing many of their central, commercial streets during the past decade, with positive results.

Not a shopping mall by our definition, but one of the best examples of commercial and aesthetic success of lineal form in this country is the Riverwalk (Paseo del Rio) in San Antonio. Initially limited to a mere walk along the concrete bank of the overflow bend in the San Antonio River, the walk was part of a 1930's Works Progress Administration program for safety and beautification in the city. Recognizing its potential for commercial enterprise, private funding developed a kind of shopping mall along the corridor, and today it ranks as one of the city's major tourist attractions. From woodsy greenery, past a grassy amphitheatre of ever changing musical fare, to waterfront shops, decked verandahs and tree shaded outdoor cafes, the strolling pedestrian takes respite within the city from the roaring traffic above him. Like the lower walks along the banks of the Seine River in Paris, the Riverwalk provides an escape from the intensity of modern urban life which swirls above it. San Antonio's economic resurgence in tourism is unquestionably tied to this unique urban experience (pp. 200-201).

The other kind of shopping mall is in reality a newer version of the shopping center. Entitled 'mall' by its inventors, it differs only in having its central pedestrian way under one roof, with shops lining the sides. In this way it resembles a covered downtown street, similar to the previous examples, but its location is that of the shopping center, with its attendant enclosure of parking acreage.

The major limitation of the mall—its open ended lineal quality—has led recently to to some promising half measures. For example, the transit mall, now being implemented in Brooklyn, Chicago, Portland, Vancouver, Santa Barbara and Santa Cruz, California, to name a few, merely limits vehicular access to public transportation systems. The street is still a street with all its implications of high speed traffic, noise, and noxious fumes, but without parking requirements or passing lanes there is more space available for benches, plants, and other pedestrian pleasures. Moreover, the passing traffic is regular, predictable, and can be accommodated at attractively designed gathering points which act as rest areas as well as bus stops.

Portland's transit mall, the largest and most successful to date, operates one-way systems on two parallel streets for a distance of eleven blocks each. When completed it is expected that 230 buses—one third of the city's fleet—will move through the two malls each hour at peak periods of the day.

The Civic Mall. The term 'mall' is of course more accurately applied to those long, green promenades of pre-industrial European cities. Derived from the French Formal garden design of the 17th century, like the *tapis vert* (green carpet) of Versailles, the mall was translated into urban form in the expansive Neoclassic era, as illustrated by the Avenue des Tuileries, Paris and London's Pall Mall.

Unlike boulevards, the mall is considered to be primarily for pedestrian use, the best example of which in the United States is the Capitol Mall in Washington, D.C., originally conceived in 1791 by Pierre L'Enfant. Most of the credit for the design as we know it today belongs however to the 1902 McMillan Commission team (Frederick Law Olmsted, Jr. in particular) who substituted a wide green promenade, heavily bordered in shade trees, for L'Enfant's Grand Avenue. Unlike the original plan it carries vehicular traffic only on its perimeters, making it a six hundred foot wide median, enclosed in allees of American Elm trees, five across on either side.

The mall stands alone today in American cities, a triumph of Neo-classic space—a *tapis vert* more than two miles in length, terminated by the capitol on the East and the Lincoln Memorial on the West, the last half mile of which is replaced by a reflecting pool which shames the Taj Mahal. To complete the scheme, a North-South cross axis runs from the White House to the Jefferson Memorial, across a broad sweep of open greensward, crossing on the golden section and marked there by the placement of the Washington Monument.

The only discrepancy in this monumental Neoclassic accomplishment lies in the fact that the Washington Monument itself, that magnificent reminder of Sixtus V's obelisks of Rome, actually stands some 300 feet east of the crossing of the two sight lines. The explanation for this peculiar departure from symmetry lies in the engineer's report during the first phase of construction in 1848, which determined that the subsoil at the crossing location was unstable for such a structure (555 feet high). Perhaps if the report had been ignored, in the aim of achieving visual perfection, a kind of 'leaning tower of Washington' might have resulted—probably a worse infraction of symmetry.

Pierre L'Enfant, the French engineer whom George Washington selected to design 'Federal City' in 1791, did not conceive of either the Washington or Jefferson monuments, the latter coming into realization during the depression years and finally dedicated on the banks of the Tidal Basin in 1943. The McMillan team, having addressed itself to the project for over two years and producing at last the definitive solution, was also doomed to achieving only partial success. Today's Capitol Mall, although conceived at once, in a single ingenious stroke, has needed most of our two hundred years of existence as a nation, to reach its present realization. And it continues unfinished—unrealized, at least according to one of its more noteworthy exponents of late, Nathanial Owings. In his grand plan of 1966, the mall received an additoinal six acre reflecting pool beneath the Capitol, and extensions of the western pools that lie along the East-West axis. Considerable architectural revamping along the mall and Pennsylvania Avenue were called for, as well as a National Square at the terminus of Pennsylvania—just before the eastern facade of the White House. These plans were abandoned in favor of a new scheme by the Pennsylvania Avenue Development Corporation, which retains the existing hotel and small spaces as terminus. The National Square, with the White House as the major and final terminus to the avenue, would have been a far superior solution.

The most significant and far reaching aspects of Owings' Mall revitalization plan actually occur on Pennsylvania Avenue, with the introduction of a series of buildings of uniform height facing the street across double rows of trees. To achieve a terminus of some power and meaning, the hotels at the west end are razed and incorporated into the area of Pershing Square in order to create National Square, while at midpoint on the avenue (Eighth Street) a cross-axis is proposed, from the National Archives through Pennsylvania Avenue *and* the Mall, terminating at the Federal Aviation Agency block. The crossing at the Mall would be marked by a reflecting pool (p. 121).

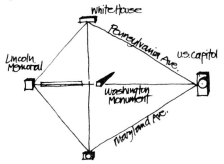

In criticizing Pennsylvania Avenue, architect Paul Rudolph states: "its flanking buildings are not sufficiently dense to define the space of the street. There is no defined beginning or end. The diagonal intersections with the gridiron call for special forms of buildings not yet evolved, nor is the height of existing buildings great enough for the width of the avenue. The avenue acts as a barrier between the commercial and federal city". Rudolph also correctly scores the awkwardness of triangular spaces which occur when diagonal and grid intersections are not creatively handled. As for the Mall itself, he proposes architectural connections to prevent the space from 'leaking out' between the present freestanding buildings.

The Owings plan answers most of Rudolph's criticisms (*Architectural Forum,* Jan. 1963), with one major exception. Maryland Avenue, the other diagonal sight line, which balances and encloses the Mall, terminating *visually* at the Jefferson Monument, remains pathetically undeveloped—in reality and in plan. Rudolph would locate a new Supreme Court building on axis, coinciding with a cross-axis from the proposed National Square (p. 121).

Civic design at this scale is complex and difficult to manage, as was certainly true in Haussmann's day as well, but perhaps even more so in the democratic framework of today's society. Everyone has a right to be heard. We are less willing to destroy a man's livelihood than they were in the Paris of Napoleon III. The efforts to create a mall scheme in St. Louis of the proportions and magnitude of Washington and Paris, are therefore worth reviewing.

A river front town established at the landing site of the French adventurer, Pierre Laclede, in 1764, who intended it as a fur trading outpost for New Orleans, St. Louis evolved a typical 'T' plan—a front street (Broadway) above the levee paralleling the river, and a main street (Market) running perpendicular and away from the river, the juncture of the two becoming the crux of commercial activity.

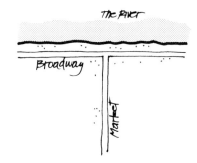

The significance and visual impact of Market and Broadway have been maintained and strengthened over the past two centuries by the commercial and municipal architecture fronting them, including the old and the new courthouses, Union Station, Kiel Auditorium, the Wainwright Building (by Louis Sullivan, 1891), and the beginnings of a mall adjacent to Market Street. In 1964-5 the 'T' plan was further emphasized by the erection of Eero Saarinen's

magnificent stainless steel arch (1948 Competition) which soars 630 feet above the banks of the Mississippi River, clearly symbolizing St. Louis as the 'Gateway to the West'. Anchored in the greenery of the Jefferson National Expansion Memorial Park, the arch spans the thrust of Market Street, looking west toward lands only dreamed of by Thomas Jefferson and those who knew America's future lay in that direction. In 1803, the year United States made the Louisiana purchase from France and thereby doubled its size overnight, St. Louis was indeed the frontier of the nation and the gateway to the West. From here Meriwether Lewis and William Clark set out to explore and record the area of the Missouri River to its source. From the standpoint of scientific exploration it ranks second only to Charles Darwin's adventures on board the Beagle a couple of decades later. Lewis and Clark returned to St. Louis in 1806 bringing the first documentation of this vast, unknown area reaching to the Pacific Ocean. This is what the arch is all about. In 1904 the Louisiana Purchase Exposition was held in what is now Forest Park (p. 177). 1764, 1804, 1904 and 1964 are significant dates in the city's history. Since 1964 city planners and selected urban designers have labored to bring the dream of a Gateway Mall to completion. In 1967 Hideo Sasaki's design for the mall was selected in a national competition. This plan called for the removal of all buildings in the path of the proposed mall, a block wide area, save for the 1851 Courthouse, which anchors the mall on the east, and the Civil Courts Building on the west end. Two small squares, the Serra sculpture area and the Kiener Plaza supply the base for each. West of the Civil Courts Building, the mall continues outward for another eight blocks to its west end terminus in front of Union Station at Aloe Plaza, where Carl Milles' famed sculpture group, 'The Meeting of The Waters', is located. It is easily his most important work outside Europe, and a most fitting conclusion to the Gateway Mall. Unfortunately a design scheme of the early 1970's, in attempting to introduce greenery and more seating area around the fountain containing the sculpture group, constricted the size and shape of the pool to the point of greatly diminishing the impact of Milles' superb work (p. 206). The Sasaki plan for the eastern portion of the mall remains on paper. Good or bad, it was shelved in favor of a scheme done in 1976 by Hellmuth, Obata and Kassabaum which realigned

Market Street to run through the center of the mall, curving out and around the two judicial anchors. In the same year a plan by Richard Claybour was introduced which preserved many of the buildings in the path of the mall, strengthening the position of owners and preservationists and leading to the controversy which has embroiled planners and alderman to this day. In 1979 and 1980 both Sasaki and HOK were brought back for the purpose of preparing further schemes, and in 1982 a private landholders corporation bent on preserving several old buildings in the path of the intended continuation of the mall to the river, brought Claybour and Sasaki together to produce yet another scheme, this one obliterating the mall concept altogether, replacing it with a series of pedestrian spaces that wind through a complex of enclosing structures.

Each successive scheme has had something of a deleterious effect on the mall concept—as well as on the weary officials who have grappled with it for the past two decades. In 1965 with the erection of the arch it probably seemed clear enough sailing. But the history of the planning of Gateway Mall goes back far beyond that date, all the way to the 1904 world's fair, with new schemes proposed every decade or so—to the arch competition of 1948 and the Market Street Mall concept of Russell Mulgardt in 1954, which first delineated the arch and mall relationship.

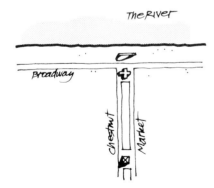

And where does the Gateway Mall proposal stand today? The business leaders and commercial interests appear to have won at last. In a 1982 scheme by Hellmuth, Obata and Kassabaum a series of six story office buildings were planned for the length of the eastern portion of the mall (between the old Courthouse and Civil Courts Building), sparing only the Serra Sculpture court and Kiener Plaza. The controversial historic buildings in the path of the mall (the Buder Building, Title Guaranty and Western Union Building) will all be demolished, ending forever the myth that they possess aesthetic and/or historic value, in favor of replacement architecture—not open space at all! The sugarcoating of this questionable proposal is the Redevelopment Corporation's intention of erecting the new low-rise buildings *only on the north half of the mall.*

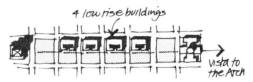

The effect of the scheme is to reduce the width of the mall by half, but more importantly to throw the axial sight line—through the courthouses and the arch itself—out of symmetry. Worse yet, the Redevelopment Corporation (comprised of downtown business leaders) in October of 1982 requested that HOK's six story buildings to be erected along the north side of the mall be allowed to grow—to perhaps 17 stories or more. True, Gyo Obata's proposed low-rise buildings are unpretentious at best (p. 207), but taller buildings on a mall narrowed by half are certain to have a negative effect spatially. Leone Battista Alberti considered the importance of that relationship long ago (p. 78). We can only hope that the 'half mall' scheme flounders, and that one of the older and better mall plans is resurrected. (Drawings and synopsis on pages 202-207, with thanks to W. Davis van Bakergem, Washington University's School of Architecture, for his assistance.)

While urban designers have been struggling with city fathers and landholders for decades in St. Louis, we should bear in mind that L'Enfant was sacked in 1792, only a year after the drawings for Washington were finished, for causing buildings to be removed which stood across the straight lines of his axial avenues; and Haussmann as well, in 1870 for failing to compromise with existing vested (and powerful) interests. Perhaps Daniel Burnham, the driving, dynamic spirit of Chicago's turn-of-the-century re-organization, is unique in having emerged unscathed from the wars of large scale civic design making.

Burnham's 1909 plan for Chicago came on the heels of his 'White City' world's fair of 1892–3, the site for which became Jackson Park, as pre-arranged through the determination of Frederick Law Olmsted, the fair's co-planner. Similar to Haussmann's grand neoclassic scheme for Paris and L'Enfant's concept of 'Federal City', Burnham's plan for Chicago resulted from a radial overlay of a traditional gridiron street system, with radial squares, in the best tradition of the neoclassic planners, at the major intersections—marked there in true Baroque fashion by obelisk, elaborate fountain sculpture and the like. Burnham was nothing if not a true exponent of the Sixtus V, L'Enfant, Haussmann tradition. His plan called for a centric government complex, from which radiate the major avenues of the city. In addition, the principal axial street, Congress Avenue, was to connect the civic center with the waterfront and newly planned yacht harbor, enclosed in a Bernini-like sweep of arcaded pavillions.

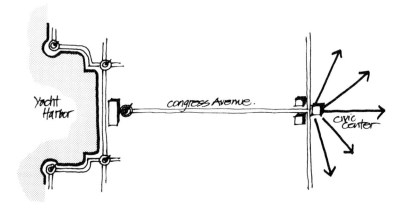

Harnessing the disorganized city which at that time was already sprawling aimlessly along the lake shore, was indeed a Herculean endeavor, and to Burnham's credit much of his plan was actually accomplished. The civic center complex with its six radiating avenues failed to materialize, but the development of the harbor and is principal axis, Congress Street, have been realized, along with Lake Shore Drive and Michigan Boulevard, which parallel the lake,

as planned, and the string of parks along the lakefront proper (p. 226), as well as the necklace of 'boulevard parks' which connect along the city's west side.

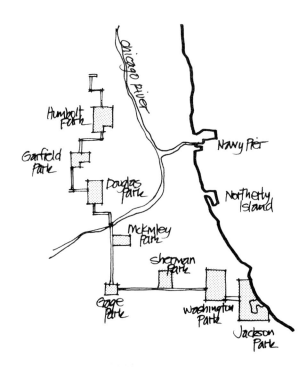

Although the yacht harbor was never completed as conceived by Burnham and his associate, Edward H. Bennett, Congress Street (now Eisenhower Boulevard), Grant Park and Buckingham Fountain remain the definitive elements forming the east-west (perpendicular) axis to the lake, as Michigan Boulevard and the parks define the parallel. Of course, the similarity to the urban structure of St. Louis is obvious.

In recent years Chicago has added measurably to the quality of urban space, with the Daley Plaza opposite City Hall in 1978, and the First National Plaza in 1979—the latter being more successfull as a noontime gathering place in pleasant weather. The Daley Plaza, a straight forward, unimposing space in the angle of the City Hall and its annex possesses no particular design merit, save for the Picasso peace sculpture, which dominates and thereby controls the space. On the other hand, First National Plaza, which boasts a ceramic tile enclosing wall decorated by Marc Chagall, is a modestly pleasant place due to the enclosing elements themselves—the bank building, the carefully articulated planters and the Chagall wall. Moreover, the plaza itself is depressed several feet below street level, stepped down to an inner space augmented by a large spray fountain. When Chagall arrived for the dedication he discovered that by leaving the top of the six foot wide wall undecorated he had denied his work to the office workers above, so at age 90 he painted the top portion for their exclusive benefit. (pp. 226–227).

These new public spaces, along with the Federal Building Plaza and its bright orange 'Flamingo' sculpture by Alexander Calder and a tiny space with sculpture by Joan Miro, form a sequence of small commercially oriented squares along Dearborn Street, each with its unique work of art. Parallel to Dearborn, State Street has recently been upgraded as a fashionable transit mall, with widened sidewalks, benches and planters, and elaborate glassed enclosures for bus passengers.

With the very latest modern architecture, like the Sears Tower, the Xerox Building and the John Hancock Building, Chicago remains at the forefront of the Modern movement—the Post-modern movement as well (if indeed such faddish counter movement enterprise is ever given serious recognition).

Certain to come as a surprise to some, Los Angeles possesses a very distinct six block mall (one half mile) of a primarily administrative nature, called the Paseo de Los Pobladores and including the Court of Flags and the Music Center, and terminated by City Hall at one end and the Water and Power Building, with its elaborate fountains, at the other. The mall is enclosed by a heavy brigade of courthouses and civic buildings for the most part, but includes as well three performing theatres and a skyscraper Art Deco city hall of some distinction.

Cross axis to this is the Los Angeles Mall, described on page 151, combining administrative, social and commercial activities into a 'T' shaped plan of significant order. Although some of the enclosing structures are unprepossessing at best, there exists over all a blithe informality that tends to excuse both the heavy handed and the capricious. Most importantly it projects a sense of urbanity—of being in the center (although detractors may still maintain that Los Angeles has no center).

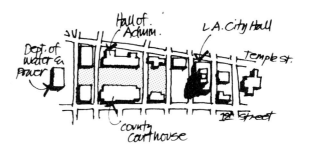

Philadelphia's Market Street performs a similar function to its St. Louis namesake, running perpendicular to the Delaware River and connecting the harbor area to the city center. William Penn's 1681 plan for the city is based on a gridiron system, the heart of which is comprised of four green squares arrnaged in a rectangle, one mile by one half mile, with a fifth square at the center representing the heart of government.

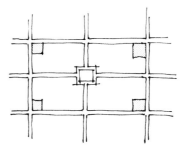

Unlike Savannah, the squares are set *inside* rather than across the primary circulation, with the principal north-south and east-west axes intersecting at the center, where the monumental French Renaissance city hall rises. On top the dome Ben Franklin's statue placidly surveys the city below (although post-war skyscrapers now rise above his eye level).

The city hall stands just over a mile from the riverfront, on the Market Street sight line which penetrates the heart of the old colonial section, now well on its way towards a complete historic restoration by the National Park Service. Across this sight line lies Independence Mall, on the western edge of the restoration area. Less than a half mile in length (three blocks), the mall does not carry the force or significance visually comparable to the four preceding examples. Indeed, Market Street alone possesses the potential for grand scale impact, with Independence Mall performing as a secondary cross-axis.

Nonetheless, Independence Mall marks the edge of the historic area, gives the city open space where its is badly needed and acts as a setting for Independence Hall, a beautiful and uniquely significant building in American history. In front, the mall consists of a series of symmetrically arranged spaces in each of three blocks—first, a trio of fountains framed by avenues of trees; in the second block a single large spray fontain framed by arcaded stoa-like structures, and a *tapis vert* the width of Independence Hall through the center of the facing block, this also formally enclosed by several rows of matching trees. All three segments hold together easily through the agency of symmetry and axial alignment. Altogether the system is properly subordinant to and supportive of Independence Hall, the real star of the show, the only questionable element in the mall complex being the rather grand, non-functioning stoa arcades of the middle block. (p. 195).

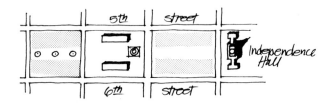

With the construction of the Benjamin Franklin Parkway, the city's only major diagonal street, the Philadelphia Museum of Art became visually connected to city hall, in the manner of radial

planning. High on a bluff above the Schuylkill River, the massive, classic structure dominates the city in somewhat the way the Parthenon and the Acropolis dominate Athens.

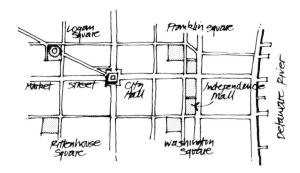

In order to facilitate vehicular traffic, Logan Square, the northwestern corner of the four original Penn squares, became a circle, in the manner of a radial hub. The Ben Franklin Parkway and Logan Circle are Philadelphia's only concessions to radial planning.

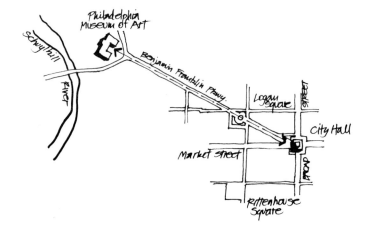

Philadelphia, St. Louis, Los Angeles and Chicago—and particularly Washington, D.C.—represent sincere and monumental efforts to impose a designed structure over the face of a city's center—to establish a recognizable, even unique physical character. The examples from the past—Paris, Rome, Lisbon—have been noteworthy models for neoclassic revivalists to emulate. Unfortunately, classic precepts, with all their need for formalism, symmetry, geometry, sight lines, termini and grandly overblown scale are too often the only conditions permitted by the rules governing civic art. Physical structure, recognizable, tangible and measurable, are necessary conditions of urban design, but there are other pathways to its achievement—while at the same time avoiding the mire of amorphous, chaotic and meaningless form, so often the rule in urban growth. The civic mall has been a tool since the 17th century for combatting ill-planned growth, but by its nature of augmenting and emphasizing *avenue* and *circulation* it has no doubt added to sprawl, and the sense of movement over place. Identifying *place,* in respect to focus, has been another kind of problem.

The Refurbished Town Center. Following the great London fire of 1666, Christopher Wren developed an effective method for establishing visual urban order by designing singular and easily recognizable spires to rise over the city's churches. Each identified a parish, a neighborhood, and acted in conjunction with others as a kind of compass whereby one could orient himself in the congested, medieval complex of curving streets. Urban order and a sense of spatial structure have always existed, as we know, in organic and empirically developed villages, towns and cities. When small enough, a town needed little more than its walls, market square and church to give it urban structure. Wren's visual connectors served to extend eyeball range of the man in the street—in a less formal manner than Sixtus V had employed in the Rome of 1598. John Nash used another kind of visual system to connect central London to Marlebone Park (later Regent's Park) along several otherwise unrelated streets.

But as cities grew larger and more complex, and as heretofore homogenous architecture gave way to individualized and greatly varied facades, street level visual orientation began to fail. Tall buildings without singular distinction began to block out our views toward St. Paul's Cathedral, or Ben Franklin atop city hall. And even with an unobstructed view, distance must eventually become a limiting factor to visual connection—as anyone who has ever tried to orient himself in Los Angeles readily understands.

At some point designers may choose to employ a larger visual scale and the elements of nature in order to achieve some semblance of organization. For structure, parks with their great masses of trees, hills, ridges, steep valleys and of course rivers; for orientation, the mountains to the north, the harbor and coastline, the sun. While Paris, Washington and Rome have inspired urban designers like Daniel Burnham to seek solutions in neoclassic tradition, some, like Christopher Wren, will attempt to work with the fabric on hand, or create new patterns to fit changing behavioral trends and technological advances. The British and Scandinavian new towns are such an example. In United States, Reston, Virginia and the greenbelt towns of the 1930's have shown us that urban order need not be limited to hard-edged symmetry to succeed. In established cities the empirical process can be effectively employed in design, if a careful and sensitive analysis of the existing urban fabric is first undertaken. Such an analysis preceded the structural evolution now reaching completion in the historic center of Guadalajara, Mexico.

Once the colonial capital of the indian slave trade in Mexico, Guadalajara has recovered from its bloody and rebellious history to become one of the most progressive and beautiful cities of Latin America. Such progress has resulted in spite of a rapid growth rate which has seen the city's population increase more than ten fold in the last fifty years, as industry began to lure the *campesino* into town in much the same manner as Manchester attracted the country people of England's midlands a century earlier. The population explosion since the 1940's continues, but Guadalajara has learned to deal with it, through the practical application of long-range planning programs which have resulted in good lower income housing, ample parks and public spaces, rail and air terminals and most importantly, a cooperative exchange between local government and banking interests. More recently that spirit and the city's long established civic pride have continued to produce solutions to complex growth problems.

Toward this end planners and urban designers have attacked congestion in the old city center by developing a plan which has pedestrianized many of the narrow secondary streets, converted the arterials into a one-way traffic system and constructed underground parking in the area. An improved public transport system and air pollution devices on all vehicles are needed to complete the modernization of the downtown area.

The 17th century architecture of the center, including the cathedral, the governor's palace and a dozen lesser structures, remains intact for the most part and serves as a guide to present and future planning. Bold, solidly neoclassic in the Spanish tradition, the remnants of the old colonial city have endured the onslaught of 20th century urban flotsom to the point of nearly disappearing under a plethora of aluminum storefronts, billboards and uninspired architecture—until the city's restoration and modernization program began to take hold.

Due primarily to the efforts of architect Ignacio Diaz Morales in the early 1960's, the program of revitalization began with the development of the four squares that frame the cathedral—the spiritual heart of the city. In typical Roman cross plan, each arm of the basilica is faced by a discreet public space, the largest of which acts as the link to the *Plaza Tapatía,* the name for the complex of new squares which form the commercial heart of the city.

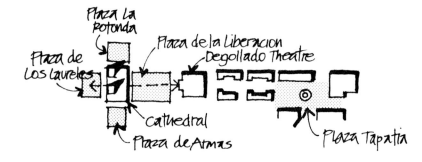

This is the *Plaza de la Liberación,* linking the two most important colonial structures, the cathedral and the Degollado Theatre, on the primary visual axis of the city center. Extending this axis to the west locates its terminus in front of the cathedral in the *Plaza de Los Laureles,* and to the east it carries to the arched entry of a newly constructed municipal building.

The four block area has been cleared of all but a few significant colonial structures so as to allow for the development of this series of spaces, wich eventually link together with the *Hospicio Cabanas* (a 17th century orphanage converted to a museum) and the *Mercado Liberdad* (built in the late 1950's).

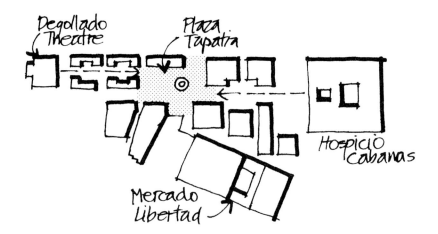

At this point a major problem developed for the planners. The *Hospicio,* perhaps the third most important colonial building in Guadalajara with its classic dome and lantern, acts as terminus to a second major axis *(Avenida Morelos)* paralleling the first. Further complicating matters are two diagonals, the alignment of the *Mercado* and the main thoroughfare through the city, *Avenida Independencia*—both of which impact on the plaza axes.

In order to carry out the pedestrian access and sight lines along the parallel east-west axes, the entire structural system, including all of the new buildings which enclose the plazas, had to be raised to bridge *Independencia,* and to maintain control of the vertical changes. There is a drop of some twenty feet from cathedral to *Mercado.* To mark the point where *Independencia* passes diagonally under the *Plaza Tapatía,* the designers have located a prominent piece of contemporary sculpture in a fountain complex, acting as a pivotal hinge to the divergent sight lines, like hands on a clock face. This fulcrum performs the awesome task of centering all three axes visually, as well as balancing them.

The other diagonal, the *Mercado,* is altogether a different kind of problem, and had to brought into linkage by use of another design technique. Below the level of the primary east-west sight line which bridges *Independencia,* the *Mercado,* on its own axis, is reached by an elaborate stairway which acts as part of a three-stage transition in line and form. First, recognition of the *Mercado* (to the south) is made by a setback in the line of the new buildings which frame the plaza.

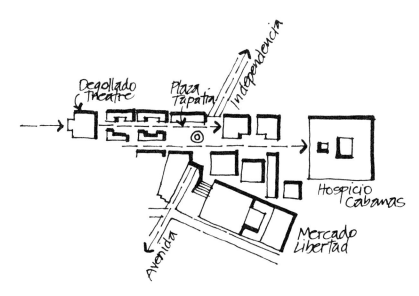

This has the effect of swinging the center of interest away from both axial termini and toward the *Mercado.* The stairs themselves act as a transition, vertically as well as in form, and finally the small plaza in front of the *Mercado* accepts a transitional shape to accommodate the three otherwise unrelated sides.

The elevated parts of the plaza system assist in providing access to the 2000 car parking area directly beneath it. Delivery and service to the buildings on the plaza is accommodated underground as well.

While the series of new open spaces through central Guadalajara ranks as a casebook study in solving linkage to disparate urban elements, it is perhaps most successful at the pavement level, where the acid test of parks and public spaces is finally made. Here we see *Tapatía* already proving itself day in and day out, Sundays and evenings when the stores are closed, as well as on regular shopping days when the new stores are full of customers. The key to *Tapatía's* popular success lies in its balanced mixture of religious, commercial and municipal facilities—and of course its gathering spaces. The map on page 228 identifies the buildings, both historic and newly completed. Thus the behavioral factors re-inforce the solution—as elements in the design as well as factors in design determination.

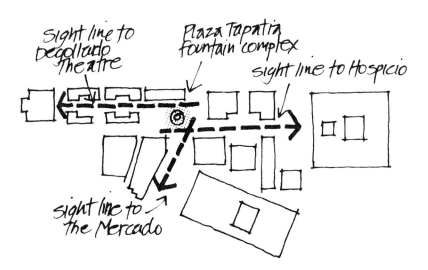

The new buildings are not in themselves noteworthy, resembling shoe boxes with the wrong sized lids, and even the more important new buildings tend to be theatrical, as elements in a giant stage set. They take on a single purpose character and as a result seem obvious, prepossessing and undistinguished—all the more aggravating when so readily comparable to the vastly superior colonial buildings at their shoulders.

The skyline however is correct, and infinitely more significant when viewed as a total concept. The uninterrupted flow of horizontal line and space is all the more powerful visually when finally and dramatically stopped by designed termini. It is the opposite from Wilshire Boulevard, Los Angeles where individually distinguished buildings march along side by side, creating no sense of overall spatial harmony.

This grand series of spaces, encompassing the best in both empirical and rational design processes, are named (from east to west) *Plaza Lopez Portillo, Plaza Hospicio, Paseo Hospicio, Plaza San Juan de Dios, Plaza Tapatía, Paseo Degollado, Plaza de la Fundación, Plaza de la Liberación, Plaza Rotondo, Plaza de las Armas,* and *Plaza de los Laureles.* In sharp contrast with the new buildings, the details of the new plazas—planters, fountains, sculpture, furniture, paving patterns and materials, flowering plants, trees and decorative motives are well defined and effective. *Plaza Tapatía* itself is stiffly formal and badly needs the eventual tree growth to reduce its present starkness in order to provide some sense of overhead, human scale and balance with the apparently excessive paving. Likewise, *Plaza de la Liberación*'s simplistic formalism provides little reason to pause there. On the other hand the attenuated *Paseo Degollado,* which links *Tapatía* and *Fundación,* is richly decorated, offering a variety of intimate sitting alcoves, changes in level, whimsical fountains bedecked with frogs in a glossy send-up of a Renaissance garden, and masses of contrasting plantings. Perhaps the best single element of decor in the entire complex is the surprise terminus of the *Plaza Lopez Portillo,* unexpected until one reaches the very end of the severely formal *Plaza Hospicio.* Rounding the corner to the south one is drawn to explore the hidden garden, anticipated by a glimpse of densely planted trees. And of a sudden he finds himself in the path of a raging stampede of wild mustangs, beautifully captured at full scale in glistening steel. It is the tribute to Jose Lopez Portillo, ex-president of Mexico who must be accorded the credit for his support and sustaining interest in this vast project.

The lessons of Guadalajara and the several United States examples cited here teach us that by knocking down a few old buildings of questionable historic or aesthetic value—in true empirical fashion—and opening up the clogged arteries at the center, a revitalization of a city's structure can be accomplished. Most American cities originally possessed space at their centers but during the period of industrial expansion when the manufacture and transport of goods laid claim to all available inner city space, warehousing, railroad terminals and stations, switch yards, sidings and round tables replaced traditional market centers—just as witnessed in British and European cities a few decades earlier.

Now, railroads and their terminals are in turn under attack. The former culprits in the destruction of pre-industrial buildings and market places, they are themselves the objects of controversy in preservationist schemes, especially in the West and Midwest.

Eastern cities with more tangible pre-industrial traditions worth preserving have retained pieces of the past in sufficient form to be restored. Williamsburg, Savannah and Philadelphia, as noted earlier, have taken steps to insure and reaffirm their 18th century character. In resurrecting the past we can only hope that the designers and planners involved are also cognizant of the needs of the future, which as a matter of simple deduction maintains the same requisites for human scale, tree-lined streets and a pleasant urban environment. The charm of Williamsburg does not devolve from atavism but from a restoration of human values and aesthetics, dimensions and materials—and an absence of technologically related *bric-a-brac,* overkill signs and lighting, and unnecessarily wide streets—for starters.

The restoring of open space to impacted urban centers does not obligate us to seek nostalgic solutions in design. Pittsburg has produced Mellon Square, one of the new breed of contemporary geometric spaces—with a jangly diamond paving pattern to boot (p. 223), and has restored the Golden Triangle area (the point of land at the confluence of the Monongahela and Allegheny Rivers) with plazas and gardens. Boston, St. Louis and New Orleans have cleared riverfront slums and replaced them with parks and civic spaces. In San Francisco the old Ghirardelli Chocolate Factory and surroundings have been converted into a complex of shops and restaurants around an open space which accommodates both contemporary and historic detailing (pp. 208-209). Likewise, the Faneuil Hall Marketplace in Boston has undergone major restoration which retains the colonial architecture and overall open space organization while tolerating modernizing trends. More importantly, in San Francisco as well as Boston, human scale and pedestrian orientation have been preserved and enhanced.

For a while it almost seemed that we had extended to ourselves the luxury of discarding cities in the same manner as we divest ourselves of clothing, automobiles and even homes—when they no longer suit our needs. The frontier mentality of the last century certainly encouraged Americans to move on when the soil seemed worn out or conditions no longer suited their needs. And well into the 20th century we have continued to walk away from jobs, homes, families, cities that were no longer what we wanted them to be. Some of us still try to live by frontier mentality, piling our trash and old cars out back, mistrusting of neighbors within sight, but for most of us the city at least can no longer serve as our collective rubbish dump. Revitalization begins with the removal of decay at the center. Waste of any kind is expensive, and wasted space at the city's heart is the most expensive of all.

New town centers. Perhaps the best way to achieve a sense of spatial scale and variety in the modern marketplace is to plan it from scratch—with the development of an entirely new town. The British planners have had considerable success, notwithstanding a few notable setbacks, in rediscovering the grand art of ideal city design, but unlike their Renaissance predecessors they have usually carried through to construction. British new towns, like those that followed on the continent, have always been provided with a central market space (town centre), clearly identified and always taken for granted (Englishmen normally give directions to tourists which are based on a relationship to the town centre). Pedestrian access to the centre is usually provided without the necessity of crossing streets or "car parks," and service to the stores and shops is often underground. Circulation of all kind is thereby separated, adding to both the efficiency and aesthetics of the complex.

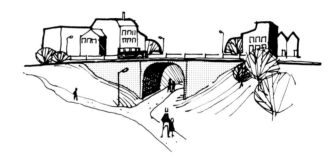

Based generally on the "garden city" concept of Ebeneezer Howard, published in 1898 under the title *Tomorrow,* British new towns since that time have been built with careful respect for public open space. Planning of new towns in Britain differs from continental versions in two significant ways: they are low density, allowing for ample centric space as well as generous public residential space; and they have been planned to develop into independent economic entities—self-sufficient, with their own commercial and industrial base.

Continental new towns, particularly as developed in Scandinavian countries, are semi-independent generally, having been developed like satellites around the parent city. The individuality of each is maintained by green buffer areas of park or farmland, but

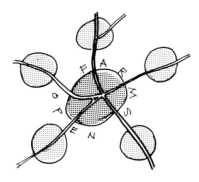

they are tied to their parent by an umbilical rapid transit system which allows merchandise and working commuters to move easily back and forth.

The Scandinavian new town center *(centrum)* is perhaps more rigidly defined than the British example, allowing perhaps for less flexibility, or "settling in," which only common usage and the passing of years can provide. Furthermore, the British designers have never been satisfied with any purely objective set of proportional rules, which may account for Crawley's town centre being too "tight" and Harlow's being too open—so much so that space seems to lose its containment and its sense of scale. Stevenage, perhaps Britain's best planned new town, possesses a good spatial balance in the town centre, with sight line termini, axes, variable spatial containers and a vertical accent to mark its nucleus.

The concern for flexibility and growth in new town centers has been a perplexing one for urban designers who are finding that careful and precise form in the central square—as sought by Re-

naissance rule givers—is difficult to achieve, even with the aid of the sophisticated measuring and prognostic machinery in use today.

Urban space takes shape through a series of adjustments—the source of light, numbers of people and their circulation patterns—all of the things mentioned in chapter one, and more. At best the square acts as a stage or a backdrop for the real drama taking place there, and as Goldfinger theorizes, awareness of spatial order and a sense of enclosure are usually subconscious. The *activities* matter more than the space, and it is for that reason alone that empirical order need be recognized—that enclosure not be allowed to dictate function irrevocably, or until the walls fall down. In Farsta, a satellite of Stockholm, the designers of the *centrum* have made an attempt to allow for physical change, in an expeditious manner. Aluminum awnings and other types of facade screens are bolted to the structure in such a way as to allow for periodic replacement—and a fresh, new look to the downtown. This self-conscious attempt at empiricism may seem somewhat naive, since the foundation of empirical design is not planned obsolescence, but organic adjustment to changing conditions and needs. Even by the strictest interpretation, empirical change will not occur until conditions so dictate.

The Social Factor

Finally, it is necessary to say something about those urban spaces which are not directly associated with civic or commercial uses—the squares which act primarily as places for interaction—neighborhood spaces for example—or as a simple relief against the hard gray geometry of modern cities.

The small park or green square of today's sprawling cities makes little impression on the overall urban fabric. It is neither a central organizing force, like the system of squares at Nancy, nor the economic nucleus, as in the British and Scandinavian new towns. It does, however, occasionally provide the city with exciting and imaginative form. The small neighborhood or downtown square can make a major difference in the assessment of a city's overall qualities for living.

These smaller open places have tended towards either an informal, natural design base, or the geometric, classic form. Pershing Square in Los Angeles began in a natural state, as a sort of park, was changed at the turn of the century to reflect Spanish heritage by providing an open central space, then redesigned in 1950 to allow for an underground parking garage, with the resulting formality above ground reminiscent of seventeenth century France. It was changed again in 1962—not so much to eliminate a simplistic design—which looked for all the world like two dice on a billiard table—but to overcome a *social* problem, the oldsters and winos who were allegedly disturbing patronage to adjacent business enterprise. The square retains its formality, with the loiterers moved to the center, away from the serious-minded who move about their business on the square's edges. Its counterpart in San Francisco, Union Square, retains its original classic symmetry, including the traditional vertical symbol, while citizens of all stripe lie about the grasses verges when the sun is out (pp. 217, 220–221).

After World War II this either-or approach to design (natural vs. classic formality) began to disappear from the small square, with examples like Mellon Square in Pittsburgh, which is hard surfaced and geometric, but informal and asymmetrical in design. This new approach to the design of small downtown squares has been successfully carried out in the Los Angeles Civic Malls, East and West, by landscape architects Bridgers, Troller and Hazlitt, and in Portland's Fountain Square by Lawrence Halprin. The latter is probably the ultimate in socko design impact, but it belongs in a hot, dry climate instead of Portland, where its roaring cascades and waterfalls combine with the near eternal rain and mists of the Pacific Northwest to create an unceasing reminder of dampening discomfort.

In a nation as independent as ours, where cities sprawl out of control over the landscape, and where little effort at limitation seems possible in the reorganization and renovation of downtown spaces—in scale with the city as a whole, then perhaps the value and impact of these smaller, detached squares can be fairly measured. They

are, in a real sense, the best we have in America in the way of public open space. Their purpose or impact can never be measured in terms of the *Piazza San Marco's* relationship to Venice, or *Hei'jokyo's* meaning to Kyoto. But the fresh, imaginative design work which continues to appear, even to replace older ones, is an encouraging sign of recognition and appreciation in this country for public institutions and for good design. Nor should we overly concern ourselves about the loss of some time-honored square. It is not the *space* which has been removed, only the *form,* and we cannot truly judge the decision which brought about a change until we compare the loss with the gain. Surely everything must fall in time, and what form the replacement takes is our only method of determining whether or not the urban order has progressed or declined.

History will determine the real value of our design efforts—in respect to those things which our works have replaced. And history will surely mark the late twentieth century in United States by our apparent need to intensify architectural competition. As our buildings reach out to grab attention from others, the American city street begins to resemble an out-of-step chorus line, each structure dancing to its own rhythm, while trying to outwiggle its neighbor.

In an age when architects feel they must prove their artistic mettle by continually inventing new wall planes and roof lines, the idea of structural harmony is hard to achieve. History also shows us, however, that when architectural arrangement is harmonious rather than in violent conflict, then the overall composition of streets and enclosed spaces will be more sedate, aesthetically balanced, and a kind of architectural language will emerge. Many European, oriental and Latin cities have such a language, as do most rural towns and all primitive villages. The efforts of a dedicated urban design team in Guadalajara are demonstrating that an architectural language—even in the technological atmosphere of our telecommunications age—can evolve, just as Daniel Burnham in Chicago and L'Enfant, Olmsted and Owings in Washington have struggled to prove. In order for the architect to understand the role his building is expected to play in the overall structure of the city, he must first understand and accept the words of Paul Rudolph:

> Civic design is the art of assigning roles to every element of a city, coordinating them so that they form the total environment, providing a three-dimensional framework for adding and subtracting in such a way that every act respects, augments, enhances and allows the original great idea to fulfill itself.*

Our urbanized society of today is capable of bringing people together with lightning speed and clarity of purpose, and capable as well of developing the great ideas by which cities themselves may become more useful and livable. As *designers,* and not as social reformers and urban ecologists, we must forge the challenge of creating and maintaining urban form that is essentially and lastingly *human* in scope and purpose, regardless of the technological changes in materials and their applications. It is Rudolph's *great idea*—once fixed and understood—which should not change. In such a way a city's future is assured—not in spite of change, but because of it.

A future which includes an inner urban framework of human scale, architectural harmony, and a spirit of individuality without conflict is a future where urban space can be readily integrated—not as oases of relief within a gridiron of cultural and aesthetic desiccation, but as parts within the changing harmony of a balanced whole—a city of life.

Architecture Forum, Jan. 1963.

The park is a place to catch the sun on a fine day, feel cool breezes on your face, the grass with your toes. Notice how the earth yields beneath you—as pavement never does. (James Gilray)

A place to meditate, to feel the earth beneath your feet, to be alone.

(London. St. James's Park)

Lucca, Italy
The 16th Century walls, still intact, form the basis for a greenbelt circling the old city, and providing town folk with their only urban park.

Edinburgh. The steep slopes below the castle became the city's first park—after urban growth began to develop below. (Ill. London News)

Life in manufacturing towns by mid-19th century was harsh and recreational opportunities for working classes were generally limited to riverbanks, commons, public streets—and 'gin mills'. (Illustrated London News)

Nottingham. The newly constructed mills.

Manchester. Dogfighting in the area of Salford.

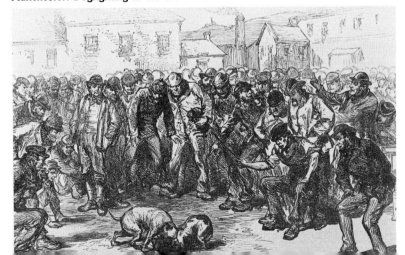

London. Sailors on leave enjoying a brief respite in the common.

Paris and London. Warm Spring days brought the fashionable to the parks, prior to their being opened to the working classes about 1850. Police guarded the entrances to prevent the unseemly and ill dressed from entering. (Ill. London News)

London. Kew gardens in early summer.

Paris. The season at Bois de Boulogne.

London. Kensington Gardens.

Left: London's Spitalfields.
Above: Rioting for better working conditions, New Cross.

In working class areas violence began to erupt as a result of crowded, unhealthy conditions, long working hours with low pay, and lack of recreation open space. (Ill. London News)

London: Hampstead Heath. Park violence was largely abated by 1872, when a mixture of classes appears together in this illustration.

London. Working people attempting to enter Hyde Park on a summer afternoon are repelled by Police. This scene is from August, 1866.

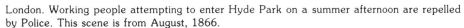

London. St. James's Park. The city's most popular Royal Park in an 1841 aerial view showing the recently completed re-design by John Nash and John Repton. In this view the Horse Guard Parade grounds appear on the left, the new lake (with island) at the right and Westminster Abbey directly behind. The buildings of Parliament are still some 50 years in the future. (Ill. London News)

Right: the lake today

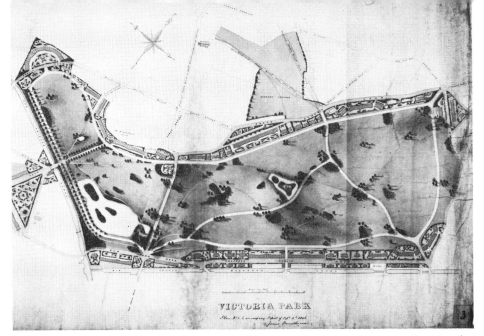

Above: A new park in the industrial midlands, complete with Romantic 'ruin' and name tags on newly planted trees. (Ill. London News)

London. Victoria Park. The city's first working class park, located in the crowded east end, designed by James Pennethorne in 1841, re-designed in 1846.

Lower right: Birkenhead Park, across the river from Liverpool this is considered to be the first important park to accommodate all classes, designed by Joseph Paxton in 1843.

Below: An early attempt at providing play equipment, London, 1855. (Ill. London News)

Chicago. Jackson Park. The grounds of the World's Columbian Exposition, translated into a city park by Frederick Law Olmsted at the close of the fair. (Chicago Park District)

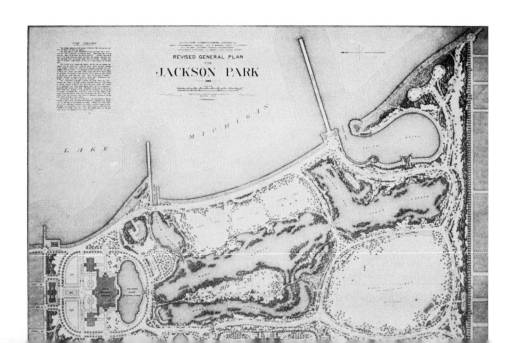

San Francisco. Palace of Fine Arts Lagoon. The terra cotta rotunda is a remnant of the city's 1915 Panama-Pacific International Exposition. (S.F. Convention and Visitors' Bureau)

Below: Chicago. Grant Park. Part of Daniel Burnham's 1909 plan for the city's restoration. (AIA) Journal

St. Louis. Louisiana Purchase Exposition of 1904. Today the site includes Forest Park and Washington University, on the city's western edge.

The Grand Basin from in front of Festival Hall in 1904, and as it looks today. (Jefferson Memorial)

In St. Louis, Chicago, San Diego and San Francisco International expositions have proved to be successful sites for city parks. In some instances remnant structures have become useful park additions.

St. Louis. Aerial Panorama of 1904 fair, looking SW by H. L. Wayman.

Below: Plan of Forest Park, located on site of fairgrounds. The Grand Basin (center left) is one of the few remaining features of note. The Pavillion and Jefferson Memorial were built in 1914 out of fair's profits and the administrative complex became Washington University.

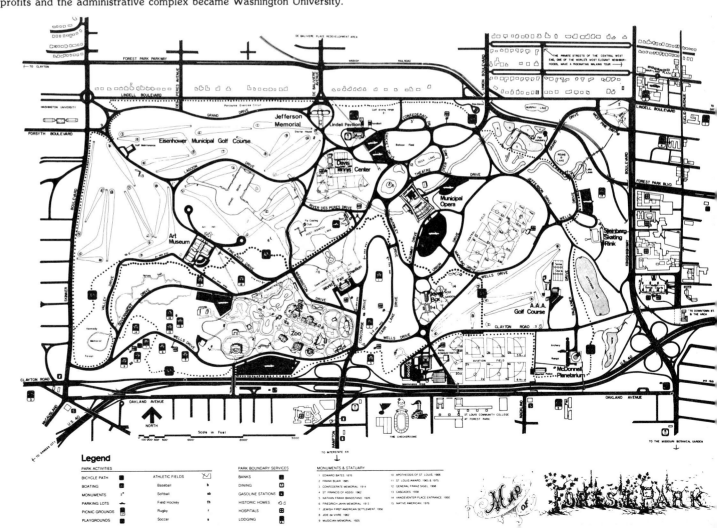

Amsterdam.
The Bos (The Woods).
(Dienst Publieke Werken)

Trails through the park. The large park of 500 acres or more, when properly designed to limit vehicular penetration, allows the urban dweller many opportunities for rural and wilderness experience. Skating, cycling, hiking through snow or casual strolling are features usually reserved to only the larger city parks.

Chicago. Jackson Park (Chicago Park Dist.)

Paris. Parc Floral.

Geneva. Parc Anglais.

Osaka. Tennoji Park (H. Soda) Note European influence on this Japanese city park.

Rome. Villa Borghese

Some parks retain much of the formal geometry of an earlier heritage, which is often out of touch with today's needs for flexibility in design.

Amsterdam. Darwin Park. (Dienst Publicke Werken)

And some parks are self-consciously geometric in a contemporary idiom. But is flexibility improved?

Amsterdam. Vondel park. (Dienst Publieke Werken)

Park activities vary greatly, depending upon age and interests of participants. Park design must reflect variations and include flexibility of purpose in order to allow individuals and groups to create their own fun.

Paris. Bois de Vincennes.

Amsterdam. The Bos (Woods). (Dienst Publicke Werken)

London. St. James's Park.

Los Angeles. Venice Athletic Beach (H. Boltz)

Stockholm. Blackberg Play-park. (Göste Glase)

Stockholm. Vasaparken (Bildarkivit)

Paris. Bois de Boulogne.

Seattle. Freeway Park. An excellent example of 'found' space, it literally hangs above the busy Interstate freeway which traverses the city. As such, it often surprises those who would expect the areas around high speed motor ways to be unusable as parks. The roaring concrete waterfall imitates the water power of the Pacific Northwest, and also helps to mask auto noises. (Seattle Parks & Recreation Dept.)

A park is a personal place—along a riverbank of a seemingly endless woodland meadow, where one can be alone amongst others.

Stockholm (Gosta Glase)

Stockholm. Humlegarden (P. Blom)

A park can be a dull, forboding place of warning signs and regimented picnic cages. Who insists on watching us, regulating our recreation, scrutinizing our pleasures?

Paris. Bois de Vincennes.

Pomona, California. Ganesha Park.

(James Gilray)

(History of Kotohira)

(from Ito's 'Minka')

(T. Uesugi)

Temple towns in ancient Japan. These drawings from old manuscripts illustrate typical urban activities in the development of temple towns.

Note characteristic methods of enclosure of town houses, and the immediate relationship between street and house—of exterior to interior. This remains a carefully guarded trait in Japanese urban life.

High density living is accommodated here by symbolizing a sense of space, leading to the development of two aspects of spatial organization—through simplicity and complexity.

Kyoto Daitokuji Temple

Zen Buddhism and the tea ceremony aim at creating fusion between man and nature, through natural law. The open and closed spaces, changing direction of approach with every change in scale, serves to emphasize dynamics of space and circulation. Compare this method with Renaissance and Neo-classic methods of spatial interruption to signify spatial or directional change.

Kyoto (T. Uesugi)

Kyoto. Street scene.

The primary development of urban space in traditional Japanese cities is linear—along major commercial thoroughfares. In order to maintain their vitality and usefulness as space, the automobile and other motorized vehicles must be prohibited. Compare with the development of pedestrian malls in United States, after World War II.

The traditional Japanese equivalent to the church or Cathedral parvis of European towns is the space provided as entry to the temple (right), or that alloted to the traditional shrine (below). In the latter case the shrine acts as a common public square, in use and variety of function, and the symbolic monuments act as elements of vertical relief and directional devices.

Kyoto. Asakusa Kannon (T. Uesugi)
Kyoto. Common shrine (T. Uesugi)

The city of Phoenix's new cultural center includes primarily a symphony hall and convention center (flat roof on left, both photos). The bridge permits an increase in pedestrian flexibility without disruption of vehicular access.

Phoenix. Civic Center Plaza (Director).

Underground parking needs have unfortunately restricted tree planting to these small containers (below), making protection against the desert sun virtually impossible, and sunglasses an absolute necessity.

San Francisco. Civic Center (right) The great dome of the city hall stands as terminus to the primary axis, reinforced in Neoclassic manner with fountains, formal walkways and avenues of formally aligned trees to act as enclosure to the corridor.

(San Francisco Convention and Visitors Bureau)

Albany. Empire State Plaza (right). Completed in 1979, the complex of domino-like buildings exemplifies the 'new geometric' in modern rational civic order. Note the contrast in scale reflected by the Gothic Church which remains a part of the downtown skyline.

(Patrick Sturn)

Philadelphia. Independence Mall. (Phil. City Pl. Com.)

In classic tradition Independence Mall stands across the central sight line, terminating the long axis. The series of formal, lineal spaces here reflect a continuing eclectic spirit in American city planning. Note the *tapis vert* (green carpet), reminiscent of Versailles (right), which permits a clear view from facade to fountain. In lieu of taller structures the cupola might yet serve as a visual reckoning point, just as Christopher Wren's church spires served 17th century London (left).

Philadelphia. Independence Mall (Philadelphia City Planning Commission).

Riverside, California. The Mall.

The reconstituted downtown commercial street—now a pedestrian mall. Here landscape architects Eckbo, Dean, Austin and Williams have supplied infinite variables in texture, form and direction in order to provide slow moving pedestrian traffic with a variety of experiences, as well as to create stopping places and spatial connections to enclosing store fronts.

In the series of photos to the right the historic Mission Inn is approached by way of the Mall, the lantern above its dome serving as a directional finder for pedestrians, reminiscent of historic precedent.

(Janice Wilkman)

Below: The Transit Mall allows vehicular traffic to continue through, but by eliminating parking it is able to widen and vary the pedestrian areas. (Santa Cruz, Ca.)

Pomona, Ca. The Mall. No longer
pedestrianized, the Mall concept has seen
the return of the auto, and parking as
well (right and p. 198 above).

This facade was exposed when adjacent
structure was removed. The result is an
unplanned, unexpected triumph of tromp
l'oel street graphics in true empirical
method.

San Antonio, Texas. El Paseo del Rio

The Riverwalk provides relief from the noise and congestion of the immediate urban surroundings. Originally a WPA project of the late 30s, intended to provide protection against periodic flooding of the San Antonio River, it is now considered to be the city's major attraction and prime reason for San Antonio's growing prominence as a tourist center.

The sketch above depicts suggestions for beautification occurring in 1966. Opposite: Same area prior to beautification

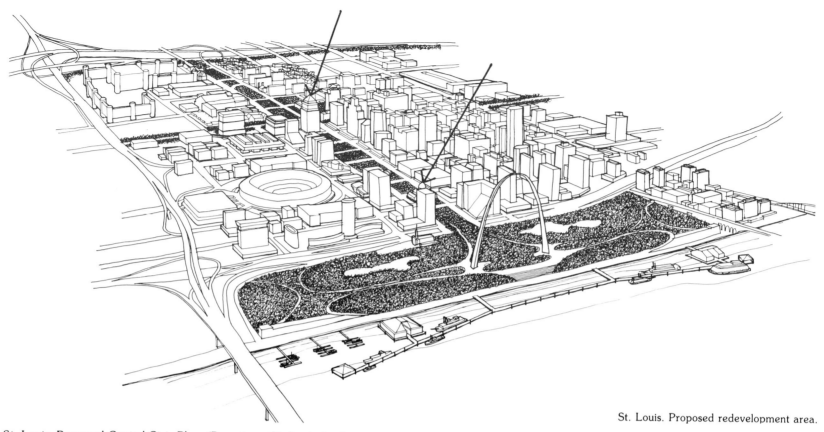

St. Louis. Proposed redevelopment area.

St. Louis. Proposed Central Civic Plaza (Downtown St. Louis, Inc.)

The sketch above illustrates the Gateway Mall, from the Mississippi River to a point beyond Union Station. The area which remains to be cleared lies between the Civil Courts Building and the old Courthouse (arrows). The grand concept, comparable to Haussmann's Paris or L'Enfant's Washington, terminates in the riverbank, under Saarinen's arch in the center of Jefferson Expansion Memorial Park. (opposite page)

St. Louis. Gateway Mall.

Left: The proposed mall bordered by Market Street (left) and Chestnut Street (right) from the top of the arch looking west, away from the river. Union Station at the end of the mall can be seen at top, center. The Buder Building and Title Guaranty Building (Opposite Wainwright Building) are scheduled for demolition, with the old Courthouse (foreground) and Civil Courts Building to remain as anchors to the eastern portion of the mall.

Ground level. The massive Centerre Bank Building tends to unbalance the scheme, well before the mall's completion.

Right: Mall looking east, towards the river from the top of the Civil Courts Building. In the foreground the Telephone Building and behind it the Buder and Title Guaranty buildings block view to Old Courthouse. (Hellmuth, Obata, Kassabaum)

Below: Market Street looking east from the base of the Civil Courts Building.

St. Louis. Gateway Mall. The west end of the mall, anchored by Union Station (above) and Aloe Plaza with its celebrated sculptural fountain by Carl Milles, 'The Meeting of the Waters' (below).

St. Louis. Gateway Mall. The 1982 plan by Hellmuth, Obata and Kassabaum which replaces the various interruptive buildings with four low-rise structures along the north side of the mall. The result is an unpleasing imbalance which destroys the harmonious setting of the arch and the old courthouse (see plan). Despite the pressures of business interests it is doubtful that such an ill-conceived plan will find acceptance.

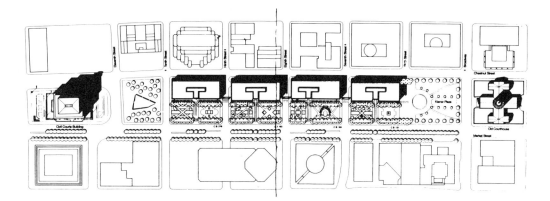

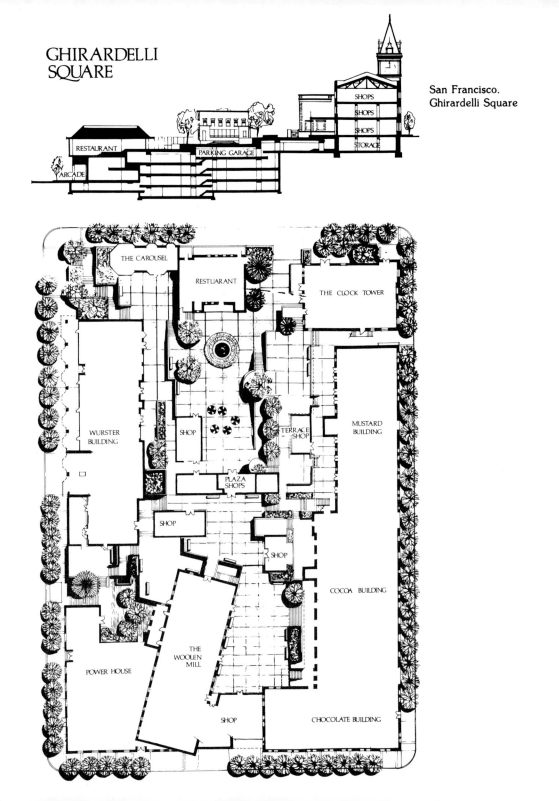

GHIRARDELLI
SQUARE

San Francisco.
Ghirardelli Square

RESTAURANT

PARKING GARAGE

ARCADE

SHOPS

SHOPS

SHOPS

STORAGE

THE CAROUSEL

RESTUARANT

THE CLOCK TOWER

WURSTER
BUILDING

SHOP

TERRACE
SHOP

MUSTARD
BUILDING

PLAZA
SHOPS

SHOP

SHOP

COCOA BUILDING

POWER HOUSE

THE
WOOLEN
MILL

SHOP

CHOCOLATE BUILDING

San Francisco. Ghirardelli Square. (S.F. Conv. & Visitors Bureau)

Nostalgia and great variety in texture and form make this a prime tourist attraction. Its human scale, as well as surroundings, are major factors in its success.

Valingby, Sweden. Centrum. The first of Stockholm's post-war satellite cities has a central commercial space resembling many American shopping centers, but as a city center it reinforces centric organization, while the shopping center typically weakens the 'downtown' commercial structure by competing.

The open space *centrum* in Stockholm shown here is largely taken up by fountain display—an odd choice in this cold, wet climate. The main underground station linking satellite cities to the center of Stockholm is directly below fountains.

Newport Center. Fashion Island.

The shopping center attempts to capture much of the scale and vitality of 'downtown' and often succeeds—although far removed from the city's center. In the case of Fashion Island—commercial hub of Newport Center, near Los Angeles, the growth of surrounding professional, light industrial and housing development give it the basic qualities of a 'new town.' In most cases however, the shopping center, unlike the new town center, is a decentralizing factor in city development.

Montclair, California. Montclair Plaza. The enclosed shopping mall, product of the seventies, provides a great variety of shopping, eating and entertainment opportunities under a single unvarying roof. Like its forerunner the postwar shopping center, the mall continues the decentralization of cities by catering to the desire for independent mobility. Surrounded by the resultant parking sea, it isolates itself from the fabric of urban order.

Santa Cruz, California (left). The Transit Mall provides for a widened pedestrian way, with space for passive recreation and plants as well as vehicular traffic—at the expense of on-street parking.

Fresno, California. The Fulton Mall. Before and after views of the mall by Garrett Eckbo that revolutionized the designing of pedestrian corridors. The six block area of Fulton Street, including the crossing streets, was developed to enhance mobility of foot traffic and variety of experience, and at the same time reduce the impact of otherwise monotonous linear space. Opened in 1964, after nearly ten years of planning, the Fulton Mall is a pioneer in the experimentation of returning pedestrian life to the urban core.

Tidyman Studios

Tidyman Studios

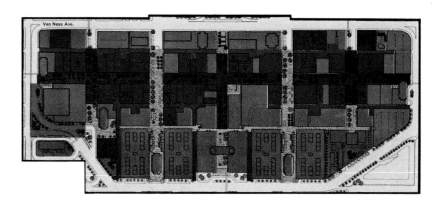

Tidyman Studios

Tidyman Studios

Los Angeles Mall. From the top of City Hall looking west to the Power and Light building which acts as terminus.

Left: Pershing Square in the 1950's when the design encouraged seating on the perimeters. (Also opposite page, lower left.)

1887 (L.A. planning dept.)

1950 (L.A. planning dept.)

Los Angeles. Pershing Square.

The photo (above left) dating from 1887 shows the new Victorian Architecture on Bunker Hill in the background. By the 1950 photo (above right) the present architectural enclosure has been established, though the square still shows the early plaza design (changed in 1950)

The third photo (below left) shows the square as it looked from 1950-65. It was redesigned again (below right), primarily to move sidewalk orators and bench squatters inward, in order to keep the sidewalks clear for business people. Note the shrinkage of usable area (between 2 and 3) with the addition of underground parking. The Buckminster Fuller dome (lower right) honored the 1981 city's bicentennial.

1956 (L.A. planning dept.)

1976

Los Angeles. Civic Center Mall (South Mall).

The civic center malls, including Bowron Square (right) have given the heart of the city a series of pedestrian spaces, surprising visitors who imagine Los Angeles to be a totally auto-oriented jumble of freeways. Conceived in the 'new geometric' form of asymmetric balance, the spaces make use of traditional vertical elements for balance and emphasis. Note the totem fountain (center, rear) and the "Triforium" (left foreground), a vertical symbol which provides both music and a light show. The pedestrian bridge (lower right) connects Bowron Square with the South Mall, (opposite page).

San Francisco. Union Square.

A Neoclassic design, complete with centric masculine symbolism and balance, the square over a parking garage in the heart of the city's shopping district is successful in attracting a broad range of visitors, sitting on bench and wall or lying across the sloping formal turf areas to catch the noontime sun. (S.F. Convention and Visitor's Bureau)

The square actually slopes or is stepped upward to the center column in order to accommodate the roof of the subterranean parking garage. This requirement, as in Phoenix's Civic Plaza and Los Angeles' Pershing Square, necessarily limits the size, quantity and placement of trees.

Pittsburg. Mellon Square (Fred P. Swiss)

Located in the center of a high density commercial area of the city, the square offers spatial relief while reinforcing the surrounding gridiron with an informal geometry of its own. The design is by landscape architects, Simonds and Simonds.

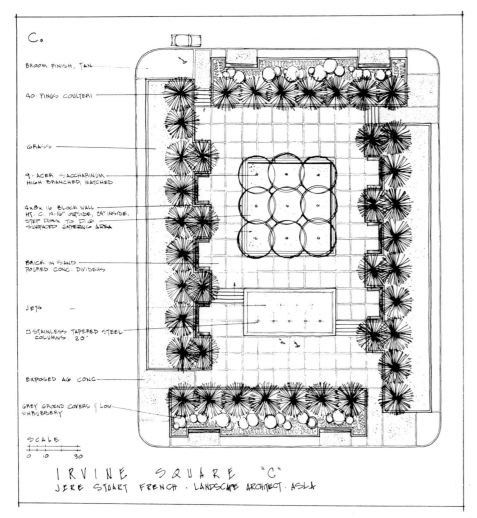

C.

BROOM FINISH, TAN

40· PINUS COULTERI

GRASS

9· ACER SACCHARINUM
HIGH BRANCHED, MATCHED

4×8×16 BLOCK WALL
HT. C. 19-16" OUTSIDE, 29" INSIDE.
STEP DOWN TO D.G
SURFACED GATHERING AREA

BRICK IN SAND
POURED CONC. DIVIDERS

JETS

□ STAINLESS TAPERED STEEL
COLUMNS, 20'

EXPOSED AG CONC.

GREY GROUND COVERS & LOW
SHRUBBERY

SCALE
0   10   30

I R V I N E   S Q U A R E   "C"
JERE STUART FRENCH · LANDSCAPE ARCHITECT · ASLA

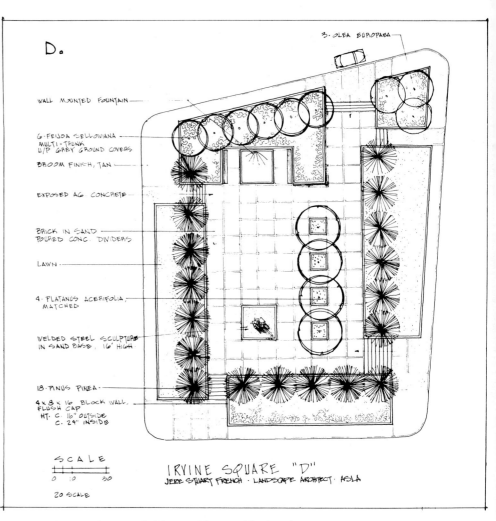

D.

3· OLEA EUROPAEA

WALL MOUNTED FOUNTAIN

6· FEIJOA SELLOWIANA
MULTI-TRUNK
U/P GREY GROUND COVERS

BROOM FINISH, TAN

EXPOSED AG CONCRETE

BRICK IN SAND
POURED CONC. DIVIDERS

LAWN

4· PLATANUS ACERIFOLIA,
MATCHED

WELDED STEEL SCULPTURE
IN SAND BASE, 16' HIGH

18· PINUS PINEA

4×8×16 BLOCK WALL,
FLUSH CAP
HT. C. 16" OUTSIDE
C. 24" INSIDE

SCALE
0   10   30

20 SCALE

I R V I N E   S Q U A R E   "D"
JERE STUART FRENCH · LANDSCAPE ARCHITECT · ASLA

Two prototype plans by the author for higher density condominium developments in Orange County, California. The neighborhood squares shown here are intended as local gathering places, or spatial nodes identifying different residential complexes, similar in purpose to the residential squares of 18th century London and Edinburgh.

Portland, Oregon. Fountain Square.

Two views of landscape architect Lawrence Halprin's fantastic water display, seen on an unusual sunny day. The theme might better serve in Los Angeles where the coolness of rushing water is nearly always welcome.

(L. Rudolph Barton)

Chicago. Daley Plaza. (left) from City Hall, with City Hall annex on left. The plaza includes Pablo Picasso's 'Peace Sculpture' as its prominent feature, but is otherwise lacking in design organization and has proven to be unsuccessful as a public gathering place. (Mart Studios, Inc.)

Chicago. The lakefront from Grant Park (right). The Sears Tower is extreme left in skyline. (Murphy, Inc.)

Chicago. First National Bank Plaza. Completed by Perkins and Will in 1969 the Plaza has been generally successful in attracting noon and after work crowds, due in part to a regularly scheduled calendar of musical events during the warmer months. Part of the revitalization of the loop area, it features a box-like wall decorated by Marc Chagall (bottom of aerial photo) and a variable centric fountain. The certain key to its success in attracting pedestrians lies however in its recessed floor plane and adroit separation from external and vehicular circulation.

(Perkins and Will)

Guadalajara, Mexico. The Plaza Tapatía and related urban spaces which form the newly built central pedestrian core of the city.

Above left, The Plaza de las Armas with its 19th Century bandstand opens the south face of the cathedral.

The Paseo Degollado, left center, represents the primary axis connecting Plaza Tapatía with Plaza Fundación and the Degollado Theatre.

Plaza Tapatia from the air, below left, flies over Avenida Independencia, the spiraling sculpture acting as vertical balance and fulcrum of the intersecting sight lines.

Below, general plan of the plaza complex, completed 1983. The parallel axes of Cathedral and Hospicio, together with the alignment of Independencia and the Central Market (lower right) required a sophisticated approach to design. Some of the architecture remains incomplete.

(City Planning Dept.)

GUIA GENERAL DE LA PLAZA TAPATIA

Presidencia municipal
Plaza de los laureles
rotonda de los hombres ilustres
catedral
Plaza de armas

Plaza de la liberacion
Palacio de gobierno
congreso del estado
Palacio de Justicia
teatro degollado

sta. ma. de gracia
edificios comerciales
Plaza tapatia
san Juan de dios
mercado libertad

Plaza Tapatía, looking east towards the spiral fountain. In this view (right) both parallel termini are visible, the entrance to the unfinished government hall and the dome of the Hospicio.

Adjacent to the Hospicio (lower right) the surprise conclusion to the series of squares appears, the Plaza Lopez Portillo, dedicated to the former President and his love for horses.

A typical pedestrianized street (below) in the central re-development area.

Plaza Tapatía, Guadalajara (left). Pomona, California Civic Center (right).

In order for geometric and axial organization to be successful and overall harmony of function and form must be attained.

Above, axial design, requires a terminus, as in Plaza Tapatia but missing in Pomona (Ca.) Civic Center.

Left, Cleveland's Municipal auditorium is poorly related to new addition, and to the agitated diamond/triangle theme of the plaza.

City of Cleveland, Burlot photo service.

The following plates of urban spaces referred to in text were drawn to scale by landscape architecture students at California State Polytechnic University, Pomona.

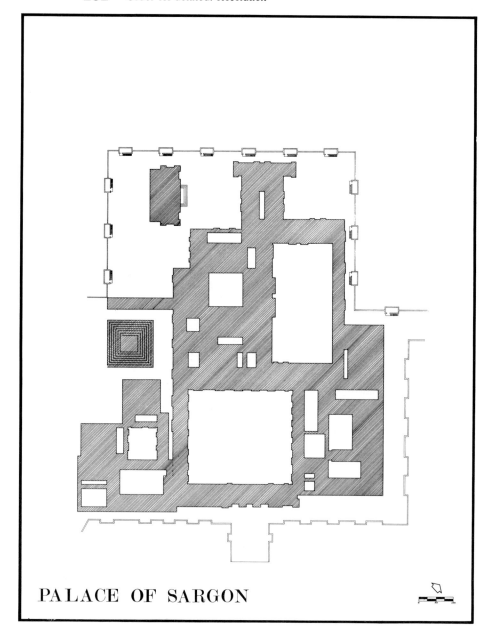

PALACE OF SARGON

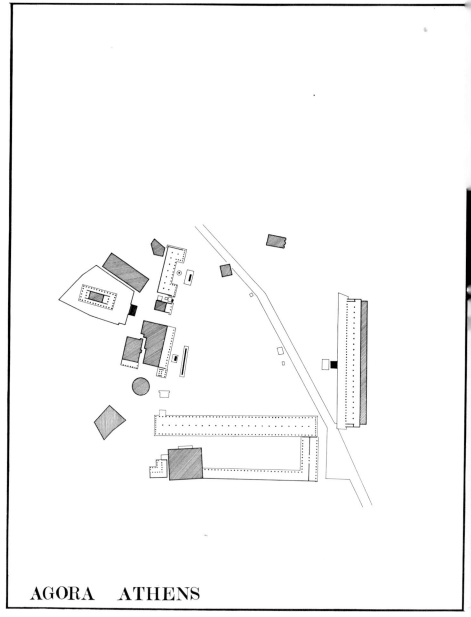

AGORA ATHENS

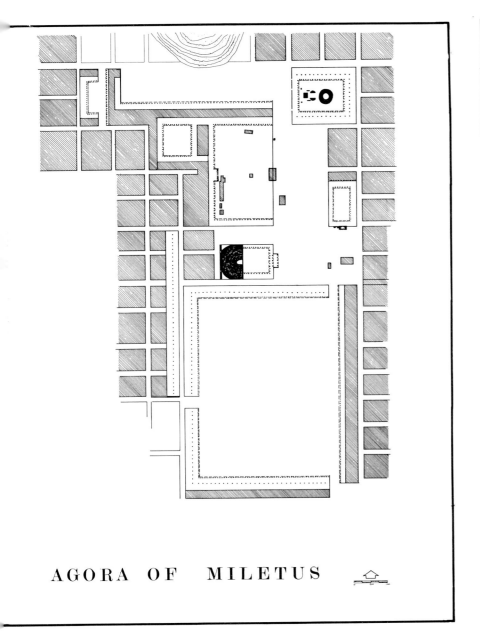

AGORA OF MILETUS

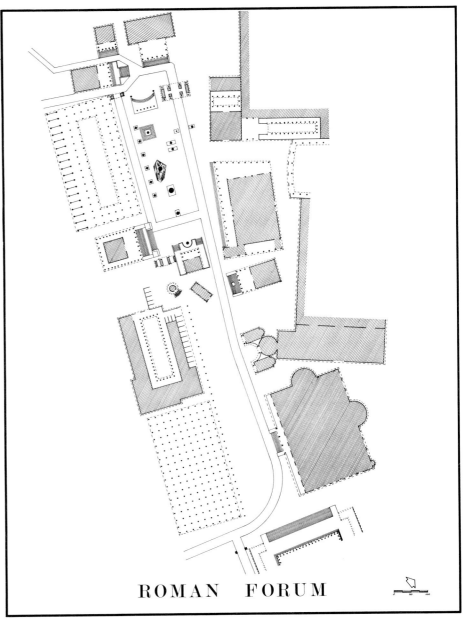

ROMAN FORUM

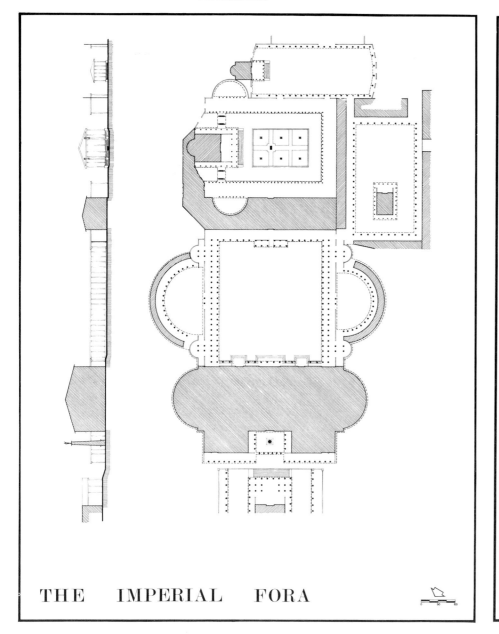

THE   IMPERIAL   FORA

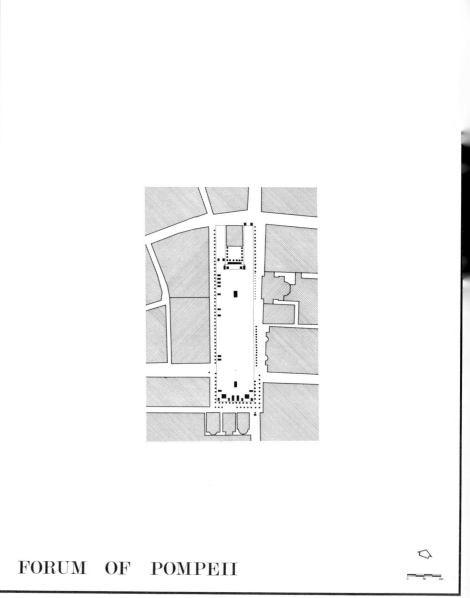

FORUM   OF   POMPEII

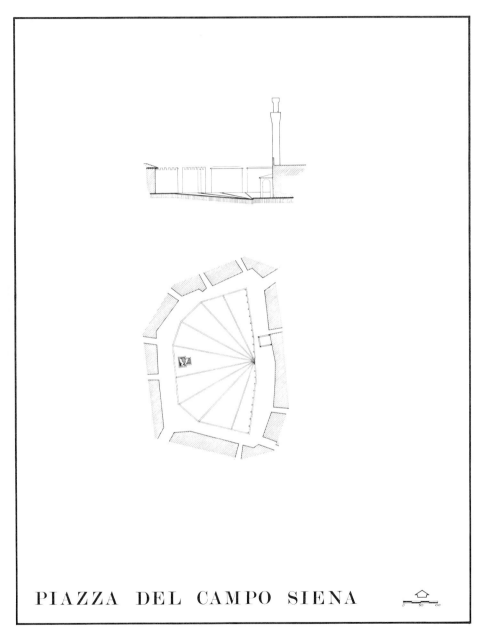

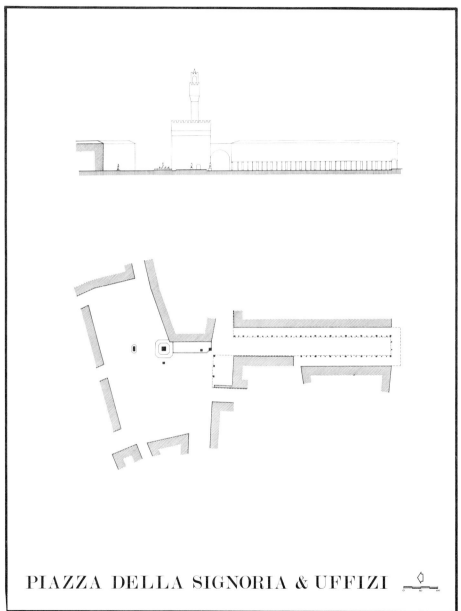

PIAZZA DEL CAMPO SIENA

PIAZZA DELLA SIGNORIA & UFFIZI

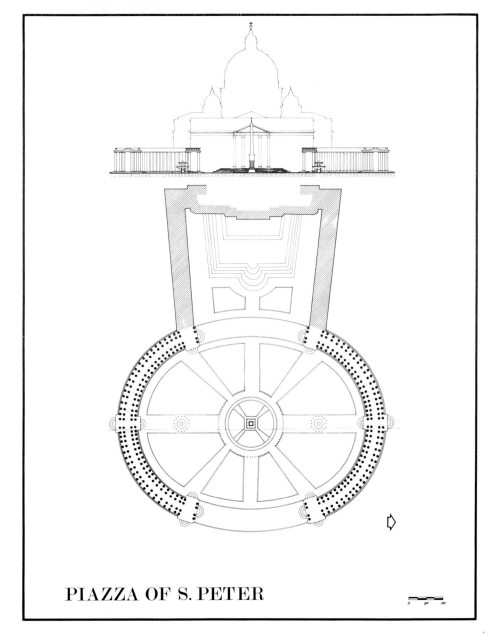

PIAZZA OF S. PETER

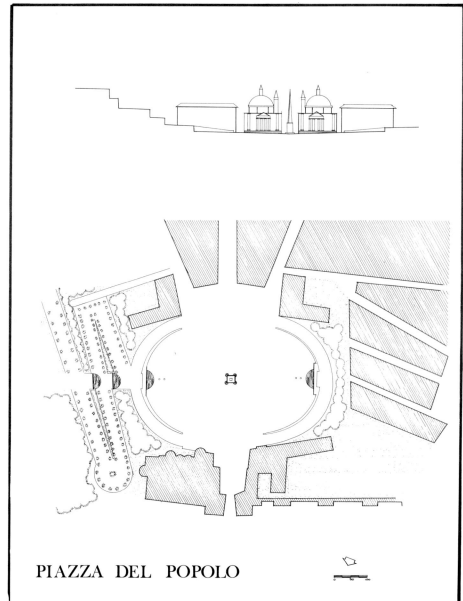

PIAZZA DEL POPOLO

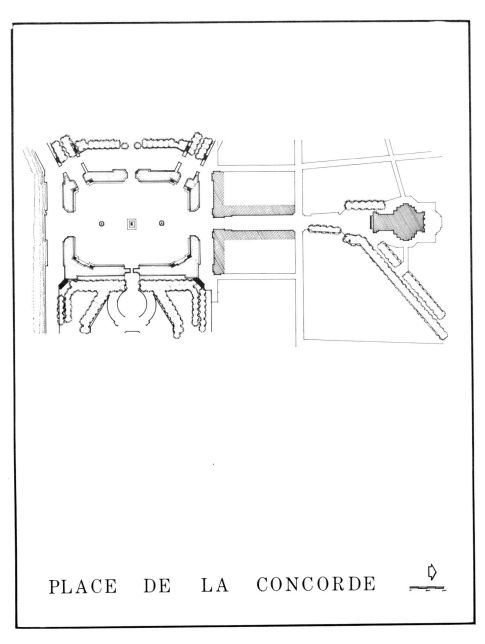

PLACE DE LA CONCORDE

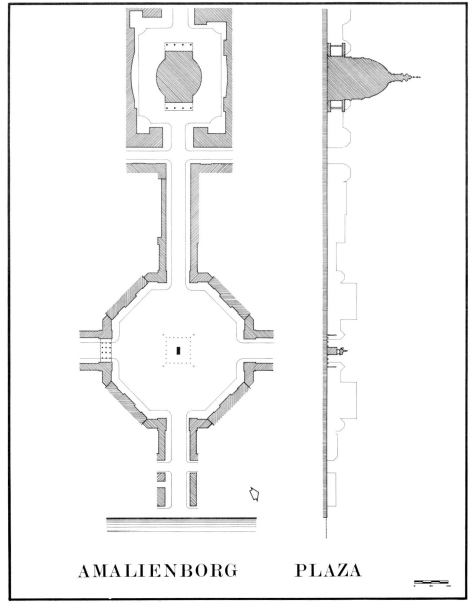

AMALIENBORG PLAZA

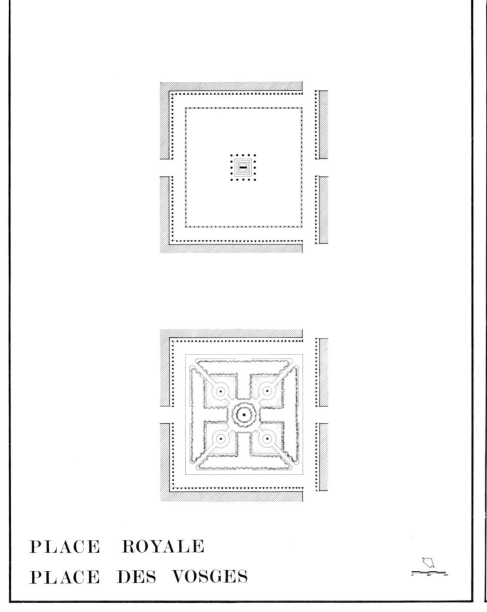

PLACE ROYALE
PLACE DES VOSGES

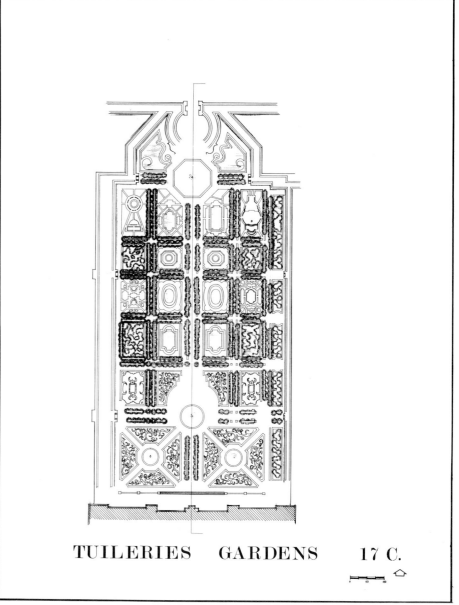

TUILERIES GARDENS 17 C.

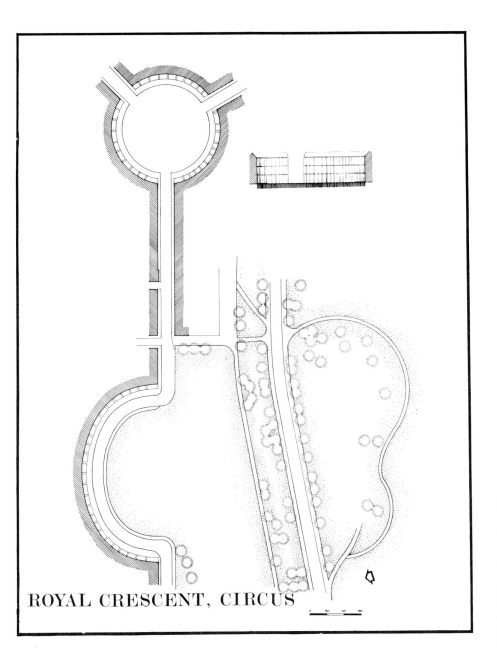

ROYAL CRESCENT, CIRCUS

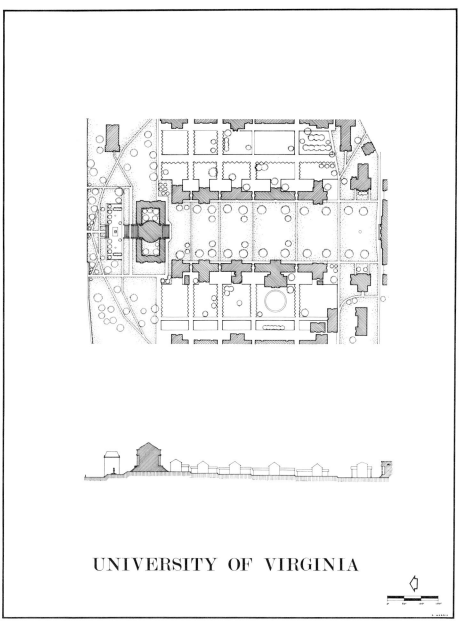

UNIVERSITY OF VIRGINIA

One, two, three or four people making public seating fit their own.

Bibliography

Countless inquiries and many years of reading went into this small book, but I am listing below only those to which I have made direct reference or which I consider to be of particular value to the reader who is sufficiently interested in further reading on the subject.

Alberti, Leone Battista. *Ten Books of Architecture* (Engl. Tr. by James Leoni, 1726). London: Alec Tiranti, 1955.

Argan, Giulio C. *The Renaissance City*. New York: George Braziller, 1969.

Ashihara, Yoshinobu. *Exterior Design in Architecture*. Tokyo: Shokokusha Publishing Company, 1976.

Bacon, Edmund. *Design of Cities*. New York: Viking Press, 1967.

Betjeman, John. *English Cities and Small Towns*. London: W. Collins, 1943.

Boyd, Andrew. *Chinese Architecture and Town Planning*. Chicago: University of Chicago Press, 1962.

Brooke, Christopher. *The Structure of Medieval Society*. London: Thames and Hudson, 1971.

Cameron, N. and B. Brian. *Peking: A Tale of Three Cities*. London: Harper and Row, Publishers, Inc., 1965.

Chadwick, George. *The Park and the Town*. London: The Architectural Press, 1966.

Clark, Kenneth. *Civilization*. London: Harper and Row, Publishers, Inc., 1971.

Cullen, Gordon. *Townscape*. London: Van Nostrand-Reinhold, Publishers, 1961.

de la Croix, Horst. *Military Considerations in City Planning: Fortifications*. New York: George Braziller, 1972.

Department of City Planning. *City Planning of Kyoto*. Kyoto City, 1962.

Fraser, Douglas. *Village Planning in the Primitive World*. New York: George Braziller, 1972.

Giedion, Sigfried. *Space, Time and Architecture* (5th ed.). Cambridge, Massachusetts: Harvard University Press, 1970.

Goldfinger, Erne. "The Sensation of Space. Reprinted by Michigan State University, 1954.

Gunn, Clare. *Cultural Benefits from Metropolitan River Recreation—San Antonio Prototype*. College Station, Texas: Texas Water Resource Institute, 1972.

Hall, Edward T. *The Hidden Dimension*. New York: Doubleday and Company, 1966.

Hegeman, W. and E. Peets. *Civic Art*. New York: The Architectural Book Company, 1922.

Kusumoto, K. *Kurashiki*. Tokyo: Asahi Newspaper Company, 1972.

Lane, Mills. *Savannah Revisited*. Savannah: Beehive Press, 1973.

Lynch, Kevin. *The Image of the City*. Cambridge, Massachusetts: MIT Press, 1960.

Mumford, Lewis. *The City in History*. New York: Harcourt, Brace and World, 1961.

Mumford, Lewis. *The Urban Prospect*. New York: Harcourt, Brace and World, 1968.

Okakura, Kakuzo. *The Book of Tea*. Rutland, Vermont: C. E. Tuttle Company, 1956.

Olmsted, Frederick Law. *Civilizing America* (ed. S. B. Sutton). Cambridge, Massachusetts: MIT Press, 1971.

Palladio, Andrea. *The Four Books of Architecture* (Tr. by Isaac Ware, 1738). New York: Dover Publications, 1965.

Saalman, Howard. *Haussmann: Paris Transformed*. New York: George Braziller, 1971.

Saalman, Howard. *Medieval Cities*. New York: George Braziller, 1972.

Shimamura, N. and Y. Suzuka. *Townhouses in Kyoto*. Kyoto: Kajima Shuppan, 1971.

Tange, Kenzo. *Katsura*. New Haven: Yale University Press, 1972.

Toynbee, Arnold. *Cities on the Move*. London: Oxford University Press, 1970.

Waley, Donald. *The Italian City Republics*. New York: McGraw-Hill Book Company, 1969.

Wycherley, R. E. *How the Greeks Built Cities*. London: Macmillan, 1962.

Wittkower, Rudolph. *Architectural Principles in the Age of Humanism*. London: Warburg Institute, University of London, 1949.

Zevi, Bruno. *Architecture as Space*. New York: Horizon, 1957.

Zevi, Bruno. *Towards an Organic Architecture*. London: Faber and Faber, 1950.

Zucker, Paul. *Town and Square*. New York: Columbia University Press, 1959.

Index